GLOBAL GOVERNANCE AND DEVELOPMENT

THE INITIATIVE FOR POLICY DIALOGUE SERIES

The Initiative for Policy Dialogue (IPD) brings together the top voices in development to address some of the most pressing and controversial debates in economic policy today. The IPD book series approaches topics such as capital market liberalization, macroeconomics, environmental economics, and trade policy from a balanced perspective, presenting alternatives, and analyzing their consequences on the basis of the best available research. Written in a language accessible to policymakers and civil society, this series will rekindle the debate on economic policy and facilitate a more democratic discussion of development around the world.

OTHER TITLES PUBLISHED BY OXFORD UNIVERSITY PRESS IN THIS SERIES

Fair Trade for All
Joseph E. Stiglitz and Andrew Charlton

Economic Development and Environmental Sustainability
Edited by Ramón López and Michael A. Toman

Stability with Growth
Joseph E. Stiglitz, José Antonio Ocampo, Shari Spiegel, Ricardo Ffrench-Davis, and Deepak Nayyar

The Washington Consensus Reconsidered
Edited by Narcís Serra and Joseph E. Stiglitz

Capital Market Liberalization and Development
Edited by José Antonio Ocampo and Joseph E. Stiglitz

Industrial Policy and Development
Edited by Mario Cimoli, Giovanni Dosi, and Joseph E. Stiglitz

Time for a Visible Hand
Edited by Stephany Griffith-Jones, José Antonio Ocampo, and Joseph E. Stiglitz

Debates on the Measurement of Global Poverty
Edited by Sudhir Anand, Paul Segal, and Joseph E. Stiglitz

Overcoming Developing Country Debt Crises
Edited by Barry Herman, José Antonio Ocampo, and Shari Spiegel

Good Growth and Governance in Africa
Edited by Akbar Noman, Kwesi Botchwey, Howard Stein, and Joseph E. Stiglitz

The Economic Development of Latin America since Independence
Luis Bértola and José Antonio Ocampo

Law and Economics with Chinese Characteristics
Edited by David Kennedy and Joseph E. Stiglitz

Intellectual Property Rights
Edited by Mario Cimoli, Giovanni Dosi, Keith E. Maskus, Ruth L. Okediji, Jerome H. Reichman, and Joseph E. Stiglitz

Global Governance and Development

Edited by

JOSÉ ANTONIO OCAMPO

OXFORD
UNIVERSITY PRESS

OXFORD
UNIVERSITY PRESS

Great Clarendon Street, Oxford, OX2 6DP,
United Kingdom

Oxford University Press is a department of the University of Oxford. It furthers the University's objective of excellence in research, scholarship, and education by publishing worldwide. Oxford is a registered trade mark of Oxford University Press in the UK and in certain other countries

First Edition published in 2016

Published in the United States of America by Oxford University Press
198 Madison Avenue, New York, NY 10016, United States of America

British Library Cataloguing in Publication Data
Data available

Library of Congress Control Number: 2015959800

ISBN 978–0–19–878594–1

Preface

This book addresses the interrelated issues of global governance and of cooperation with developing countries—or development cooperation in short. The two issues are, of course, closely interrelated, not only because support for developing countries has been one of the major objectives of global cooperation since the creation of the United Nations (UN), but also because such support has been increasingly linked with other objectives of international cooperation, including the provision of Global Public Goods (GPGs) and the realization of global social and environmental goals set by UN Conferences and Summits since 1990, and their predecessors in the decades before. To this we must add the inclusion of economic and social rights in the Universal Declaration of Human Rights and its development in the 1966 International Covenant on Economic, Social and Cultural Rights and related human rights instruments. These objectives are furthermore related to the broad determination, set in the Preamble to the United Nations Charter, to "promote social progress and better standards of life in larger freedom."

As this indicates, the United Nations has been and continues to be at the center of global cooperation. Several of the chapters in this volume emphasize the importance of the United Nations as the apex organization in charge of global intergovernmental cooperation. This is reflected in the 2030 Development Agenda and the associated sustainable development goals (SDGs) that succeeded the Millennium Development Goals (MDGs) set in 2000. Some of the SDGs deal with GPGs, notably those related to the protection of our ecosystem. In turn, the agreement that the SDGs will be universal and thus binding for developed and developing countries alike relates to the fact that the economic, social, and environmental goals set in the SDGs—the three dimensions of sustainable development—are indeed global in character.

The way the global agenda has been set reflects the fact that "development" has been used in UN debates in two different, though interrelated senses: to refer to the global development objectives set in the UN Charter, Conferences and Summits, but also to cooperation with developing countries. Of course, development in that dual sense goes beyond the United Nations. To start with, sustainable development, in its broad sense, is essentially a responsibility of national governments. In the area of development cooperation the world depends not only on global organizations—the UN system, including the World Bank Group—but also on regional organizations—regional and sub-regional development banks, in particular—and on bilateral and plurilateral official development assistance. In the latter case, aside from the traditional cooperation between developing and developed countries (North-South in now traditional terminology), there is a dynamic world of cooperation among developing countries (South-South) and multiple partnerships involving civil society, foundations, and other private actors.

* * * * *

The first part of the volume discusses global governance issues and their relation to the 2030 Development Agenda. Chapter 1, of my authorship, deals with international cooperation in general and its relation to the UN system. I start by defining three basic objectives of international cooperation in the economic, social, and environmental fields: (i) managing interdependence among nations (a concept that has been captured in the concept of GPGs); (ii) promoting common social norms and standards, and the associated provision of a minimum level of social services for all world citizens, which I call universal social goods (USGs); and (iii) reducing international inequalities, in particular different levels of economic development among countries, which is the realm of development cooperation.

As I point out, this typology coincides with the historical origin of international institutions. Most mechanisms of cooperation created prior to the First World War were related to the management of interdependence (navigation treaties, managing contagious diseases, interconnections of telegraph and postal services, etc.). The creation of the International Labor Organization in the Treaty of Versailles gave birth to the second form of cooperation, but of course this form of cooperation was further expanded after the Second World War (WW2). The third form of cooperation was born in the aftermath of WW2 and was closely interlinked with the dismantling of colonialism.

Beyond their sequential historical origin, I underscore the fact that the three forms of cooperation are conceptually distinct in terms of both their demands for international cooperation and their relation to national sovereignty. The first responds to the economists' criteria of the need for collective action to avoid the under- or over-provision of the goods or services that are non-rival and non-excludable in consumption, or that generate strong externalities (positive and negative, respectively) through their consumption or production. This form of cooperation therefore relates to issues of efficiency in the provision of goods and services. In contrast, the second and third objectives of cooperation relate to equity, among citizens and among countries, respectively.

The chapter then turns into the analysis of what would be better global governance structures. In this regard, it discusses six criteria. The first two are closely interrelated: the recognition of the subsidiarity principle and the need for a "dense" network of global, regional, and national institutions rather than relying on a few global organizations. A dense network, it is argued, is both a more effective system of international cooperation and more balanced in terms of power relations. The third criterion is the need to overcome the tension between inclusiveness—and the legitimacy associated with it—and effectiveness. In international governance, a typical solution, exemplified by the G-7 and now the G-20, is for the major economies to take the lead—a process that I call "elite multilateralism"—but this is done at the cost of the legitimacy that at the international level can only be guaranteed by universal membership. For this reason, a much better model would be smaller decision-making bodies within universal organizations—i.e., a similar mechanism to how this tension is solved by representative democracy at the national level. The fourth criterion is closely related, as it refers to the need for the equitable participation of developing countries in decision making and norms-setting. The fifth is the need to design effective instruments of monitoring, accountability for, and at the end compliance with international commitments. The final criterion is the need for coherence of the system of global governance.

The rest of the chapter deals with the need for an apex organization and the role of the UN's Economic and Social Council (ECOSOC), the body that the UN Charter (weakly) endows with the responsibility to coordinate the UN system in the economic, social, and environmental fields. In the first case, the chapter analyzes the functioning of the G-20 at the leaders' level, the major recent innovation in global governance. It argues that while it helped avoid a major global depression in 2008–2009 similar to that of the 1930s, the G-20 shows overall a weak record in terms of effectiveness and faces problems of legitimacy. It thus endorses the proposal of the 2009 Commission of Experts Convened by the President of the UN General Assembly on Reforms of the International Monetary and Financial System (Stiglitz Commission) to create a UN-system-wide Global Economic Coordination Council. ECOSOC, it is argued, should play a complementary role particularly in the follow-up of major global goals like the 2030 Agenda and those set in summits and conferences, and in coordinating the actions of the UN system to help achieve those goals, as well as in some policy area. The UN's High-Level Political Forum created in 2013, offers a new promising framework to both use the political legitimacy of the General Assembly and its capacity to regularly convene heads of state with the more specialized functions of ECOSOC, which can also mobilize its elaborate network of functional, regional commissions and expert bodies.

In Chapter 2, Inge Kaul and Donald Blondin start by asserting that many contemporary global challenges possess the properties of GPGs (non-rivalry and non-excludability in consumption), or at least components of a GPG nature. However, beyond that, and beyond the changing nature of global challenges and power relations, the authors trace the root causes of current crises to what they call the "sovereignty paradox": the fact that, by holding onto conventional notions of sovereignty that lead them to shy away from international cooperation even in areas where interdependence is strong, national governments are effectively weakening their policymaking capacity. As a result, governments end up undermining the very sovereignty they seek to protect.

What this implies it that we are going through a global version of the "prisoner's dilemma": no country can succeed on its own, yet none trusts others enough to attempt effective cooperation and coordination. The critical missing link is, according to Kaul and Blondin, the lack of understanding that international cooperation actually increases—rather than reduces—the capacity to undertake effective action and thus to enhance sovereignty. They thus propose the need to move to the notion of "smart sovereignty": the concept that pooling sovereignty is the smartest strategy when there is strong interdependence.

The governance frameworks needed to manage GPGs require, in their view, differentiating four functions/criteria. The first function is to avert the risk of failure to act, both by state and non-state actors, generated by the preference for free riding in the provision of public goods. The second function is to promote global fairness, which implies that parties must have voice in matters that affect them, while striking a balance between representativeness and decision-making efficiency. The third, which is essential to transforming decision making into action, is to manage interdependence in the provision of GPGs (summation process), as well as consumption interdependence. The fourth function is to foster a balanced and coherent global public domain, within a global order in which states recognize that there have to be limits on the types of national policy freedoms they have traditionally exercised, because they are unsustainable and/or have led to costly crises. In this global domain, the authors argue, the UN has to be at the center but will need to add a global, transnational perspective to its structure and work.

Several initiatives do not meet or only meet some of these criteria. For example, increased monitoring of global issues by intergovernmental and civil society organizations has contributed to a shared normative framework—although most of the enforcement measures are being applied only to developing countries. However, the opening of space for civil society has not been accompanied by increased participation of developing countries in decision making, and shifting more responsibility and initiative to non-state actors has also frequently meant bypassing the conventional organizations. In terms of action, single-issue delivery and financing mechanisms with limited coordination have proliferated. Even more importantly, the signs of positive-sum thinking and the recognition that there are win/win strategies are barely evident in developed and emerging countries alike. More broadly, the global public domain is yet to be discovered as a "territory" that requires governance.

Overall, there are many pertinent policy initiatives, but they are still ad hoc and uncoordinated and in some cases only experimental in nature. There is therefore no coherent, effective approach to the provisioning of GPGs.

Three trends are clearly visible. First, governance has become vertically and horizontally de-concentrated, associated with the growing role of regional or national organizations and, particularly, of non-state actors. Second, while these processes have promoted more open and participatory international cooperation, they are still incomplete substitutes rather than complements to the central provision of GPGs. Lastly, governments can be counted among the more reluctant actors in international cooperation, particularly when they have to commit to global norms and standards, though they have been open to public–private partnership, as they perceive that this may reduce the amount of resources they have to contribute to international endeavors.

The central challenge is, according to Kaul and Blondin, to bring the states back in. This requires forging global consensus to break the sovereignty paradox and to generate support for the notion of mutually respectful sovereignty. This depends on global fairness, which is essential to securing broad-based support for international cooperation. Moving in this direction also requires incorporating interdependence management into the architecture of the UN—that is, a global public domain with the UN at the center. This means explicitly and systematically introducing interdependence management into the architecture of the UN system: expanding the focus of UN agencies to deal explicitly and systematically with issues of global concerns. Establishing global-issue anchor agencies or agents within the multilateral system might encourage setting-up of institutional counterparts at the national and regional levels, which would, in turn, facilitate coordination and cooperation between these different levels of governance. And in order for the UN system to perform its coordination role in a more explicit and systematic manner, the UN Secretariat could be requested to establish a new unit—an observatory of global trends, challenges, and opportunities.

Chapter 3, by Alicia Bárcena, argues in a forceful way, that multilateral development objectives and targets need to be recognized as universal in nature—and, in this sense, be "decolonized" in that they should not focus exclusively on developing countries. She starts by underscoring that two visions were put in place in the 1990s: the global market reform agenda (the "Washington Consensus") and the UN processes, which includes the UN Conferences and Summits, the Millennium Declaration, and now the design of the 2030 Development Agenda. These two parallel tracks embedded contradictory principles and thus prevented the formation of a common and broad-based approach to global cooperation. The UN track has also been disappointing in her view, because since 2000, the broad sustainable development agenda has been practically substituted by the MDGs, which are minimalistic and lack an integrated approach to development.

On top of these tensions, international cooperation faces, in Bárcena's view, two crucial problems: the incomplete character of the international agenda, and the weak institutional mechanisms for decision making, prioritization, follow-up, accountability, and, ultimately, enforceability of international commitments. There is an additional tension in the current institutional setup, which is more practical in character and relates to the protection of the mandates or interests of specific international agencies or clusters of countries.

In terms of the evolution of the international system, there have been areas of advance, notably the rise of emerging powers, but also problems, notably the worst economic crisis since the 1930s. Rising incomes in the developing world have led to success in the reduction of extreme poverty, but also to the rise of a middle class that is still vulnerable to falling back into poverty. The technological revolution is a clear advance, as it has both spearheaded globalization through lower production costs and the greater speed of communication, and brought a greater sense of participation of the world's population in global processes. In contrast, the environmental degradation has generated major challenges: it has underscored the fact that the living habits and production matrices of developed countries and high income segments of developing countries must change to ensure a sustainable growth and development path. Yet little has been done in this regard.

The 2030 Development Agenda should, therefore, according to Bárcena, reorient cooperation towards an integrated agenda that embraces economic development, social inclusion, and environmental sustainability. This agenda should, in her view, place equality at the center as an ethical principle and the ultimate goal of development. This means adopting a rights-based approach, which recognizes that all individuals are equal in rights—civil and political, as well as economic and social—and that they should have autonomy, recognition, and dignity. This requires a new equilibrium between state, market and society, in which the state would play the central role in developing and strengthening the necessary social covenants, though the balance between the three would necessarily be specific to each country.

The SDGs would be the central element of this agenda and, as agreed in the UN 2012 Conference on Sustainable Development (Rio+20), should be "action-oriented, concise, measurable and easy to communicate, limited in number, aspirational, global in nature and universally applicable to all countries." Other essential elements should be policy coherence at the international, regional, and national levels, and the recognition that development and market-oriented policies are not mutually exclusive.

One of the major issues in the implementation of the new integrated agenda would be guaranteeing the coherence between the negotiations and commitments adopted at different international forums, whether they relate to trade, climate, the environment, social issues, or finance. They also call for an equitable distribution of scientific and technological advances, for financing, and for strong multilateral institutions.

Finally, one of the most important elements in Bárcena's contribution is the emphasis she places on the role of the regional dimensions of cooperation.

Regional and sub-regional institutions are best placed to ensure the inclusion and protection of weaker players. Following the work of Elinor Ostrom, she argues that, instead of focusing only on global efforts—which remain important and part of a long-term solution—it is essential to simultaneously encourage polycentric efforts. This could be a better strategy to, for example, reduce the risks associated with the emission of greenhouse gases. This logic gives regional organizations more intellectual and political space to deal with such issues. Therefore, if cooperation faces important roadblocks at a global level, the regional level might contribute to achieving it through regional agreements, thanks to the greater homogeneity of the countries involved. In this regard, she underscores the fact that Latin America and the Caribbean have achieved a level of maturity that can enable it to propose and manage its own change and build its own regional agenda, including its ad hoc institutions for the provision of regional/global public goods.

* * * * *

The second part of the volume opens with a chapter by José Antonio Alonso on the development cooperation system. He starts by analyzing how that system has evolved in recent years: official development assistance (ODA) has tended to increase, though with a temporary reduction during the recent crisis, at a much slower rate than international private flows, and has been increasingly concentrated in low-income countries. The net effect is that the contribution of aid to the total sources of financing has become irrelevant in the case of the upper middle-income countries, but continues to be important for lower middle-income countries and, particularly, for low-income and least-developed countries, for which it continues to be by far the greatest source of international funding.

At the same time, the development agenda has significantly widened and mixed in several ways with the agenda of global and regional public goods generated by growing interdependence among countries. This fact, plus the lack of adequate elasticity of ODA, has generated the need to look for new resources to finance both aid and GPGs. These new resources have come to be called innovative sources of financing. At the same time, the number and diversity of aid providers has expanded, thanks to middle-income countries active in South-South cooperation and non-governmental actors.

Alonso contrasts these changes in the international cooperation system with the faster and deeper transformations that have occurred in the world economic system. He highlights four major changes. The first is the increasing heterogeneity of developing countries. The second is the new patterns of global poverty: the fact that we are living in a world with fewer people in extreme poverty, but with a growing number of people in the next categories, which can in many ways still be considered poor, and the fact that the poor are increasingly located in middle-income countries.

The third trend is the multipolarity generated by the growing share of developing counties in world GDP and trade, among others, with key emerging economies becoming important growth poles in their own region. The fourth is, as already indicated, the rising importance of GPGs, and the complex ways in which they interact with the development cooperation agenda. This suggests the need for an increasingly integrated perspective for both agendas.

In the face of these trends, Alonso argues that the development cooperation system faces two extreme options. The first would be to move fully into an integrated perspective, working through a differentiated agenda in accordance with the heterogeneous conditions of developing countries. The alternative would be to preserve aid as a focused policy, specialized in fighting extreme poverty almost exclusively in the poorest countries and fragile states.

The second perspective overestimates, in his view, the capacities of middle-income countries to overcome their own problems, neglecting the fact that some of them appear to be caught in middle-income traps and other vulnerabilities that may require international support. In spite of individual particularities, these traps refer mainly to three dimensions: good governance (they require more complex institutions to manage the problems of coordination that emerge in a more developed economy), financial and macroeconomic stability, and productive and technological change.

This leads him to opt for the first of these options as the desirable way forward, claiming that the general purpose of the cooperation system should be to correct the market failures that penalize the convergence of incomes between developed and developing countries, understanding that those obstacles change as countries develop. Furthermore, a perspective of this kind is, in his view, the only one that provides the adequate incentives to promote social and economic progress. These incentives are absent in a system in which only unsuccessful development is thought worthy of international support, a system that is also embedded with problems of moral hazard. What this implies is that, although aid should continue to be focused in low-income countries, the development cooperation system should also support some middle-income countries in their fight against poverty and breaking the middle-income traps.

The rise of new actors also calls for new governance structure. He analyzes in this context the advantages and weakness of the two major cooperation frameworks that have arisen in recent years: ECOSOC's Development Cooperation Forum and the Global Partnership for Effective Development Cooperation (Busan Partnership). The role of South-South cooperation should also be recognized in this structure, as well as the growing role of middle-income countries in the provision of global and, increasingly, regional public goods. More fundamentally, the aim should be, in Alonso's view, to define a new global approach to development policy that overcomes the traditional separation between donors and recipients on which the aid system has been based and establishes a new framework of common but differentiated responsibilities. In any case, he recognizes that the system could evolve in the opposite direction: a progressive loss of drive for development cooperation and the consequent relegation of international aid to a minor role in donor countries' priorities.

Chapter 5, by Bruce Jenks, analyzes the evolution of the UN's operational activities for development since its creation and the major challenges such activities face today. In the original conception, he argues, the UN system was based on the concept of communities of practice organized around specialized agencies, with ECOSOC playing loose coordination functions. However, this original conception was soon challenged by the logic of both the Cold War and decolonization. The first severely curtailed the room for international leadership, giving prominence to the UN as essentially an intergovernmental forum. The second saw the principle of state sovereignty strongly affirmed and transformed development cooperation into a mechanism for serving and transferring resources to new states.

The need for more integrated and coherent approaches to development became a recurring theme in the 1970s. The first great series of UN global conferences was then convened, but did not define a new agenda. In turn, following a series of reports that advocated for the need for an overall direction, the position of a Director-General for International Cooperation and Development was created, but divorced from real authority and access to resources. This at the end evolved into a "non-system." The allocation of resources was based on a "country-entitlement system," with resources being channeled by different agencies according to the priorities established by national governments.

The call for a global agenda came back in the 1990s, giving birth to what Jenks calls the "era of goals," and was a response to the need for a global sense of purpose after the end of the Cold War. This was reflected in the series of global conferences and summits—an amplified version of the trend initiated in the 1970s. It was also materialized in the definition of concrete, quantifiably global goals. The trend was initiated by the OECD's Development Assistance Committee, but achieved its full expression in the MDGs. This transformation also implied a major change in the nature of funding of the UN development system: in less than a decade, it was transformed from reliance on regular contributions to dependence on extra-budgetary resources.

The counter-reaction to the victory of vertical funding was the 2005 Paris Declaration on Aid Effectiveness, which again set the principle that the allocation of development resources had to be overseen and indeed decided upon by national authorities. In the UN system, the Annan Reforms instituted a better system of coordination, both in the normative area (the Executive Committee for Economic and Social Affairs) and one in the operational area (the United Nations Development Group, UNDG). The latter was mixed with managerial instruments to strengthen coordination at the country level: the UN Resident Coordinators, Development Assistance Frameworks and Common Country Assessment. The creation of two coordination mechanisms at the global level unfortunately led to a further gap between the operational and normative dimensions of the UN's work. The creation of the UNDG in turn created a trade-off between inclusiveness and the coherence that a small group of agencies can provide.

In the face of the challenges posed by the new realities of the international system, Jenks proposes a set of possible but not mutually exclusive strategies for the UN system: (i) coherence through global task forces (e.g., food, gender, HIV/AIDS), which should go beyond ad hoc task forces to drive more strategic allocation of resources within the system; (ii) country-level coherence, which has the advantage of ownership but may make it more difficult for the strategic repositioning and (wrongly) assumes that the effective delivery of resources will remain the critical lever for the UN's development system; (iii) UN system-wide governance, with two institutions playing a crucial role going forward: the High-Level Political Forum created in 2013 and ECOSOC's Development Cooperation Forum, created in 2007; (iv) deep integration of a selective and strategic character; (v) leadership by specific agencies in their own fields and by the United Nations Development Program (UNDP) for development cooperation as a whole; and (vi) changes in the financing model.

Each of the strategies has a useful contribution to make, but none of them will provide solutions on their own and must therefore be combined in creative ways. In Jenks' view, three essential elements must be taken into account. The first is that the urgent need for reform must not follow a reductionist logic, but should rather be leveraged on the rich historical legacy of the UN. The second is that for any reform process to be successful, form must always follow function. Lastly, without radical reform of the financing instruments, reform will remain wishful thinking. In the latter case, he points out that over half a century the system has been dominated by three models: financing communities of interest, transferring resources to member states, and allocating resources to goals. This last model has left the system today highly dependent on extra-budgetary resources and consequently project driven. Comprehensive reform of this model is essential to avoid going back to central funding.

The last chapter of the book, by Roy Culpeper, Stephany Griffith-Jones, and Daniel Titelman, deals with another major form of development cooperation: the role of multilateral development banks (MDBs). They start by underscoring the recognition of the role that MDBs have received in recent years in wider and ever-growing circles, as positive instruments to respond to the call for finance to serve the real economy, both to counter the procyclical pattern of private finance and support long-term development strategies. Interestingly, this is true not only of the developing world, but also the developed world, as the roles of the European Investment Bank and Germany's KfW testify.

One of the most interesting views developed in the chapter is the need to conceive development banks as a system—a "dense" institutional architecture—where synergies and complementarities exist between multilateral, regional, sub-regionals and national development banks. Thus, multilateral and regional development banks seem to perform their functions far better, such as providing counter-cyclical finance and supporting productive development, when they work closely with national development banks. Similarly, national development banks can operate better if they have the financial and technical support of MDBs.

One of the crucial roles of these institutions is their capacity to enhance access to different borrowers on an equitable basis. Most MDBs count with concessionary for relatively low-income countries and non-concessionary windows for middle-income ones, but the latter also promote access to countries with inadequate access to private capital markets and reduce financial costs. Equally important, most MDBs not only directly lend to the private sector, sometimes through finance corporations, but also use domestic private financial institutions as an intermediary for the funding of some activities, particularly lending to medium, small, and micro-enterprises. The corporations associated with MDBs can also contribute risk capital for new firms in the developing world. They are not substitutes but complements to private financial institutions.

The authors identify four basic functions that the system of development banking should provide. The first is counter-cyclical financing during crises. This function should be recognized as a central role of MDBs during the recent North Atlantic financial crisis, during which there was indeed a major increase in financing by the World Bank and the regional development banks. Such financing is complementary but distinct from the provision of official liquidity during crises by the IMF at the international level and by central banks at the national level (the European Central Bank in the euro area). Its major role is to support public-sector investment during crises and hopefully finance counter-cyclical public sector projects or support the reactivation of private sector investment. In order to enhance MDB's counter-cyclical capacity, the authors suggest that the number of instruments that are used for this purpose can be expanded. They include GDP-linked loans, counter-cyclical guarantees or loans that allow debt servicing holidays in the face of adverse external shocks, or regional guarantee agencies or funds to enable risk-sharing among neighboring countries with common interests.

The development functions are, of course, the essential reason why development banks were created in the first place. Infrastructure financing is a fundamental issue in this regard, for which there is a significant deficit in available financing. This deficit has been the center of the BRICS New Development Bank and the Chinese initiative to create the Asian Infrastructure Investment Bank. Financing of production sector development, particularly of innovative activities, has also figured into the agenda of some MDBs and has been central in the history of national development banks. And the whole development financing network plays a central role in facilitating the access of financing by small and medium-sized firms, and, more recently, supporting the development of microfinance.

Another key role of development banks is to mobilize larger resources for development, particularly to finance those developing countries that lack full access to private capital markets. One role that has received increasing attention is the blending of grants with loans from MDBs to increase financing for poorer countries. By co-financing projects with private banks, they are able to achieve additional leverage. By working collaboratively with national development banks, MDBs can also help deepen local currency bond markets. They can also be "market makers" for instruments such as GDP-linked bonds. MDBs and, particularly, regional development banks, can expand their financing of regional infrastructure.

Finally, a clearer recognition has emerged in recent years of the role that MDBs can play in the financing of global and regional public goods, specifically climate change mitigation and adaptation. Catastrophe financing is another line that could be expanded.

Looking ahead, the authors argue, financial turmoil and occasional crises can be expected, no matter how much financial reform takes place. The international community must thus have at its disposal a set of institutions in the form of well-capitalized MDBs. It could even create new institutions to support development efforts. In any case, the governance of these institutions should be at the center of the agenda, particularly to guarantee adequate participation of developing countries in their decision-making processes.

* * * * *

This volume is the product of a project undertaken together by Columbia University's Initiative for Policy Dialogue (IPD) and the United Nations Economic Commission for Latin America and the Caribbean (ECLAC). We are grateful for the support to this initiative by the Spanish Cooperation.

José Antonio Ocampo

Table of Contents

List of Figures

List of Tables

List of Boxes

List of Acronyms

AfDB	African Development Bank
AfDF	African Development Fund
AFT	Aid-for-Trade Initiative
BDC	Business Development Bank of Canada
BRICS	Brazil, Russia, India, China and South Africa
BWIs	Bretton Woods Institutions
CCRIF	Caribbean Catastrophe Risk Insurance Facility
CDRP	Common but Differentiated Responsibilities Principle
CELAC	Community of Latin American and Caribbean States
CG	Consultative Group
CGAP	Consultative Group to Assist the Poor
CIFs	Climate Investment Funds
DAC	Development Assistance Committee
DCF	UN Development Cooperation Forum
DESA	United Nations Department of Economic and Social Affairs
ECA	Europe and Central Asia
EC-ESA	Economic and Social Affairs Group
ECOSOC	United Nations Economic and Social Council
EIB	European Investment Bank
EMDCs	Emerging Markets and Developing Countries
EPTA	Expanded Program for Technical Assistance
ESMID	Efficient Securities Markets Institutional Development Initiative
EU	European Union
FDI	Foreign Direct Investment
GDP	Gross Domestic Product
GECC	Global Economic Coordination Council
GECC	Global Economic Coordination Council
GEMLOC	Global Emerging Markets Local Currency Bond Program
GNI	Gross National Income
GPEDC	Global Partnership for Effective Development Cooperation
HLTF	High-Level Task Force on Food Security
IBRD	International Bank of Reconstruction and Development

ICT	Information and Communications Technology
IDA	International Development Association
IEA	International Energy Agency
IFC	International Finance Corporation
IFFIm	International Finance Facility for Immunization
IFMC	International Monetary and Financial Committee
ILO	International Labor Organization
IMF	International Monetary Fund
IPF	Indicative Planning Figure
IPGs	International Public Goods
IPRs	Intellectual Property Rights
LAC	Latin America and the Caribbean
LDCs	Least Developed Countries
LICs	Low-Income Countries
LMICs	Lower Middle-Income Countries
MDBs	Multilateral Development Banks
MDGs	Millennium Development Goals
MENA	Middle East and North Africa
MICs	Middle-Income Countries
MPTF	Multi-Partner Trust Fund
NDB	New Development Bank
NDBs	National Development Banks
NTDS	Non-Traditional Development Assistance
O&M	Operations and Maintenance
ODA	Official Development Assistance
OECD	Organization for Cooperation and Development
OECD/DAC	Organisation for Economic Co-operation and Development's Development Assistance Committee
OWG	Open-Ended Working Group
OWGSDG	Open Working Group for Sustainable Development Goals
PPP	Purchasing Power Parity
PPPs	Public Private Partnerships
R/MDB	Regional/Multilateral Development Bank
R2P	Responsibility to Protect
RDBs	Regional Development Banks
REDD	Reducing Emissions from Deforestation and Forest Degradation

SDGs	Sustainable Development Goals
SIDBI	Small Industries Development Bank of India
SIDS	Small Island Developing States
SMEs	Small and Medium Enterprises
SSC	South-South Cooperation
SWFs	Sovereign Wealth Funds
Taiwan SMEG	Small and Medium Enterprise Credit Guarantee Fund of Taiwan
TOSD	Total Official Support for Development
UMICs	Upper Middle-Income Countries
UN	United Nations
UNASUR	South-American Union of States
UNCTAD	United Nations Conference on Trade and Development
UNDFC	Development Cooperation Forum of the United Nations Economic and Social Council
UNDG	United Nations Development Group
UNDP	United Nations Development Program
USGs	Universal Social Goods
WSS	Water and Sanitation Services
WTO	World Trade Organization

List of Contributors

José Antonio Alonso is Professor of Applied Economics at the Faculty of Economic Science of the Universidad Complutense of Madrid. Formerly Director of the Complutense Institute for International Studies.

Alicia Bárcena is Executive Secretary of the UN Economic Commission for Latin America and the Caribbean (ECLAC). Formerly UN Under-Secretary General for Management and Chef-de-Cabinet of the Secretary-General.

Donald Blondin is an independent consultant on public policy issues, with a special focus on issues of European regional cooperation and consumer protection.

Roy Culpeper is Senior Fellow, School of International Development and Global Studies, University of Ottawa. Formerly President of the North-South Institute, Ottawa.

Bruce Jenks is Adjunct Professor at School of International and Public Affairs at Columbia University. Formerly Assistant Secretary General at the United Nations Development Program (UNDP) responsible for UNDP's resource mobilization.

Stephany Griffith-Jones is Financial Markets Director, Initiative for Policy Dialogue, Columbia University. Formerly Professorial Fellow Institute of Development Studies, Sussex University.

Inge Kaul is adjunct professor at the Hertie School of Governance, Berlin. Formerly director of the Offices of Development Studies and the Human Development Report at UNDP, New York.

José Antonio Ocampo is Professor at the School of International and Public Affairs and co-President of the Initiative for Policy Dialogue at Columbia University. He is also Chair of the Committee for Development Policy of the United Nations Economic and Social Council (ECOSOC). He has been Under-Secretary-General for Economic and Social Affairs of the United Nations, Executive Secretary of the UN Economic Commission for Latin America and the Caribbean (ECLAC), and Minister of Finance of Colombia.

Daniel Titelman is Director of the Economic Development Division at the United Nations Economic Commission for Latin America and the Caribbean (ECLAC).

Part I

Global Governance: Institutions and Priorities

1

Global Economic and Social Governance and the United Nations System

José Antonio Ocampo

In recent years the world has experienced a remarkable contrast between strong adverse economic, social, and environmental trends, and the weakness of the international system of governance to manage them. These adverse trends include, among others, the global effects of the North-Atlantic financial crisis,[1] the threats generated by climate change, and the growing income inequality that affects a large number of countries. In the face of these challenges, the response of the international community has been weak. The major innovation during the recent economic crisis was the creation of the Group of 20 (G-20) at the leaders' level. However, this ad hoc intergovernmental group poses many questions of legitimacy and—after a good start, in which it helped the world avoid another Great Depression—its effectiveness has been mixed. In turn, the European system of governance, the most developed in the world, has shown many weaknesses and even a regression during the recent crisis to a dominantly intergovernmental process, led by the most powerful countries in the European Union.

This chapter takes a broad look at the system of global economic and social governance. "Economic" is understood in a broad sense, to include also environmental sustainability. Its focus is on the UN *system*, understood also in broad terms and thus encompassing the specialized agencies (including the International Monetary Fund [IMF] and the World Bank) and the World Trade Organization (WTO), which should formally become part of the UN system. We also refer in several parts to the UN *Organization,* defined as the UN Secretariat, Funds, and Programs—i.e., those organizations that are under the direct mandate of the UN General Assembly. The chapter is divided into six sections. The first considers the objectives of international cooperation. The next two analyze the essential dilemmas and challenges posed by the design of the system of global governance. The fourth and fifth consider the role of an apex organization and of the UN Economic and Social Council

(ECOSOC) in terms of guaranteeing the coherence of the system. The last presents some conclusions.

1 THE OBJECTIVES OF INTERNATIONAL COOPERATION

Following Ocampo (2010) and United Nations (2010, ch. VI), it is possible to differentiate three basic objectives of international cooperation in the economic and social fields:

- Managing interdependence among nations
- Promoting common social norms and standards, and the associated provision of a minimum level of social services for all world citizens
- Reducing international inequalities, in particular different levels of economic development among countries.

This typology coincides with the historical origin of international institutions. So, most mechanisms of cooperation created prior to the First World War were related to the management of interdependence: navigation treaties, controlling the spread of contagious diseases, interconnections of telegraph and postal services, the first treaties on intellectual property rights (IPRs), cooperation on statistical information, etc. The creation of the International Labor Organization in the Treaty of Versailles gave birth to the second form of cooperation; to a lesser extent, the League of Nations also made contributions in this field, although its overriding objectives (and failures) were political. These two forms of cooperation were further expanded after the Second World War (WW2). The third form of cooperation was born in the aftermath of WW2 and was closely interlinked with the dismantling of the colonial order.

Of course, all forms of international cooperation blossomed after WW2 and became more elaborate with time. In the first field, it includes, among others, the creation of the IMF in 1944, GATT in 1947, and WTO in 1994 (after the failed creation of ITO in the 1948 Havana Charter), and the late arrival of cooperation in the environmental field, which started with the United Nations Conference on the Human Environment held in Stockholm in 1972. The second includes the design of an elaborate decentralized system of specialized agencies, funds, and programs of the UN system, as well as the inclusion of economic and social rights in the 1948 Universal Declaration of Human Rights, their further development in the 1966 International Covenant of Economic, Social, and Cultural Rights, the approval of a multitude of UN conventions in the social field, and the principles and plans of action agreed since the 1970s in the UN conferences and summits. The third includes, among many others, the early reorientation of the International Bank for

Reconstruction and Development (the main pillar of the World Bank group) from European reconstruction to financing developing countries, the launch of official development assistance (ODA), and UN technical cooperation in the late 1940s, the creation of the World Bank's International Development Association (IDA) in 1960, and the inclusion of the principle of "special and differential treatment" in trade agreements, under the leadership of the United Nations Conference on Trade and Development (UNCTAD), created in 1964.

But beyond their sequential historical origin, the three forms of cooperation are conceptually distinct in terms of both the demands for international cooperation and the relations with national sovereignty. The three also have their parallels in the systems of national governance. The first is the only one that responds to economists' criteria of the need for collective action to avoid the under- or over-provision of the goods or services that are non-rival and non-excludable in consumption (these being the attributes of what welfare economics defines as public goods), or that generate strong externalities (positive and negative, respectively) through their consumption or production. So, cooperation in this domain relates to issues of (economic) *efficiency*, whereas those that relate to the second and third objectives of cooperation relate to *equity*—equality of citizens and of nations, respectively (see Table 1.1).

At the national level, the demand for collective action to avoid such under- or over-provision is reflected in the assumption by the state of the responsibility for supplying or regulating the provision of these goods and services, but the collective action problem can and is usually solved by different forms of communal or private (generally non-for-profit) cooperation. At the international level, the demand for collective action to manage interdependence requires in this case handing in or, better, *sharing* national autonomy—"responsible sovereignty" in the terms of Kaul (2013) and Kaul and Blundin (2016), a term that is further discussed in Section 1.2.

Table 1.1 The objectives of international cooperation

	Global Public Goods (GPGs)	Universal Social Goods (USGs)	Development Cooperation
Objective	Managing interdependence	Promoting common social norms and standards	Reducing international inequalities
Basic aim	Efficiency	Equality of citizens	Equality of nations
Demand for cooperation	Collective action to manage interdependence	Adopting and monitoring common norms and standards	Asymmetric rules, transferring financial resources, enhancing policy space
Relation to national sovereignty	Responsible sovereignty	Traditional sovereignty, embedded in universal values	Traditional sovereignty, within the limits of interdependence

Looking at it in greater detail, the first form of cooperation embraces at least four issues: (i) the provision of "pure" global/regional public goods in the economists' sense of the term (non-rival and non-excludable); (ii) goods with significant externalities; (iii) managing of the global/regional commons; and (iv) shared infrastructure and networks (critical for telecommunications and, prior to them, the postal system).

In the second form of cooperation, the call for collective action is *not* associated with externalities or the *technical* attributes that economists define as intrinsic to public goods. Furthermore, it is consistent with the principles of national sovereignty in the traditional (Westphalian) sense, as nation-states (and/or local governments within them) continue to play the essential role in managing the associated public domain, though subject to their commitment to abide by universally-agreed norms and standards.

In this case, the origin of "publicness" is the definition by society of certain goods, services, or rules as worthy because of their inherent *social* rather than *technical* attributes. They refer to those goods and services that society decides should be guaranteed to all independently of their capacity to pay, and the rules that citizens should respect in their interaction with each other (e.g., non-discrimination, protection of weaker members of society, etc.). They can also be seen as the definition by society of certain realms in which citizens are equal by the nature of being citizens. Therefore, the concept relates to Musgrave's (1959) definition of "merit goods" or what ECLAC (2000) defined as "goods of social value" rather than to the economists' concept of public goods. In their provision or the enforcement of the associated rules, the nation-state continues to exercise full autonomy, though following internationally-agreed principles/norms. So, it rather responds to the concept of "sovereignty embedded in broader values and principles"—the concept that, as Jenks (2016) argues, was at the center of early post-WW2 conceptions of international cooperation.

In turn, the third form of cooperation is also related to the demand for equality, but in this case of equality among *nations*. Its counterpart at the national level is policies adopted to reduce inequalities among countries' regions. It encompasses both the transfer of financial resources (at the national level essentially through the fiscal system) and also the definition of preferences in economic regulations or taxation for the benefit of the less advanced regions. Similarly, at the international level, it involves a transfer of resources (ODA or the European cohesion funds, for example), special credit channels for developing countries, or rules that create preferences for them.

As in the previous case, the traditional concept of sovereignty prevails in this form of cooperation. Furthermore, it can be argued that, to the extent that lower levels of development and the economic interdependence generated by globalization reduce the room for the effective exercise of sovereignty, international cooperation should aim at enhancing such sovereignty—thus increasing the "policy space," to use the concept that was coined in UN (particularly UNCTAD) debates.

This area of cooperation is related to mitigating the asymmetries that characterize the international economic system. In this regard, three contemporary asymmetries should be underscored: (i) the technological and productive, which relate to the fact that technological progress is highly concentrated in a few developed countries and its diffusion is imperfect and made costlier by intellectual property rights (IPRs); (ii) the financial and macroeconomic, which relate to the fact that the global monetary system rests on national/regional currencies from developed countries and that there is a significant degree of financial market segmentation, which limits the room of maneuver of developing countries to adopt counter-cyclical macroeconomic policies; and (iii) the asymmetries in the degree of mobility of factors of production, in particular limited mobility of unskilled labor vs. skilled labor and, particularly, of capital (Ocampo 2001).

Under these conditions, rules that do not take into account these asymmetries will tend to reproduce or deepen international inequalities. For this reason, the international system has agreed that global rules (in trade, investment, finance, and IPRs) should follow the principle of "special and differential treatment" for countries at lower levels of development. But the scope of this treatment has been very limited in practice and its effectiveness has been weak. The UN also developed around the 1992 Rio Earth Summit the principle of "common but differentiated responsibilities." This is a better concept, as it underscores the different responsibilities and capacities that countries at different level of development have to contribute to global action, but also recognizes the responsibility that developing countries have in an interconnected world. Furthermore, it can be said that the latter should be equally "differentiated" in a world in which the developing world is increasingly diverse.

The concept of "global public goods" (GPGs) derived from the economic literature[2] does not encompass all forms of international cooperation. There are two alternatives in relation to this concept: to restrict its use to the first form of cooperation, or to use it in a broader sense to encompass the three forms of cooperation. The latter alternative tends to coincide with the use of the concept of "public goods" by non-economists, particularly in the political and even the popular discourses. These discourses define as "public" those areas that nations/citizens define as of general interest, therefore belonging to the public domain.[3] However, I will follow here the first of these options, defining GPGs in a broad sense and thus including goods with significant externalities, as well as global commons and infrastructure. This implies that, aside from GPGs, there are two other objectives of international cooperation: the provision of universal social goods (USGs) and development cooperation (understood as cooperation with developing countries).[4]

Needless to say, globalization has certainly strengthened the need for cooperation to manage interdependence—the first dimension—but has also generated challenges in the other two dimensions, notably the limitations of the "policy space" that nation-states have in an increasingly interdependent world to provide USGs and to adopt certain economic policies (e.g., counter-cyclical macroeconomic policies or some types of industrial policies). In turn, in all areas, international cooperation faces two crucial problems: (i) the incomplete character of the international agenda and (ii) the weak mechanisms for monitoring, accountability, and ultimately, enforceability of international commitments. I will look carefully at the second issue below and concentrate on the first one here.

This problem includes an incomplete set of institutions and asymmetry between the agenda and instruments for action. Needless to say, the incomplete character of the agenda reflects power relations. This bias is reflected in the different degree of development of international organizations in at least three ways: the nature of decision-making processes (which also follow different models in different organization), inadequate financing, and the different degrees of autonomy given to different organizations, particularly in relation to most powerful countries, including the power and autonomy of the Secretariats[5] of different international organizations.

For example, the incomplete map of cooperation in the first domain is reflected in the fact that there are areas where cooperation is accepted and relatively well developed (contagious diseases, international trade, and transportation rules), others in which there are agreements but also significant gaps (climate change, global macroeconomic and financial stability), and some in which there are no or very limited cooperation (economic migration and tax cooperation, for example). There also are "transnational private regulations," many times imposed by powerful private parties through practice or contracts (e.g., labeling and quality standards) and even endorsed by states (e.g., accounting standards) or international institutions (e.g., "best practices" in certain areas) (Cafaggi and Pistor 2013). More generally, vacuums in the intergovernmental "regulatory space" will tend to be filled by powerful nations or powerful private actors. Migration norms may be the best example of the first type; accounting standards and even the management of the internet, of the second.

The UN system has been at the center of all forms of cooperation, again encompassing the Bretton Woods Institutions (BWIs). The BWIs and WTO have, of course, a central role in the first and third. Any meaningful reform of global cooperation must, therefore, have the United Nations system at the center.

2 THE ESSENTIAL DILEMMA OF COOPERATION IN AN *INTER*NATIONAL SYSTEM

As it is widely recognized, the basic problem of all forms of *inter*national cooperation is the contrast between globalization and the national (or even local) domain of politics. This generates the unsettled relation that exists between globalization and the nation-state, which is essential to the questions regarding the nature of sovereignty raised in Section 1. The challenges this issue poses can be illustrated with a contrast between two "paradoxes" that have been proposed in the literature to analyze this relation: Kaul's (2013) "sovereignty paradox" and Rodrik's (2011) "globalization paradox."

Kaul defines the sovereignty paradox in the following terms: governments "are losing policymaking sovereignty, because they hold on to conventional strategies of realizing sovereignty, which may make them shy away from international cooperation. But, in policy fields marked by GPG-type challenges and interdependence, such behavior actually undermines rather than strengthens states' policymaking capacity" (Kaul 2013, p. 34). To overcome this problem, she proposes—following a tradition in this field—the notion of responsible sovereignty, defined as sovereignty exercised in a way that is fully respectful of the sovereignty of others. On this basis, she proposes three essential commitments to guarantee a more effective multilateralism: (i) to voluntarily strengthen national-level management of cross-over spillovers, (ii) to protect any state's sovereignty if it comes under attack (with issues such as financial contagion, viruses, illicit trade, or cyber-security), and (iii) to cooperate in meeting global system risks (Kaul 2013, Box 2.3, p. 55).

In turn, Rodrik defines the globalization paradox as the result of the fact that "we cannot simultaneously pursue democracy, national determination, and economic globalization" (Rodrik, 2011, p. xviii). In his words: "Democracies have the right to protect their social arrangements, and when this right clashes with the requirements of the global economy, it is the latter that should give way," and therefore, "A thin layer of international rules that leaves substantial room for maneuver by national governments is a better globalization" (Rodrik, 2011, p. xix).

The problem with both formulations is that they are partial. In terms of the typology presented in Section 1, they apply to different domains of international cooperation. Kaul's responsible sovereignty should certainly be the rule in the first domain (GPGs), but it is unclear whether it applies to the second (USGs) or the third (development cooperation). In those two domains, and particularly since the nation-state is and will continue to be the space of political citizenship, the international system should not only respect national sovereignty in the traditional sense, but actually enhance the policy space of countries that have been traditionally constrained (economically and politically) from fully exercising it.

At the same time, however, when the exercise of national sovereignty can adversely affect other countries, because of interdependence (the domain of GPGs), full sovereignty in the traditional and Rodrik's sense cannot prevail.

So, the international system should be fully respectful of national decisions and of diversity of the international community that they generate, but such respect of sovereignty can only be exercised *within the limits of interdependence*. This is what has been clearly accepted in the trading system, which implies, for example, that subsidies should be internationally regulated and their exercise can be contested by countries that are negatively affected by other countries' use of them. It has been equally accepted in the realm of exchange rate management, where countries are free to choose the exchange rate regime they prefer, as long as they avoid "manipulating" it to the detriment of others. Similar principles should clearly apply to other areas, where they have so far not been accepted—for example, in relation to IPRs, investment rules, tax, or energy policies.

The complexity of this issue has, of course, increased due to two factors: the incomplete character of international arrangements—including the associated bias of the agenda and actions generated by world power relations—and the fact that globalization may weaken nation-states and therefore their capacity to exercise their "policy space" in social and economic development. Both generate strong arguments in favor of Rodrik's position: international governance structures should not constrain and should aim at enhancing the "policy space" of nation-states to promote social cohesion and economic development.

In any case, the fact that interdependence weakens the space of nation-states, and that such space may not be fully recreated by the best international arrangements, means that in the long run it is necessary to build democratic spaces of an international/global character as part of a (certainly slow and partial) transition to a *trans*national order. But so far the efforts in this area have rendered at best partial results, as reflected in the European debates regarding the "democratic deficit" of its regional institutions—a deficit that may have increased in recent years.

In this regard, the best development at the global level is the role that global civil society plays in enhancing international cooperation, a role that has been captured by the UN Intellectual History Project's concept of the "three UNs": the intergovernmental, the Secretariat, and civil society (Jolly et al. 2008). Of course, the international role of civil society predates the creation of the UN, as it includes, among many others, the anti-slavery movement, the struggle of the sequence of socialist internationals for better labor standards, the fight of the international feminist movement for the women's right to vote, and the most recent international movement to enhance the rights of indigenous peoples. In any case, it is an incomplete development, both because international civil society is not entirely a democratic force (in particular, its representatives are not elected by the full citizenship) and because at the global level it is still largely dominated by civil society organizations from the developed countries.

3 BUILDING A BETTER GLOBAL GOVERNANCE STRUCTURE

The need for international cooperation in the three realms that have been identified, and the tensions that are inherent in international cooperation, pose a series of demands on the international system. These demands help to define six criteria to design a better global governance structure—and, by parallelism, to analyze the strengths and weaknesses of current structures.

The first criterion is that any system of international governance should be based on *strong subsidiary principles*. This concept was coined in European debates but has a long history in the practice of federalism at the national level. This principle not only involves respect for the policy space of nations but also the use—indeed, the reinforcement—of national state capacities to implement international agreements, rather than the creation of organizations that replace national decision making and policy implementation.

At the same time, the international system is a complex one, as it encompasses countries of very diverse sizes and levels of development. For this reason, the regional dimension is important, particularly to strengthen the voice of the weak nations and to create additional mechanisms to cooperate with them. This is again based on old federalist principles: regional and subregional institutions give stronger voice and a sense of ownership to smaller countries. These institutions are, therefore, more likely to respond to their demands. For this reason, *a dense network of global, regional, and national institutions* is both a more effective system of international cooperation as well as one that is more balanced in terms of power relations. This is the second criterion for a better global governance structure.

The third is the need to *overcome the tension between inclusiveness—and the legitimacy associated with it—and effectiveness*. The main concern in this regard is that smaller decision-making bodies are generally more effective, both for consensus building and for implementing a set of agreements. The major challenge is, of course, how to avoid existing power relations from dominating those smaller bodies, thus eliminating the voice of small and less powerful countries. Many analysts (particularly defenders of the G-7/8 and G-20) tend to assume that effectiveness requires small bodies dominated by the most powerful countries and that representative bodies are inherently ineffective. This is implicit in Bradford and Lim's (2011) formulation of this dilemma as a "trade-off between achieving legitimacy as a representative body and achieving legitimacy as an effective body." But this view is in sharp contrast to the traditional democratic principles' claim that more representative institutions are ultimately more effective, particularly because of their capacity to generate stable consensus. Furthermore, given the fact that different actors may have different interests in the issues of the global agenda, a "variable geometry" of decision-making bodies according to the issues in the global agenda may be a better structure than one in which decision making is always in the hands of the most powerful countries.

The international community has resolved the tension between inclusiveness and effectiveness in several ways. The worst model (which does not belong to the economic and social sphere) is, no doubt, the veto power granted to the five permanent members of the UN Security Council, which can be characterized as a fossilized system of exclusion. It can further be argued that it has not been a very effective decision-making body and that the abundant reform proposals on the table are unlikely to make it more effective. The alternative UN decision-making rule used by the General Assembly—"one country, one vote"—is clearly the most inclusive and has facilitated consensus building, but frequently leads the powerful countries to disregard the associated decisions. In particular, in relation to economic issues, it has led to what Toye and Toye call the "twin-track system": "The UN General Assembly provides a world forum where economic ideas, interests and policy proposals are presented, discussed, and negotiated. Its authority is, and can continue to be, a moral authority [...] Once the process of UN discussion and negotiation produces agreements, however, their implementation is delegated to executive agencies in which the countries that will foot most of the subsequent bills place their confidence" (Toye and Toye 2004, p. 280). However, their inclusive character implies that, under any arrangement, the UN General Assembly and ECOSOC should be recognized as the most open and democratic and, therefore, as the most appropriate forums for debate and consensus building.

The model followed by the BWIs mixes weighted voting and constituencies—and thus, power relations—with universal participation. Power relations are embedded in quotas/capital, which follow a "one dollar, one vote" principle. Although they have not become fossilized, as in the UN Security Council, the process of redefining them has been slow, painful, and certainly incomplete in recent years. It is mixed with a small share of basic votes that follow the "one country, one vote" principle, and which have been increased in recent reforms to protect small and poor countries. In turn, universal participation is pursued through a constituency system, which allows all countries to have a voice in decision making through the constituency to which they belong. An appropriate use of this system, which would require a dynamic estimation of quotas/capital according to agreed criteria with a larger share of basic votes, may provide the best way to mix representation with recognition of power relations. Such criteria would tend to deviate in significant ways from those currently in use and could change from one organization to another, as reflected in the different criteria used in recent IMF and World Bank reforms.

Another interesting model is the WTO model, based on consensus building through a system of "concentric circles," to use the term coined by the former WTO Director General Pascal Lamy.[6] It is a bottom-up approach, in which negotiations are made among representatives of certain coalitions, which should then respond back to those coalitions (and in this way, it is supposed to be transparent). It is an inclusive system, as all delegations are included in the negotiations and have to be part of the final decision, which should be based on the principle of consensus. In practice, however, this system has proven to be relatively ineffective in terms of decision making and includes elements of inequality, particularly arm-twisting against weaker members.

The model that I have called "elite multilateralism" (Ocampo 2011) is certainly suboptimal relative to the previous two. This model has been followed by the G-7/8 and in financial regulation (the Basel Committee on Banking Supervision) for some decades, and it is now used in the G-20 and the Financial Stability Board. As we will see in relation to the G-20, it has only been partly effective, involves areas of major conflicts of interests for its members and is ad hoc and exclusionary in its composition. It generates, therefore, significant problems of legitimacy. This implies that formal representative institutions (treaty-based organizations) should be preferred to ad hoc intergovernmental grouping (Gs), which can nonetheless play a role in consensus building in representative institutions—if we want, as part of a process of "concentric circles."

A major form of exclusion has historically been the inheritance of the unequal economic and political (colonial) order upon which the current institutions were originally built and which tended to discriminate against developing countries. So, the fourth criterion of better institutional structures is the *equitable participation of developing countries in decision making* and, particularly, *economic* decision making. A central issue in this regard is the unfinished process of increasing "voice and participation" of developing countries in the BWIs. Beyond that, however, this criterion refers to the place that the UN occupies in the international order. As the de-colonization process proceeded in the post-war years, the UN became the organization in which developing countries had the broadest participation and strongest voice; for that basic fact, it is their preferred forum. This is also true of civil society. For both reasons, the UN should not be sidelined in economic debates, as it is clearly the most open global forum for debate and consensus building.

In rethinking the role that developing countries should play in the global order, the Rio principle of "common but differentiated responsibilities" should be the guide. However, with the increasing heterogeneity of developing countries and the rise of some of them to leadership at the global level, the system has become more complex. The major "emerging economies" clearly have growing responsibilities in the global order. The addendum of "and respective capabilities" to said Rio principle introduced by the UN Framework Convention on Climate Change have thus acquired increasing relevance. In any case, the responsibilities of major emerging economies have to be differentiated from those of major developed countries, as they still are developing countries (as reflected, for example, in their technological dependence or the high share of low-productivity agents or sectors in their economies) and, given existing arrangements and past history, have a differentiated role in certain areas (for example, they do not manage global reserve currencies and have contributed much less to climate change). What all this means is that although major emerging economies cannot be treated simply as weaker partners (as the older principle of "special and differential treatment" implied), they should not be considered partners with equal responsibilities or capabilities to those of developed countries.

A fifth demand on the system of governance is the need to design *effective instruments of monitoring, accountability for, and compliance with international commitments*. Again, the world system of governance has struggled to find appropriate instruments to fulfill this demand. The best developed is, no doubt, the WTO dispute settlement, which has created an international judicial body to guarantee compliance and allows countries to retaliate against those who do not fulfill their obligations. The major weakness of this framework is the unequal capacity to retaliate that different countries have. Another strong mechanism has been the Montreal Protocol, which is clearly recognized as a model for environmental agreements. According to existing analysis, its specific advantages were the clear identification of chemical substances that affected the ozone layer, the availability of technological alternatives, the limited time horizon the agreement involved, and full respect to the differentiated responsibilities of developing countries (they were given more time and financing to adjust).

International conventions are an intermediate case. When they have become national law, in principle the domestic judicial system is in charge of guaranteeing their implementation—a principle that may, of course, operate in an imperfect way in many national settings. Beyond that, the international reporting to and monitoring through the treaty bodies (committees) create a mechanism to check compliance with the conventions' provisions. The monitoring of core ILO and human rights conventions are the best examples. The pressure exercised by these bodies may have some effects, but they only exercise moral sanctions, whose effectiveness has proven to be weak. An additional and perhaps more effective mechanism may be the pressure exercised by international and national civil society on governments to comply with the conventions.

Peer review is another intermediate framework. It is extensively practiced by the OECD, and has been introduced by the African Union and the Human Rights Council, with less effectiveness. It was also proposed after the 2005 UN Summit for the follow up by ECOSOC of global summits and conferences but it was only accepted in a diluted version (as the voluntary presentations that came to be known as the "Annual Ministerial Reviews").

Well-developed surveillance mechanisms include IMF Article IV consultations and WTO's "Trade Policy Reviews," but their recommendations are again non-binding, although under exceptional circumstances, they could lead to limited sanctions. As a result of the criticism that Article IV consultations may reflect the views of the most powerful countries, and in any case exercise only weak influence upon them,[7] there has been an attempt to increase their profile and make them more "candid" and "evenhanded" since the North-Atlantic financial crisis. Several mechanism of multilateral surveillance have also been added: the "Consolidated Multilateral Surveillance Report," the "spillover reports" for the "systemic 5" (U.S., U.K., Eurozone, Japan, and China), the "External Sector Reports," and the obligation of 25 jurisdictions with systemically important financial sectors to undertake Financial Sector Assessments Programs. It remains to be seen whether this more elaborate monitoring apparatus will make its influence felt. In the case of the WTO, of course, the "Trade Policy Reviews" are matched by an effective dispute settlement mechanism.

In the UN, the follow up to the Millennium Development Goals (MDGs) was a significant innovation in terms of monitoring, which has been supported by the World Bank's "Global Monitoring Reports." The follow up of the MDGs included not only a well-developed statistical information system and periodic global evaluations, but also high profile national evaluations. This system could be used to develop an improved system to monitor the Sustainable Development Goals (SDGs) that are the core of the 2030 Development Agenda approved by the UN General Assembly in September 2015, which could thus include global monitoring, high-profile domestic monitoring and debates, and peer reviews in the context of ECOSOC.[8] Again, pressure from international civil society and the rising number of follow-up mechanisms that civil society has put in place are a very important complement to these intergovernmental processes.

Beyond some specific cases already mentioned, the Secretariats of different organizations play an essential role in terms of independent monitoring and (sometimes) implementation of approved decisions. Of course, Secretariats also perform an additional function: providing neutral technical support to individual countries, which is particularly important for the weaker members of world organizations. Furthermore, independent Secretariats usually go beyond these functions to advance novel initiatives, help mediate disputes, and identify the common ground on which global agreements might be forged.

Given the relation between sovereignty and governance structures outlined in Sections 1–2, the nature of accountability for international commitments also depends upon the objective of cooperation we look at. Compliance is critical in relation to areas that involve interdependence. As there is a strong role for traditional sovereignty in the second and most of the third areas of cooperation, monitoring and non-binding accountability mechanisms—peer reviews, committees that follow up the implementation of conventions, and high-profile national debates—are more appropriate instruments. However, when the second form of cooperation involves some form of rights (prohibition of slavery, basic labor rights, non-discrimination against women, children's rights), the global community should design a stronger form of accountability. Indeed, this new accountability could be understood as a sort of "responsibility to protect," the principle that has been agreed upon in the political area. Compliance may also be essential in relation to some of the elements of the third objective of cooperation, particularly when they involve rules that guarantee differential treatment for developing countries.

The final demand on global governance is the *coherence of the system*, again of the broader UN system and the WTO. However, this should *not* be understood as a centralized coordination mechanism, as this would be impossible to implement in a system that was designed to be radically decentralized. Similarly, the different governance structures in place imply that some level of duplication may be appropriate. For example, it would be a major mistake to eliminate UN debates on global financial and trade issues, based on the idea that these issues are under the responsibility of the BWIs and WTO, respectively. As already pointed out, the fact that the UN General Assembly and ECOSOC are the most open forums implies that they can play a useful role in giving voice on these issues to actors (including both small countries and civil society) that would have a weak voice in other contexts. In contrast, the proliferation of new issue-oriented agreements may have some virtues in terms of ownership of these processes by the relevant actors and the efficacy that is associated with that ownership, but run the risk of further undermining the coherence of a system.

The idea of strengthening the coordination mechanisms is behind several proposals to create an apex organization, the most recent being that by the Commission of Experts Convened by the President of the UN General Assembly on Reforms of the International Monetary and Financial System (referred to as the UN Stiglitz Commission) (United Nations 2009). On top of that, ECOSOC is endowed by the UN Charter to serve as the basic instrument of coordination of the UN system. We will take a look at both in Sections 3–4, in the first case together with an analysis of the capacity of the G-20 to fulfill its self-designated mandate. There is also an interagency mechanism, the Chief Executives Board (CEB), that plays a coordination role, but this will not be analyzed in this chapter.

4 A GLOBAL ECONOMIC COORDINATION COUNCIL

The proposals to create an apex organization with the capacity to direct and coordinate the UN *system* have been on the agenda for the past two decades.

In 1992, the UNDP's *Human Development Report* proposed replacing ECOSOC, which it deemed "too large and unwieldy," with a 22-member Development Security Council, with three basic functions: (i) designing global policy frameworks in all key economic and social areas, providing a policy coordination framework; (ii) preparing a global budget of development resource flows; and (iii) providing a policy coordination framework for the smooth functioning of international development and financial institutions.[9] The term "Economic Security Council" was coined three years later by the Commission on Global Governance (1995). In both cases, the idea was to replace ECOSOC with the new body.[10] Similarly, the 2006 High-Level Panel on System-Wide Coherence proposed the creation of a Global Leaders' Forum of ECOSOC (also called L-27, as it would be made up by half the membership of the Council) (United Nations 2006, par. 59). Others have simply proposed reforms to reinvigorate the existing ECOSOC, to a large extent under the assumption that the Council has already been given by the UN Charter the responsibility to coordinate the system.

The most interesting recent proposal was that made in 2009 by the UN Stiglitz Commission to create a Global Economic Coordination Council (GECC). According to this proposal, the GECC would meet at the Heads-of-State level (like the current G-20) and would enjoy the formal support of a subset of existing UN system entities—the UN Secretariat, ILO, IMF, and World Bank—as well as WTO. It would also have the capacity to interact with and direct all parts of the system, broadly understood to include all the specialized agencies like the World Bank Group and the IMF, as well as WTO, which would be brought into the system. It would be a small decision-making body (or bodies, if we eventually add ministerial bodies), which would combine the participation of systemically important countries with universal representation. This would be guaranteed with a constituency system similar to that of the BWIs, with weighted votes that would mix the two ingredients previously mentioned: basic votes and economic weight. In terms of former proposals of a UN Development or Security Council, there are, therefore, two basic differences in the GECC proposal: representation based on constituencies, and the creation of a new institution instead of an evolution of the existing ECOSOC, which would continue to function in a parallel institution and as one of the principal organs of the UN *Organization*.

The capacity to coordinate the system would imply that the GECC would direct and coordinate all institutions that are part of the UN *system*, as well as identify areas of cooperation among them. It would also have as special responsibilities the identification of gaps in the current system of cooperation (e.g., the absence of a restructuring mechanism for sovereign debt, or effective instruments of international cooperation in tax matters) and of spillovers among the areas of responsibilities of individual agencies that would need attention (e.g., environmental effects of trade policies and social effects of budgetary policies). It would leave to the more specialized bodies the specific decisions in their area of work, but it could also convene ministerial meetings to handle some issues. For example, although some global monetary decisions could be left to the International Monetary and Financial Committee (IMFC), some broader global economic decisions may require new (one time or recurrent) ministerial meetings or bodies, mixing finance ministers with those in charge of other aspects of economic affairs (e.g., those directly related to the issues of domestic production, such as industry ministries).

Weighted voting would be a difficult principle to accept by those countries that defend the UN principle of "one country, one vote," as well as the balanced regional representation in elected bodies. However, the GECC proposal recognizes the fact that no relevant system of global economic government can operate without the most important countries being part of the decision-making body. Otherwise, they would simply tend to ignore its decisions. Of course, the specific weighting mechanism would have to overcome the problems of representation that the BWIs currently face. The gain for smaller countries is, of course, that the powerful members of the international community would be coordinated by a representative universal body in which they have voice, rather than by one that the powerful countries appoint (or more accurately, self-appoint).

According to this proposal, ECOSOC would continue to be the intergovernmental organ in charge of the economic, social, and environmental responsibilities given to the UN *Organization*. As we will see in Section 5, specific and highly important global functions could be conferred upon this Council, reinforcing its current role. The UN General Assembly will also continue to play an important role in global economic governance, reflecting its capacity to serve as an effective mechanism for consensus building and generating new ideas for international cooperation. In this regard, the convening of UN summits and conferences has been one of the most important developments. The UN Secretariat will also continue to play an important role, through its main departments: the UN Department of Economic and Social Affairs (UN-DESA), UNCTAD,[11] and the UN regional commissions. The UN has also made important contributions to these debates through convening high-level technical groups, such as (in the area of global finance) the Zedillo and Stiglitz Commissions (United Nations 2001 and 2009, respectively).

As recent international negotiations have shown, it may be difficult to reach agreement on most of the issues that are of crucial importance for the world. Negotiations can also lead to the least common denominator, which would be seen by many as a disappointment. In this context, as Ocampo and Stiglitz (2011) have proposed, the GECC could facilitate the creation of initiatives of "adhesion," where a large body of countries would lead cooperative actions in some area of global or regional concern, and others would join in at some later date. The GECC would, of course, also perform a crucial role exploring and developing areas of common interest and finding partial or broader bases of agreement in critical yet controversial areas, which would then be adopted by the decision-making bodies of other organizations (e.g., the United Nations Framework Convention on Climate Change in relation to climate change issues, or IMFC and the IMF Board in relation to the reforms of the international monetary system).

A basic question pertains to the relation between this body and the G-20 as a Leaders' Forum, the major innovation introduced in global governance during the recent North-Atlantic financial crisis. This is particularly important, as the G-20 took the decision at the September 2009 Pittsburgh Summit to designate itself as, "the premier forum for our international economic cooperation" (G-20 2009, par. 19). Needless to say, the creation of this body was a step forward in relation to the G-7/8, as it recognized the role that emerging economies play in today's global economy and the shifting global economic power relations associated with that fact. In turn, for emerging economies, coordinating actions with major industrial economies continues to be essential, given their vulnerability to adverse shocks from developed countries and their still-limited capacity to replace the old engines of world economic growth.

The G-20 has played a positive role: through coordinated expansionary policies, it avoided another Great Depression; it launched the initiative to strengthen financial regulation worldwide, giving that responsibility to the Financial Stability Board (previously Forum), which coordinates the efforts of a series of specialized bodies, which now include all G-20 as well as other members; it approved the largest issue of Special Drawing Rights (SDRs) in history, increased the resources available to the IMF, and promoted a reform in the capital/quotas and voting power of the BWIs; it created the most promising mechanism of macroeconomic policy consultation among major economies; and it avoided the repetition of the protectionist trends that destroyed the world trading system in the 1930s.

However, its record has been mixed. Ocampo and Stiglitz (2011) analyze its performance from the point of view of five principles that should underlie a good system of international governance: leadership, effectiveness, representation (which is the basic source of legitimacy), capacity to coordinate the system, and reliance on a secretariat that independently monitors, and in some cases implements, the approved decisions. Based on these criteria, they come to the conclusion that the G-20 fulfills only the first criterion and partly the second and fourth. But it is not well endowed with the other characteristics that are essential for the body that should be the "premier forum for international economic cooperation."

Two of these issues deserve specific attention, particularly to evaluate the aforementioned tension between inclusiveness and effectiveness. In this regard, effectiveness was remarkable in the early years of the G-20 as a leaders' forum, reaching the April 2009 London Summit. But the early "Keynesian consensus," which had been the source of that success, broke down in the June 2010 Toronto Summit, reflecting the rise of the view that austerity was the road to a stable world economic recovery. Early evaluations showed that its effectiveness waned dramatically (see, for example, Woods 2011). When seen in the light of the outcomes of the global economy in 2012 and 2013, it is clear that it has been unable to generate its most important commitment: "strong, sustainable and balanced global growth" (G-20 2009, par. 13). Furthermore, the mission creep that characterizes rotating secretariats—in which each host adds issues that it considers relevant, in an attempt to place its seal on the agenda—have meant that its effectiveness has been further eroded through time.

It can be argued on strong grounds that the legitimacy associated with representation cannot be substituted in any way, as it is essentially derived in the international system, as in all modern democracies, from universality. The problem arises from limited membership and, in particular, the ad hoc method by which the Group has chosen its members.[12] This implies that it may not be the adequate body to discuss certain crucial issues, as the relevant actors may not be members. This includes, for example, issues related to least developed countries, none of which is a member, or even cooperation with developing countries, as the UK aside, of the most committed international donors (e.g., those that meet the UN official development assistance target) are not members.[13]

Furthermore, the way it operates tends to delegitimize the governance processes of other organizations. For example, when the G-20 reached an agreement in Seoul in November 2010 to reform the IMF's quota and voting shares, the G-20 members that represent constituencies in the Fund Board did not take into account the views of other members of their constituencies. The Board thus ended up endorsing the decisions of the most powerful countries while escaping the institutional constraints of having to take into account the views of less powerful Fund members. This generated a great paradox: the G-20 ended up eroding the governance principles of the institution that it has the most help to strengthen: the IMF. The Group's mission creep is thus likely to further erode the institutional structures that the world has so painfully built up after WW2.

The most important question relates to how to move forward. The strongest defendants of the G-20 (e.g., Martin 2011) argue that it should just be a "steering committee," particularly one that facilitates changes that generate a consensus among the most powerful countries. However, this would imply major changes in the way it operates, in particular avoiding sidestepping into the mandates and governance structures of representative international institutions.

A better perspective is to recognize that formal and informal mechanisms play a complementary role. As Dervis (2011, p. 195) has argued: "Both are needed. The informal gatherings can be more flexible, they can allow leaders or ministers to develop closer personal relationships. This setting allows relatively bold proposals to be made...." Interactions between formal and informal processes do play an important role in global governance, as they do in national politics, but such interactions would be better conceived as elements of the consensus-building efforts that lead to decisions within formal international institutions—i.e., as part of a system of "concentric circles" of consensus building, to use again Lamy's concept. This is, for example, the role that the Group of 77 plays in the United Nations, and the Group of 24 in the Bretton Woods Institutions. Informal dialogues are indeed very useful building blocks in formal institutional decision making. Furthermore, the interaction between formal and informal processes works best when it facilitates a variable geometry of informal dialogues, as not all countries are equally relevant for specific international decisions.

The essence of the argument is, therefore, in the words of Ocampo and Stiglitz (2011, p. 4), "[N]o matter how 'representative' a given informal dialogue is, or how powerful its members are, it can never substitute for regular multilateral decision making within formally constituted international organizations. If they attempt to do so, the informal bodies end up generating serious problems of legitimacy, tend to amplify the inequalities in decision making power among constituent members, and can eviscerate existing more democratic—and more functional—governance structures."

For this reason, the G-20 should be seen as a transition to a more representative, and thereby legitimate, mechanism of international economic cooperation. The Stiglitz Commission proposals may be seen as one way of legitimizing the G-20 by transforming it into a GECC. It is also the view of the Palais Royal Initiative on reforms of the international monetary system, which proposes a three-level governance structure for the global economy that would have at the top a reformed G-20 based on a constituency system (Palais Royal Initiative 2011, p. 24).

An intermediate solution by Dervis (2011) is to move to an institutionalized L-20+ as a global council that oversees, in an informal way, global economic governance as a whole. But formal governance, resulting in international binding decisions, will take place in the treaty-based organizations. This L-20+ would be made more representative by including members from regional groupings. In his own words, a formal global leaders' council (say a GECC), "may still be an ideal objective, but it is probably more practical to make the L-20+ into something resembling such a global council while keeping it informal" (Dervis 2011, p. 209).

5 ECOSOC

Chapters IX and X of the UN Charter define the role of UN cooperation in the economic and social field, and the mandates, functions, and structure of ECOSOC. They give the Council two major responsibilities. The first relates to the analysis and policy recommendations in "international economic, social, cultural, educational, health, and related matters." In this regard, "It may prepare draft conventions for submission to the General Assembly and call conferences on matters falling within its competence" (Art. 62). In more recent times, the Council has assumed a complementary role in the follow-up of the major UN summits and conferences in the economic and social and related fields. The 2012 UN Conference on Sustainable Development (Rio+20) gave an explicit mandate to exercise this function seeking "a balanced integration of the three dimensions of sustainable development"—economic, social, and environmental (United Nations 2012, par. 83).

The second relates to the coordination of the UN system. In this regard, the Charter determined that ECOSOC, "may co-ordinate the activities of the specialized agencies through consultation with and recommendations to such agencies and through recommendations to the General Assembly and to the Members of the United Nations," and can enter into agreements with the specialized agencies, "defining the terms on which the agency concerned shall be brought into relationship with the United Nations" (Art. 63). These agreements, nonetheless, need the approval of the General Assembly. In this regard, it exercises an oversight function, which includes the capacity to request reports from the specialized agencies, including "on steps taken to give effect to its own recommendations" (Art. 64). This coordination and oversight applies in particular to the UN Funds and Programs, which are part of the UN Organization but are not mentioned in the UN Charter, as they are later creations. Equally, the Charter does not mention humanitarian affairs, an area in which ECOSOC came to be the main mechanism of coordination at the global level. Beyond this objective, the Council has undertaken for some time the task of convening global debates on development crises and emergencies, with the objective of contributing in this way to a timely and effective global response.

Aside from these main analytical and policy functions, on the one hand, and coordination and oversight functions, on the other, the Charter also gives ECOSOC the mandate to interact with the Security Council on issues of responsibility of the latter—today called issues of security and development—and in the human rights fields. The first of these functions was made extensive to the interactions with the Peacebuilding Commission, when it was created in 2005. The second was effectively eliminated with the creation of the Human Rights Council in 2005. Finally, the Charter gives ECOSOC the possibility of consulting with non-governmental organizations, which in practice has meant that it serves as the main channel of communication between NGOs and the UN Organization.

The Council has a wide array of subsidiary bodies to deal with specialized matters, created according to Art. 68 of the Charter. The composition of these subsidiary bodies has changed over time. There are three types: functional commissions, regional commissions, and expert bodies (some of which are made up of government experts, whereas others serve in their personal capacity). So, ECOSOC is itself a system, which is very loosely coordinated—if at all. Some of these bodies, it can be added, function better than the Council itself, and the annual meetings of some of them are truly the major annual gatherings in their fields. Some involve a massive mobilization of civil society (e.g., the Commission on the Status of Women or the Permanent Forum on Indigenous Issues). Others operate effectively as the apex global bodies for debate and decision making in certain fields (e.g., the Statistical Commission) or the only mechanism of international dialogue on critical issues (e.g., the Committee of Experts on International Cooperation in Tax Matters).

In relation to both of its major mandates, but particularly to the first, there is a significant duality in relation to the responsibilities of ECOSOC and the General Assembly (GA). This comes from the Art. 60, which indicates, "Responsibility for the discharge of the functions of the Organization set forth in this Chapter [on economic and social cooperation] shall be vested in the General Assembly and, under the authority of the General Assembly, in the Economic and Social Council." According to Rosenthal (2007), this article, which almost characterizes ECOSOC as a subordinate and not a principal organ, has its origins in the fact that the Dumbarton Oaks Proposals worked out in 1944 by the allies emerging from WW2 actually proposed ECOSOC as a subordinate body, before the debates in San Francisco transformed it into a principal organ.

In practice, this duality has been understood frequently as the GA having the main policy responsibility, with ECOSOC being in charge of coordination. But this is not entirely correct. In the policy area, ECOSOC and its subsidiary bodies are quite active, at least or even more than the GA. On the other hand, in the coordination function, although the Executive Boards of the Funds and Programmes of the UN Organization are elected by ECOSOC,[14] the GA Resolution 48/162 of 1994 states that the Boards are, "subject to the authority of the Council" (Art. 21) but are mandated, "To implement the policies formulated by the Assembly and the coordination and guidance received from the Council" (Art. 22). Similarly, the main report on the operational activities on development at the country level, the quadrennial (previously triennial) comprehensive policy review, is presented both to the GA and ECOSOC and is defined as a policy instrument, "through which the General Assembly established key system-wide policy orientations for the development cooperation and country-level modalities of the United Nations system" (GA Resolution 67/226 of 2012). In practice, what the existing duality implies is that major policy *and* coordination/operational issues are discussed twice, in different parts of the ECOSOC system and in the Second and Third Committees of the GA, in a way that simply duplicates the debates.

So, the duality has stronger roots, and it is no doubt associated with the sense that the General Assembly is the main *political organ* and has universal membership (a characteristic that ECOSOC lacks). For this reason, instead of creating an ECOSOC leaders forum, as had been recommended by many, the model adopted for the follow-up at the 2012 Conference on Sustainable Development was a High-Level Political Forum, of a universal character, which will be convened by the General Assembly every four years at the Heads of State level to provide political leadership, whereas the regular follow-up would be undertaken by ECOSOC during its annual ministerial meetings (GA Resolution 67/290 of 2013). This is a novel model, which will hopefully exploit the recognized comparative advantages of the GA and ECOSOC while overcoming duplication.

If coordination by ECOSOC of the activities of the Funds and Programs is loose, the situation is even worse in relation to the specialized agencies, which have an entirely independent governance structure. Furthermore, the BWIs do not even recognize that they are subject to such coordination and, as we have seen, the major developed economies have always given the main role in economic issues to those organizations, which they control. Furthermore, it is unclear to what extent or even whether Art. 63 of the Charter really created a mechanism of coordination of what was designed as a highly decentralized system, and whether ECOSOC has ever exercised coordination over the specialized agencies. Furthermore, the Council's decisions and resolutions are not binding on these agencies—or, for that matter, on member states. The reluctance of the BWIs to be coordinated by ECOSOC is reflected in member countries in inter-ministerial rivalries, which implies that although the Council does have strong convening power, this does not apply to economic policymakers, who prefer to work with the BWIs.

The weaknesses of ECOSOC can therefore be summarized as its ambivalent role in policy and even in coordination vis-à-vis the GA; its equally ambivalent role in economic issues associated with the preference of developed countries and even of economic policymakers from developing countries for the BWIs; its weak coordination of the Funds and Programs and even more so of the specialized agencies; and the lack of tradition of coordination of its own subsidiary bodies.

Despite these weaknesses, which are largely of institutional character, the ECOSOC system has definite advantages. They are derived, first of all, from the strong confidence of developing countries in the Council and its subsidiary bodies—though frequently in tension with their own preference for the GA as the major political organ. Given that it provides possibly the most open intergovernmental forums on economic and social issues in the world, civil society also has a definite preference for ECOSOC as a forum. With the increasing openness of the UN to the private sector, its convening power has also been manifested in this area. Further, its network of subsidiary and expert bodies is also a source of strength, as shown in the success of many of them. And, of course, the Council can always exercise its policy and coordination responsibilities better or interpret them in novel ways.

Indeed, while recognizing the weaknesses of ECOSOC, Rosenthal has argued that it, "has been quite successful in promoting the development debate, identifying emerging issues, and offering guidelines for policy makers. Many states have viewed ECOSOC as an impartial and objective meeting place where different positions and approaches can be contrasted, and implications of alternative policy prescriptions can be analyzed. It could even be argued that the non-binding nature of decisions and resolutions has been an asset in furthering the policy debate, and has contributed to the organization's considerable achievements in the development of ideas, in its advocacy role and in its ability to shape public awareness" (Rosenthal 2007, p. 143).

The potential use of the ECOSOC system in a better way was behind the 2007 reform (GA Resolution 61/16) adopted to implement the decisions of the 2005 World Summit. The first element of this reform was to give ECOSOC the central role in the review of implementation of the international development goals, including the Millennium Development Goals (MDGs). This role should be understood more broadly as the integrated follow-up and implementation of the outcomes of all major UN summits and conferences. As already mentioned, after Rio+20, this is interpreted as a balanced integration of the three dimensions of sustainable development, which would be the responsibilities of the annual ministerial meeting on sustainable development, as part of the High-level Political Forum process, as well as the new "integration segment" created in the 2013 reform of the Council (GA Resolution A/68/L.2 of 2013). However, the follow-up of major summits and conferences must be understood as a responsibility of the whole ECOSOC system, as some of its subsidiary bodies (notably the Commissions on the Status of Women, Social Development, and Population and Development[15]) have major responsibilities for the follow-up of specific conferences. The proposals presented in the mid-2000s by the UN Secretariat included the possibility of moving to a peer review process in the follow-up of the major summits and conferences, but it was significantly diluted and became only a series of "voluntary presentations," which came to be known as the Annual Ministerial Reviews (AMRs); this model will continue to be in place for the annual ministerial meetings on sustainable development.

The second major element of the 2007 reform was the creation of the biennial Development Cooperation Forum (DCF). The major idea was to serve as the hub of a series of now disparate processes of cooperation that involve North-South and South-South intergovernmental cooperation, both bilateral and multilateral, but also increasingly non-governmental actors from civil society and the private sector. As in the previous case, the Council has become multi-stakeholder forum, with weak features of mutual accountability and coordination, and for sharing best practices and lessons learned.

Based on its mandates and history, it is clear that ECOSOC should head the international system for cooperation with developing countries, continue to do so for the international humanitarian system and, most importantly, lead the follow-up of the various United Nations summits and conferences, which have developed the broadest agenda of global cooperation in economic, social, and environmental affairs (the UN Development Agenda, in short). In all of these areas, it should discuss the possibility of monitoring and eventually strengthening the mutual accountability for international commitments in the economic and social fields, possibly through peer review processes and high-profile national monitoring and debates, as outlined in the third section of this chapter. This mixes its policy and coordination role, and in the latter case it should involve a greater activity of coordination of the Funds and Programs and, at least in some areas, of the whole UN system.

In relation to policy setting and follow-up, this would imply, first of all, a responsibility to support the coherence of the UN system in the policy (and programmatic) area, analyze emerging global development challenges, and propose ways of filling the gaps in global cooperation. It would involve strengthening the monitoring and mutual accountability for UN Development Agenda. This implies that ECOSOC should also be the main organ in charge of following-up on the 2030 development goals. It would also imply strengthening the Global Development Cooperation Forum to achieve the objectives for which it was created. This means, in particular, that it should bring under its purview the agenda of aid effectiveness and thus the post-Busan process.

In turn, in relation to coordination, this implies that ECOSOC should strengthen its oversight of operational activities of the UN Organization, becoming in a sense the "board of boards" of Funds and Programs. This involves a central role in guiding inter-agency coordination, the Resident Coordinator system and the United Nations Development Assistance Framework. ECOSOC should also use its role as coordinator of the UN system more effectively, particularly in the policy areas as well as the follow-up to the UN Development Agenda. As already done with the AMRs and will now be done in the annual ministerial meetings on sustainable development, this coordination function should realistically focus on specific issues, rather than being exercised in broad terms. Finally, ECOSOC should continue to play the role of coordinator of humanitarian activities and response to specific emergencies and emerging issues.

In all of these areas, it is essential that ECOSOC should effectively function itself as a system, with a better mechanism of coordination of its subsidiary bodies that takes into account their particular specialization. ECOSOC should also continue to exploit one of its basic advantages, which is its capacity to engage multiple stakeholders: not only member States, but also civil society and the private sector.

It would be good if the reform process also addressed the main institutional issue discussed above: the duplication of functions with the GA, which, as indicated, apply both to the policy and coordination/operational functions. An ambitious reform would involve reporting directly to the Assembly and eliminating the debates in the Second and Third Committees of the GA. And, last but not least, it is essential that ECOSOC—and the committees of the GA—change their working methods, moving from speechmaking to more effective action-oriented debates. This also implies that it may be convenient to more actively use small committees, made up on the basis of constituencies, rather than rely on the larger Council or even the GA for every decision.

6 CONCLUSIONS

This chapter proposes a typology of international cooperation in the economic and social field that includes three basic objectives: (i) the provision of Global Public Goods to manage interdependence among nations; (ii) the provision of Universal Social Goods, understood as common social norms and standards and a minimum level of social services for all world citizens; and (iii) the promotion of development cooperation aimed at reducing international inequalities, in particular different levels of economic development among countries. It argues that, whereas in the first case, the concept of sovereignty should be understood as responsible sovereignty—exercising it in a way that is fully respectful of the sovereignty of others—the traditional concept of sovereignty should prevail in the second and third objectives, though subject to their commitment to abide by universally-agreed norms and standards. Furthermore, in the latter two cases, international cooperation should aim at enhancing the "policy space" of countries.

The chapter then proposes six basic criteria for rethinking the global structure of cooperation: (i) strong subsidiarity principles; (ii) reliance on a dense network of global, regional, and national institutions; (iii) reliance on small but representative decision-making bodies that help overcome the tension between inclusiveness and effectiveness; (iv) equitable participation of developing countries in decision making; (v) effective instruments of monitoring international commitments, which should guarantee compliance in the case of GPGs, rules that guarantee differential treatment of developing countries, and non-binding accountability mechanisms—such as, peer reviews or committees such as those that have been created for the implementation of international conventions in human rights—and (vi) guarantee of the coherence of the system. In the latter case, it calls for the transformation of the G-20 into the Global Economic Coordination Council proposed by the Stiglitz Commission, or a similar institution, and for the strengthening of the functions of ECOSOC in the policy area in the follow-up to global conferences, as the major development cooperation forum, and as coordinator of cooperation of the UN Organization and as an issue-oriented coordinator of the UN system.

The major opportunity for change and reinforcing multilateral cooperation comes from the transition in which the world evolves toward a multipolar order, as the result of the rise of emerging countries. This transition runs the risk of making cooperation more difficult. This requires that these countries commit to multilateralism rather than the "elite multilateralism" of the G-20, or to what Wade (2011) has called "Westphelian assertion," in which the emerging powers assert their national sovereignties in the form of "no's," which yields a low level of cooperation that may be masked by agreement on fine words. It is important in this regard that other developing countries—and notably, regional partners of the emerging powers—exercise a strong push for them to choose multilateralism over the other two alternatives, which would only generate new forms of exclusion for medium-sized and small countries. Less powerful countries would benefit (and, in fact, are already benefiting) from competition in the exercise of world power. As a strong ally of the UN, global civil society should continue to play a strong role in pushing in the same direction.

ACKNOWLEDGEMENTS

This chapter has been prepared for the IPD-ECLAC Project on Global Governance supported by the Spanish cooperation. The literature on the issues covered here is massive and so I only include specific references that discuss the issues raised in the chapter. I am grateful to José Antonio Alonso, Scott Barrett, Kemal Dervis, Eduardo Gálvez, Navid Hanif, Bruce Jenks, Inge Kaul, Katharina Pistor, Gert Rosenthal, and Dani Rodrik for very useful comments to previous drafts of this chapter. The fourth section borrows in part from Ocampo and Stiglitz (2011).

NOTES

1. This term is preferred here to that of global financial crisis as though it had global effects, the financial crisis centered in the US and Western Europe.
2. This is the concept that prevails in most discussions of international cooperation. See, for example, Dervis (2005) and Barrett (2007). See also the International Task Force on Global Public Goods (2006), which adopts, however, an imprecise definition of GPGs.
3. Kaul et al. (2003) argue, in any case, that public goods, and hence GPGs, are basically a social construct, in the sense that their reach has tended to expand through time, alongside the recognition of areas which belong to the category of public goods or have high externalities.

4. Please note that some goods that would be classified as USGs (education, health) may have public goods attributes (universal literacy, a certain level of basic education, combatting health contagion) and in this sense have GPG dimensions.
5. Following UN terminology, I use this term here to refer to the elected officials and the international civil service that administer the different international organizations.
6. See Lamy (2005) and Hoekman (2011). A graphic representation can be found in: http://www.wto.org/english/tratop_e/dda_e/meet08_circles_popup_e.htm
7. See, for example, the report of the IMF's Independent Evaluation Office on IMF surveillance in the run-up to the North-Atlantic financial crisis (IMF-IEO 2011).
8. See in this regard the proposals made by the High-Level Panel on the Post-2015 Development Agenda (United Nations 2013).
9. See UNDP (1992), pp. 82–3.
10. See also the proposal by Dervis (2005), chapter 3, and a review of several proposals by Rosenthal (2005 and 2007).
11. UNCTAD is formally a program, but its functions are similar to those of the other entities that are part of the Secretariat.
12. These problems are associated with the exclusion of some countries that fulfil the criteria of large population and GDP (the most important case being Nigeria), the fact that in given regions members are not necessarily those that meet the criteria (e.g., among Arab members) and, once again, the over-representation of Europe.
13. This was, of course, equally so, a problem of the G-7/8. One of the most interesting cases relates to the decision of the Gleneagles G-8 Summit in 2005 to write off the debt of the Highly-Indebted Poor Countries. Although agreeing with this step, the smaller European countries that met the UN ODA target of 0.7% of GNI correctly complained in the IMFC and the Development Committee that it was not the G-8's business to adopt this decision (and capture the political benefits of doing so) since no individual member of the G-8 actually met the UN target.
14. This is not entirely true of the World Food Program, half of whose Board is elected by ECOSOC and half by the FAO Council.
15. The Commission on Sustainable Development also did so, but it was eliminated as part of the 2013, which gave the follow-up to the associated Conference to the High-Level Political Forum and the major ministerial meeting of ECOSOC.

REFERENCES

Barrett, Scott. 2007. *Why Cooperate: The Incentive to Supply Global Public Goods.* New York: Oxford University Press.

Bradford, Colin I., and Wonhyuk Lim. 2011. "Introduction: Toward the Consolidation of the G20: From Crisis Committee to Global Steering Committee." In *Global Leadership in Transition: Making the G20 More Effective and Responsive*, edited by Colin I. Bradford and Wonhyuk Lim, pp. 1–10. Seoul and Washington: Korea Development Institute and Brookings Institution Press.

Cafaggi, Fabrizio, and Katharina Pistor. 2013. "Regulatory Capabilities: A Normative Framework for Assessing the Distributional Effects of Regulation." Working Paper.

Commission on Global Governance. 1995. *Our Global Neighborhood.* New York: Oxford University Press.

Dervis, Kemal. 2005. *A Better Globalization: Legitimacy, Governance and Reform*. Washington DC: Brookings Institution Press for the Center for Global Development.

Dervis, Kemal. 2011. "Towards Strengthened Global Economic Governance." In *New Ideas on Development after the Financial Crisis*, edited by Nancy Birdsall and Francis Fukuyama, chapter 8, pp. 191–212. Baltimore: The John Hopkins University Press.

ECLAC (UN Economic Commission for Latin America and the Caribbean). 2000. *Equity, Development and Citizenship*. Santiago: ECLAC.

G-20 (Group of 20). 2009. *Leaders' Statement, The Pittsburgh Summit*. September 24–25. Available at: http://www.g20.org/.

Hoekman, Bernard. 2011. "Proposals for WTO Reform: A Synthesis and Assessment." *Minnesota Journal of International Law* 20(2): pp. 324–64.

IMF-IEO (International Monetary Fund's Independent Evaluation Office). 2011. *IMF Performance in the Run-Up to the Financial and Economic Crisis: IMF Surveillance in 2004–07*. Washington DC: International Monetary Fund.

International Task Force on Global Public Goods. 2006. *Meeting Global Challenges: International Cooperation and the National Interest*. Stockholm: Final Report.

Jenks, Bruce. 2016. "UN Development Cooperation: The Roots of a Reform Agenda." In José Antonio Ocampo (ed.), *Global Governance and Development*, edited by José Antonio Ocampo, chapter 5 in this volume: Oxford University Press.

Jolly, Richard, Louis Emmerij, and Thomas Weiss. 2008. *UN Ideas that Changed the World*. Bloomington and Indianapolis: Indiana University Press.

Kaul, Inge. 2013. "Meeting Global Challenges: Assessing Governance Readiness." In *The Governance Report*, from the Hertie School of Governance, chapter 2, pp. 33–58. Oxford: Oxford University Press.

Kaul, Inge, and Donald Blundin 2016. "Global Public Goods and the United Nations," in José Antonio Ocampo (ed.), *Global Governance and Development*, chapter 2 in this volume: Oxford University Press.

Kaul, Inge, Pedro Conceicao, Katell Le Goulven, and R Mendoza (eds). 2003. *Providing Global Public Goods: Managing Globalization*. New York: Oxford University Press, Overview.

Lamy, Pascal. 2005. "Statement to Delegations." Geneva: World Trade Organization. November 10. Available at: http://www.wto.org/english/news_e/news05_e/stat_lamy_nov05_e.htm.

Martin, Paul. 2011. "The G20: From Global Crisis Responder to Global Steering Committee." In *Global Leadership in Transition: Making the G20 More Effective and Responsive*, edited by Colin I. Bradford and Wonhyuk Lim, pp. 13–15. Seoul and Washington: Korea Development Institute and Brookings Institution Press.

Musgrave, Richard. 1959. *The Theory of Public Finance*. Tokyo: McGraw-Hill.

Ocampo, José Antonio. 2001. "Raul Prebisch and the Development Agenda at the Dawn of the Twenty-First Century." *CEPAL Review* 75, December.

Ocampo, José Antonio. 2010. "Rethinking Global Economic Governance." *Journal of Globalization and Development* 1(1), Article 6.

Ocampo, José Antonio. 2011. *Reforming the International Monetary System*. 14th WIDER Annual Lecture. Helsinki: UNU-WIDER. Available at: http://www.wider.unu.edu/publications/annual-lectures/en_GB/AL/.

Ocampo, José Antonio, and Joseph E. Stiglitz. 2011. "From the G-20 to a Global Economic Coordination Council." *Journal of Globalization and Development* 2(2), Article 9.

Palais Royal Initiative. 2011. "Reform of the International Monetary System: A Cooperative Approach for the 21st Century." In *Reform of the International Monetary System: The Palais Royal Initiative,* edited by Jack T. Boorman and André Icard, ch. 2, pp. 7–26. New Delhi: Sage Publications.

Rodrik, Dani. 2011. *The Globalization Paradox: Democracy and the Future of the World Economy.* New York: W. Norton.

Rosenthal, Gert. 2005. "The Economic and Social Council of the United Nations: An Issues Paper." No. 15, February. New York: Friedrich Ebert Stiftung, Dialogue on Globalization.

Rosenthal, Gert. 2007. "The Economic and Social *Council* of the United Nations." In *The Oxford Handbook on the United Nations* edited by Thomas G. Weiss and Sam Daws, Chapter 7, pp. 136–48. New York: Oxford University Press.

Toye, John, and Richard Toye. 2004. *The UN and Global Political Economy: Trade, Finance and Development.* Bloomington and Indianapolis: Indiana University Press.

United Nations. 2001 *Report of the High-level Panel on Financing for Development* (Zedillo Report). Available at: http://www.un.org/en/ga/search/view_doc.asp?symbol=A/55/1000.

United Nations. 2006. *Delivering as One,* Report of the Panel on United Nations System-wide Coherence. General Assembly Doc. A/61/583. November 20.

United Nations. 2009. *Report of the Commission of Experts Convened of the President of the UN General Assembly on Reforms of the International Monetary and Financial System* (UN Stiglitz Commission). Available at: http://www.un.org/ga/econcrisissummit/docs/FinalReport_CoE.pdf.

United Nations. 2010. *World Economic and Social Survey: Retooling Global Development.* New York: United Nations Department of Economic and Social Affairs.

United Nations. 2012. *The Future We Want: Outcome of the United Nations Conference on Sustainable Development,* Doc. A/CONF.216/L.1, June 19.

United Nations. 2013. *A New Global Partnership: Eradicate Poverty and Transform Economies through Sustainable Development.* Report of the High Level Panel of Eminent Persons on the Post-2015 Development Agenda, May.

UNDP (United Nations Development Program). 1992. *Human Development Report: Global Dimensions of Human Development.* New York: Oxford University Press.

Wade, Robert H. 2011. "From Waning to Emerging World Order: Multipolarity, Multilateralism, the G20, the World Bank and the IMF." *Politics and Society* 39(3): pp. 347–78.

Woods, Ngaire. 2011. "The Impact of the G20 on Global Governance: A History and Prospective." In *Global Leadership in Transition: Making the G20 More Effective and Responsive,* edited by Colin I. Bradford and Wonhyuk Lim, chapter 3, pp. 36–47. Seoul and Washington: Korea Development Institute and Brookings Institution Press.

2

Global Public Goods and the United Nations

Inge Kaul and Donald Blondin

The world is confronting a lengthening list of global challenges: excessive financial volatility; global warming; the rising specters of land, water, and food scarcity; loss of biodiversity; the "end of oil"; illicit international trade accompanied by crime and violence; and cyber-(in)security; not to mention the persisting challenges of nuclear proliferation, communicable diseases, and global inequity.

These challenges have not gone unnoticed. Many have figured on national and international agendas for decades, and most have been the subject of numerous studies and conferences. By now we understand most of these challenges and we are familiar with many possible policy responses. Nonetheless, a political breakthrough does not appear imminent in any of the key issue areas.

In order to analyze and then propose solutions for this ongoing policy deadlock, this chapter takes a global public goods perspective. The central reason for this approach is that contemporary global challenges tend to possess the properties of a global public good (GPG), or at least include components of a GPG nature.[1] In line with the predictions of standard economic theory, we should therefore expect collective-action problems and associated underprovisioning. However, GPG-type challenges are nothing new, and the international community has dealt with them quite effectively before. Just think of the Uruguay Round of multilateral trade negotiations, the Kyoto Protocol, or the 1997 Mine Ban Treaty. This begs the question of why international cooperation is not more forthcoming today.

One possible factor could be that today's global challenges differ, at least in significant part, from those that we confronted in earlier decades. Another, that global power relations have changed, with an accompanying shift in actor relations. Perhaps even both of these factors come into play. Combined, they may have changed things so substantially that to gain the capacity to respond, governance systems will require more than just peripheral adjustments. Is it precisely this unmet requirement of fundamental change that is causing the current stalemates?

With that question as a starting point, the discussion in this chapter will proceed in three steps. First, Section 1 will identify what would be needed—in terms of governance requirements—in order to address more effectively today's GPG-type challenges. Working with select empirical evidence, Section 2 will then review how we have so far responded to the identified governance requirements. It will, in particular, seek to explore whether the current backlog of unresolved challenges is merely the result of "not-yet-being-there"—i.e., lagging institutional adjustment—or whether there are indications of additional constraining factors that are impeding resolution of the challenges we face. Based on this analysis, Section 3 will discuss the possible steps that could be taken to install the missing links and bring governance systems more in line with today's world.

To preview the conclusions, the analysis presented in these three sections suggests that the full complement of aforementioned factors is at work. Today's global challenges are indeed different. The world has moved from a period during which globalization was "rolled out," alongside the promise of expanded economic opportunities, to the current era, in which conventional growth paths appear unsustainable. A "rolling in" is now being demanded of states, especially with regard to cross-border externalities. This often entails difficult adjustments at a time when global power balances are shifting and unsettling the relations among states, as well as those between state and non-state actors.

However, the root causes of today's rampant crises run deeper than the altered natures of global challenges and power relations relative to those of a few decades past. Among the root causes is the "sovereignty paradox": by holding on to conventional notions and strategies of sovereignty that lead them to shy away from international cooperation even within issue areas now dominated by interdependence, national governments are obtaining precisely the unintended effects. They are weakening their policymaking capacity, especially in relation to transnational threats, which offer no respect for the notion of non-interference into states' domestic affairs; and thereby national governments are undermining the very sovereignty they seek to protect.

As a result of this behavior by states, policy responses targeting today's challenges are discernible and rising in number, but they are mostly occurring nationally and regionally, or through market-based initiatives. They are often undertaken by non-state actors. In this sense we can see both vertical and horizontal de-concentration of governance. Notably, the discernible responses are still of an ad hoc and experimental nature in many instances. Globally coordinated policy responses are missing. This analysis confirms Brown's conclusion that, "the world is stuck in a rut, acting out its own global version of the 'prisoner's dilemma'—a universe in which no major economy can succeed on its own, yet none trusts any other enough to attempt cooperation and coordination" (2013, 2).

As shown in Section 3, the critical missing links that must be put in place if the world is to escape from this rut are: first, the conceptualization and proof of a sovereignty-compatible rationale for effective—and to that end, fair—international cooperation; and second, based on that compiled evidence, the forging of global consensus on a notion of "smart sovereignty."

The concept of smart sovereignty recognizes that today's GPG-type challenges cannot be resolved unilaterally by any one nation, no matter its economic or military might. In addition to collective, multilateral action at the international level, most of these challenges also require that corrective action be undertaken at the national level by many, if not all states. Within issue areas characterized by such policy interdependence, international cooperation is thus in states' enlightened self-interest. Pooling sovereignty is, in these cases, simply the smarter strategy, because on the regional and global levels, it has the potential to allow policymaking to catch up with the border-transgressing challenges in need of rapid resolution.

Not only would the resolution of these challenges be of great benefit on a global or regional level, but, by eliminating the negative externalities, it would lift policymaking constraints on national governments and thereby strengthen, rather than limit, their national policymaking capacity. In other, non-interdependent issue areas, states would be freed to continue pursuing their own particular national interests. This is the intelligent outcome.

Because states receive recognition of their sovereignty through the United Nations (UN), the UN would also be the organization best positioned to provide them the forum they will need to reach agreement on the precise definition of smart sovereignty and on how to combine their duties of interdependence management duties associated with GPG provisioning with the exercise of national policymaking rights.[2]

As this chapter argues, to effectively take on these tasks and help member states to operationalize the notion of smart sovereignty, it would be desirable for the UN also to undergo reform. Importantly, the UN will need to add a global, transnational perspective to its structure and work. At first glance, this may seem counterintuitive given the UN's status and stated purpose, but actually it is a universal body less for its processes and work focus than its comprehensive membership. To an extent, the UN does currently deal with global challenges, but the approaches mostly originate from a country or regional perspective. Much less often does the UN approach challenges from a global-issue perspective, and it does so even less often with concern for the coherence and balance of the ensemble of issues coursing through the global public domain. This will need to change, because the sum of what countries are willing to do in respect to a global concern like climate change may not add up to what achieving climate change mitigation may actually require. Therefore, it would be desirable for the UN to be a "world body" in a dual sense: one, because its membership is universal—all countries are represented—and, two, because it is mandated to alert us to and nudge us toward recognizing planetary boundaries and fostering longer-term sustainability.

In more detail, the argument is as follows.[3]

1 PROVIDING GLOBAL PUBLIC GOODS: IDENTIFYING THE KEY GOVERNANCE REQUIREMENTS INVOLVED

The term "governance" is used here to denote the institutional arrangements and processes put in place, as well as the actions taken, in order to achieve a desired policy outcome. As governance arrangements are tools, they should fit a targeted purpose. Put differently, they should take into account the nature of the challenges to be addressed and the most desirable and feasible ways of tackling them under the given circumstances.

As noted above, many, if not most contemporary global challenges possess the properties of a GPG or have components with these attributes. Accordingly, it is important in the present context to first clarify the governance requirements posed by GPGs, especially "sticky" GPGs that are occupying critical space on national and international agendas, having become trapped in policy stalemates. Second, we ought to discuss how the global challenges associated with these GPGs could possibly be met amidst the current shifts in international power relations, specifically the intensifying trend toward multi-polarity and an insecure power balance between state and non-state. That power balance has, in recent decades, tipped in favor of the latter, in particular toward global market actors.

Taking the implications of these two aspects into account, it can be argued that an adequate provisioning of GPGs would, at a minimum, require governance arrangements that accomplish the following four functions.

1.1 Function 1: Averting Risks of Dual-state and Non-state—Actor Failure

As Box 2.1 notes, the defining property of public goods, including GPGs, is their publicness in consumption, i.e., the fact that these goods may affect anyone or everyone, for better or worse. This characteristic poses an important risk for the provisioning of these goods, because it may tempt individual actors

Box 2.1 Introducing Public Goods and Global Public Goods

Standard economic theory distinguishes between two main categories of goods: private goods and public goods.

Private goods are goods that can be parcelled out and made excludable, so that clear property rights can be attached to them.

Public goods, by contrast, are goods that are non-excludable, meaning that the goods' effects (benefits or costs) are shared by everyone.

If a good is non-excludable and non-rival in consumption, so that one person's use of the good or one person's being affected by it does not diminish its availability to others, the good is said to be purely public. Examples are peace and security. If a good has only one of these characteristics, it is impurely public. The atmosphere, for example, is non-excludable but rival in consumption, because unrestricted pollution can change its gas composition and contribute to global warming. Patented pharmaceutical knowledge illustrates a non-rival good, whose use has, at least for a limited period of time, been made excludable, so it, too, falls into the category of an impure public good.

The public effects of a good can be of different geographic—local, national, regional, or worldwide—reach; and they can span across one generation or several generations.

Global public goods are goods whose benefits or costs are of nearly universal reach or potentially affecting anyone anywhere. Together with regional public goods they constitute the category of transnational public goods.

It is important to emphasise that, in the present context, the term "good" has no value connotation. It is used as a short form for the goods or products as well as services and conditions that exist in the public domain.

Also, in most cases, publicness and privateness are not innate properties of a good, but the result of social or political choice. Therefore, it is important to distinguish between the potential and de facto publicness of a good. For example, land can be freely accessible to everyone, or it can be fenced in, be made excludable.

Globalness is a special form of publicness; and in most cases, it, too, results from a policy choice, e.g., a decision to promote free trade or financial liberalization. Thus, while some global public goods are naturally global and public, such as sunlight, many others are human-made, including the international communication and transportation systems or the goods of communicable disease control, financial stability or peace and security.

Source: This box draws on Kaul and Mendoza (2003). The interested reader may also wish to consult Barrett 2007 and Sandler 2004.

into free-riding. That is, actors may conceal their true preferences for these goods in order to wait for others to step forward and provide them. Then, when the goods emerge in the public domain, the free-riders benefit, too—free of charge.

Because some actors do succumb to this temptation to free-ride, markets will likely fail to ensure an adequate provisioning of public goods. Given that the risk of free-riding tends to increase with the number of actors involved, GPGs are especially prone to underprovisioning due to such market failure.

Another factor compounds the risk of GPG underprovisioning: at the national level, the state can intervene and potentially correct public good-related market failure due to its unique ability to create incentives and enforce compliance. At the international level, however, there is no full equivalent of state institutions. Moreover, when appearing internationally, state parties for the most part pursue national interests, which may or may not overlap with global concerns. In this sense, states are also actors with particularistic, quasi-private interests. Consequently, and as studies on international cooperation have repeatedly shown, they often succumb to free-riding temptations.

This implies that GPG-type challenges run the risk of dual actor failure: market failure and state failure.[4] Thus, one governance function would need to be averting or at least minimizing the risk of such dual actor failure in the presence of GPGs, most notably the risk of state failure. Preventing the latter is of special importance, as effective multilateral cooperation is often needed for states to "tame" globalizing markets, as well as themselves.

1.2 Function 2: Promoting Global Fairness

Alone, however, Function 1 might not suffice to bring about the level of willing participation required to make cooperation work effectively under today's poly-centric conditions, i.e., without pressure from a hegemon or club of major powers. Under these conditions, an important incentive for actors to engage in a public policy initiative is policy ownership and, to that end, process and outcome fairness.

Considering the stark differences and disparities that exist in the world, the most feasible way for parties to perceive international cooperation as fair and legitimate is probably process fairness. This means affording all concerned parties the opportunity to have a say in matters that affect them, while striking a balance between representativeness and decision-making efficiency, which, in many instances, is difficult to achieve. In the past, the tilt has sometimes been toward "club" settings (e.g., the G7/8 and now the G-20) comprising a limited number of states and justified by references to decision-making efficiency. These raise obvious representativeness concerns, but the failure of recent efforts to negotiate international agreements on climate change with more comprehensive country participation is suggestive of the likelihood of deadlock when all countries are involved in the decision-making process.

Notably, the risk of such policy stalemates due to irreconcilable differences in negotiating parties' preferences could be reduced by coupling process fairness with positive-sum thinking. The latter approach is characterized by the willingness to seek mutually beneficial bargains and broadly share the gains realized through cooperation among stakeholders, internationally and nationally. This is in the parties' enlightened self-interest because, under the prevailing conditions of openness, unresolved challenges roam the global public domain, adversely and haphazardly affecting countries and actor groups.

Hence, we can identify the second governance requirement as the promotion of process fairness coupled with positive-sum thinking. This requirement is particularly strong and urgent in respect to the "sticky" GPGs which are difficult to resolve because they tend to entail significant distributional implications. A clear example is the issue of global warming. The difficulty of achieving a grand bargain here is overshadowed only by its absolute necessity. The international cooperation required for these sticky GPGs must be designed so that it is incentive-compatible from the start—it must quickly begin to "pay," economically, politically, or otherwise.

1.3 Function 3: Facilitating Global-issue Management

While publicness in consumption is the defining property of a public good, many goods are also public in provision: They require state or non-state actors, who wish to alter the provision status or form of a public good, to pursue the cooperation of others. Thus, the interdependence that GPGs generate has two dimensions: consumption interdependence and provision interdependence.

This notion of provision interdependence is of special importance to GPGs (relative to, e.g., local level public goods), because their provision path is multi-actor, multi-sector, and, importantly, multi-level. As Figure 2.1 shows, goods of this type emerge from a summation process. National policy measures and outcomes—provided in an internationally concerted manner—tend to be the main building blocks, complemented, if needed, by international building blocks, such as an agreement defining the shared goal or an organization through which parties undertake pooled initiatives.

Consequently, effective issue management and result-orientation, i.e., actually producing the desired good in an integrated, transnational way, can be seen as a third key function of global public policy. In terms of governance arrangements, this entails recognizing the provision paths of GPGs as one of two new global spaces of policy interdependence: the global-issue space.[5] This global-issue space partially overlays the long-established policy spaces defined by geographic criteria, economic sector, and actor group. In many instances, meeting a global challenge calls for inputs from these other spaces. In turn, this may necessitate an issue manager or anchor institution to facilitate the pulling together of these diverse input threads—at both the national and the international level. To illustrate, it is not—or not only—the health sector as such that may need strengthening in order to control a disease like tuberculosis.

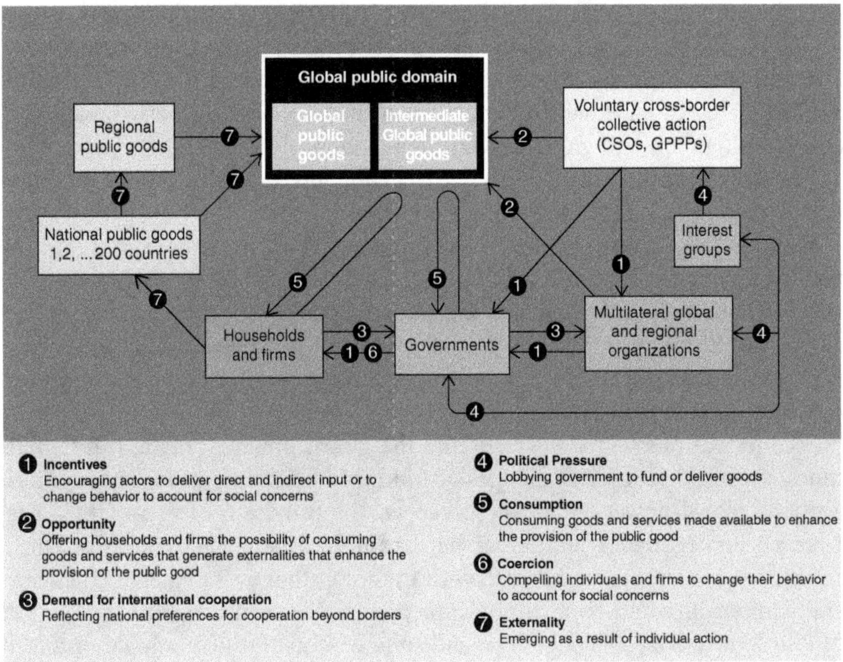

Figure 2.1 Provision of global public goods
Source: Adapted from Kaul and Conceição (2006, p. 14)

Additional policy inputs might have to come from areas like public education and information, science and technology, or international trade regulation. These inputs need to be decided upon and assembled nationally and internationally. Therefore, arrangements for "global-issue management" would need to exist nationally and internationally, on the political side as well as on the operational side of global policymaking.

An important function of global-issue management would be to draw political attention to severely underprovided issues and facilitate the actual "getting to the good": help identify possible breakthrough solutions where issues are stalemated or speed up matters where critical thresholds are fast approaching.

1.4 Function 4: Fostering a Balanced and Coherent Global Public Domain

Alongside the global-issue space there is another new global space of policy interdependence that would need to be taken into account to realize the goal of fostering more sustainable global growth and development: the global public domain. This is the overlay of the ensemble of public effects that spans across the globe. Its main components are GPGs, as well as the relationships that exist between these goods, e.g., the relationships between global health and Trade Related Intellectual Property Rights (TRIPS), or those between climate change mitigation and global poverty reduction.[6]

The global public domain requires oversight and leadership from four main perspectives. They each raise unique concerns.

First, there is the question of whose priority GPGs this domain contains. As previously mentioned, the world has been—and continues to be—marked by sharp differences and disparities, and it could be that the composition of the global public domain is such that it disproportionately, if not primarily, benefits the conventional major powers, exacerbating inter-country disparities through a biased provisioning of GPGs.

Second, various GPGs have entered the global public domain at different times, owing to specific challenges or swings in economic thought as well as evolving global power balances. Moreover, the provision of these GPGs has largely been negotiated in different venues and by different actor groups. Thus, conflicts between them may exist, with the result that overall global efficiency and equity suffer and opportunities for progress are constrained.

Third, the global challenges currently going unmet are beginning to interact and form risk clusters. As the list of these unmet challenges grows, so does the complexity, intensity, and potential impact of the risk clusters. Given the high degree of global interconnectedness today, should the clusters erupt, the resulting "debris" could rapidly spread around the world, leading to catastrophes.

And fourth, as the frequently referenced notions of "green economy" and "sustainability" suggest, the world is fast approaching critical limits, including the two-degree global warming threshold, the "end of oil," and serious inequity ratios. In other words, we have to rapidly rethink familiar growth and development paradigms—preferably within the next decade.

Thus, the current phase of the contemporary, post-1945 era of globalization differs in an important respect from the earlier, pre-2000 phase. During that first phase, states were called upon to help generate GPGs that would promote economic openness and cross-border market integration. In this often unbridled roll-out of globalization, states heeded the call. They did so, in part, because of the associated promise of enhanced access to new global opportunities, and, in part, because they were nudged into compliance by the major western powers, who acted as important drivers of globalization.

In contrast, we are now experiencing a "rolling-in" phase of globalization characterized by a constriction of externalities and reevaluation of growth paradigms. States are now being called upon to accept limits on the types of national policy freedoms they have exercised to date, because these have been linked to costly crises and appear unsustainable in the longer-run. The first

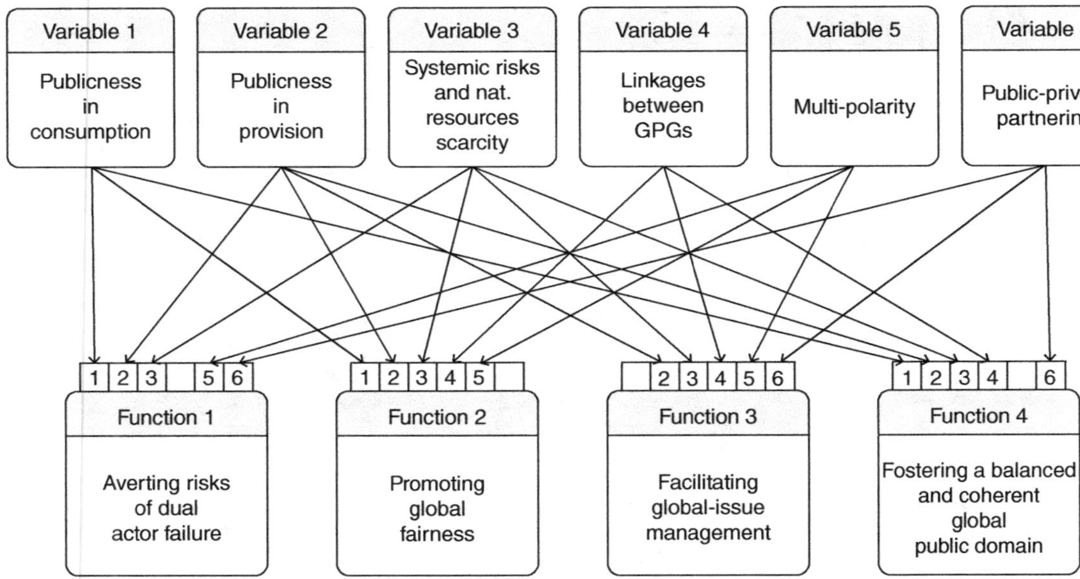

Figure 2.2 Identifying the governance requirements of GPGs

Source: Authors

signs of trouble have already made themselves felt, in the form of more volatile global weather patterns and increasing social unrest. If states individually and collectively want to maintain a full range of policy options and freedoms, now is the time for them to shift gears. They must think in terms of rolling-in cross-border externalities that emanate from unsustainable policy paths; if a business-as-usual approach is chosen, these policy paths may lead to global catastrophes.

Therefore, a fourth governance requirement prompted by today's challenges is global systemic risk and opportunity management, designed to develop a balanced structure and functioning of the global public domain.

Figure 2.2 summarizes, in graphical form, the foregoing discussion. It relates the six variables that we have considered to the four identified governance functions that must be operationalized in order for the currently needed GPGs to stand a better chance at being adequately provided. Variables 1 and 2 relate to the basic properties of GPGs; Variables 3 and 4 refer to the current provision status of GPGs; and Variables 5 and 6 reflect key features of the current overall policy context within which the requisite GPG provisioning has to succeed. As can be seen, each function responds to multiple policy demands. In addition, each function is likely to reinforce the effectiveness of the others. This means that GPG provisioning would be strengthened, if the functions were bundled so as to form a coherent policy approach.

The question to which Section 2 now turns is whether we see empirical evidence of the performance of these predicted functions. If so, what operational forms do they take and who is performing them?

2 THE PROVISIONING OF GLOBAL PUBLIC GOODS IN PRACTICE

Even a cursory review of recent policy practice in global-issue areas reveals many initiatives that exemplify one or more of the four requisite governance functions. This is not to say that these initiatives are being undertaken specifically to meet the governance functions identified in Section 1. In fact, this is most likely not the case, because the GPG notion is not yet fully established and we still lack a systematic conceptualization of global public policy. However, the governance requirements posed by today's GPGs are apparently being recognized and responded to through a mix of conventional and innovative policy approaches. Indeed, GPG provisioning is a multi-actor, multi-level process that is brimming with initiatives.

Nevertheless, many of these initiatives still appear to be of an ad hoc, uncoordinated, and often experimental nature. Thus, while a lot is happening, a coordinated multilateral approach, and thereby a "global" aspect, is generally missing from the current response pattern. This is linked to the observation that governments can often be counted among the reluctant parties in the international cooperation realm.

Before describing the current response pattern in more detail, let us first consider some of the evidence for relevant policy initiatives. This analysis will revisit each of the four governance functions identified in Section 1, namely:

- Function 1: Averting risks of dual-state and non-state—actor failure;
- Function 2: Promoting global fairness;
- Function 3: Facilitating global-issue management; and
- Function 4: Fostering a balanced and coherent global public domain.

2.1 Evidence of Function 1: Averting Risks of Dual-state and Non-state—Actor Failure

During the post-1990 era there has been a marked increase in activities aimed at monitoring and assessing the performance of countries (primarily of their governments) in an ever-wider range of issue areas. According to Bandura (2011), about 300 such performance measures existed by early 2011.

For one, governments themselves are keeping a closer check on each other through mutual monitoring and assessment of national-level compliance with international agreements. This ranges from oversight of country-level progress toward the Millennium Development Goals (MDGs) and respect for human rights, to efforts aimed at controlling international terrorism, curbing greenhouse gas emissions, and tackling excessive financial volatility. In fact, many intergovernmental organizations have strengthened their surveillance activities, focusing especially on states' management of spillover effects. Mention can, for example, be made of the national reporting under the UNFCCC (United Nations Framework Convention on Climate Change) and the International Health Regulations (IHR) of the WHO (World Health Organization), as well as the monitoring of financial spillovers by the International Monetary Fund.

In addition, states are subject to increased monitoring, reviewing, and ranking by non-state actors, including civil society organizations like Amnesty International or Transparency International, international traders and investors, and, last but not least, sovereign credit rating agencies.

According to Keohane (2012), moralism and legalism, as well as legalization, have been on the rise in the post-1990 period. Among the indications of this trend are the increased use of sanctions by the United Nations Security Council, the new norm of Responsibility to Protect (R2P), the creation of the International Criminal Court, and the Appellate Body of the World Trade

Organization (WTO). Conditionality attached to foreign aid has also increased, and it serves, in many instances, as an instrument to prod countries into compliance.

However, with the exception of the WTO's Appellate Body, most of the enforcement measures are being applied to developing countries, notably to failed and failing states. Among the more economically developed countries, mutual assessments tend to take on a gentler form. In most instances, findings of non-compliance only invite expressions of concern on the part of other states.

While pressure on state actors to cooperate is now intensifying, non-state actors, for their part, appear more readily willing to reveal their preferences and contribute to GPGs. Indicators of this willingness include the growing number of individuals and associations that engage in global advocacy, voluntary norm and standard-setting, corporate social responsibility initiatives, the creation of private foundations supporting global public policy purposes, and the volunteering of time, knowledge, and expertise. The demand for, as well as the production of, "green," "safe," or "fair price" private goods also signals a desire to contribute (Granville and Dine 2013; Hale and Held 2011; Willetts 2011). And, over time, some norms are gaining global traction. They are forming a shared—and thickening—normative framework that guides and coordinates the behavior of individual actors, especially that of non-state actors, who may have less of a territorial fixation and more of a global identity than state actors (for example, see Finnemore and Sikkink 1998 and Sen 2006).

Nonetheless, many private-sector actors still pay little, if any, heed to the externalities of the actions they take, as exemplified by the excessive embrace of risk. Yet, as the follow-up to the 2008 financial crisis has shown, it is often hesitant regulatory behavior on the part of governments that allows these actions to continue (this point is discussed in more detail during the review of evidence for Function 4). In other words, state failure frequently precedes market failure.

In sum, we see that free-riding in the presence of global public goods is being recognized and responded to by some state and non-state actors; however, in terms of reducing the risk of state failure, the outcomes appear limited. This is especially true now that many of the industrial countries are highly indebted. Due to their weak financial positions, they are dependent on market actors, some of whom prefer less rather than more government intervention, as a closer look at the performance measures identified by Bandura (2011) reveals. Within this context of limited resources and dependence on market actors, non-cooperation will in many instances be—from a short-term perspective—the less costly and, hence, preferred policy option for national governments. This path is being selected not only to comply with market expectations, but also because a shallow evaluation suggests that it allows states to retain "unbridled," uncompromised national sovereignty.

As a result, the roles of state and non-state actors have become blurred. Both actor types frequently fail in the presence of GPGs; and both sometimes intervene to push others into action. However, given the current state of GPG provisioning, we must assume that the vast majority of actors intervene only to the extent that it is in line with their particular interests, whether they be private (market actors) or public (national governments), and that no one actor has developed a full sense of responsibility for or the capacity to ensure adequate GPG provisioning.

2.2 Evidence of Function 2: Promoting Global Fairness

Turning first to the process dimension of global fairness, the days of relatively closed, "statist" international cooperation are clearly gone, as suggested by the foregoing discussion. This change did not—or not only—happen because some international agency or global leader took a deliberate decision to encourage the broader participation of non-state actors. Rather, it has been a "bottom-up" process (Kaldor et al. 2012). Over time, more non-state actors became internationally engaged and connected, sought avenues of consultation with multilateral organizations and set up their own platforms like the World Economic Forum and the World Social Forum. Although the democratic credentials of civil society organizations themselves still pose a challenge, most multilateral organizations have by now institutionalized channels of consultation with civil society (Scholte 2010).

Like non-state actors, developing countries did not sit idly by, waiting for the conventional powers to grant them a more effective voice in multilateral organizations. They, too, created their own associations, including regional and issue-specific cooperation venues, as well as their own leadership forums like the summit meetings of the BRICS.[7] And they have succeeded in influencing international agendas and negotiation outcomes (for example, see UNDP 2013 and De Lombaerde et al. 2012).

Notably, though, the outcome for the developing countries has differed from the case of non-state actors. While the latter have seen their vocal power increase dramatically on the world stage, the former have received only modest increases in their decision-making power within the multilateral organizations. Examples include quota reform in the International Monetary Fund (IMF 2014) and participation in the Leaders' G-20, which, as some analysts argue, "reflects the rising premium on an institutionalized form of an expanded dialogue as some developing countries grow to acquire systemic or near-systemic economic weight" (Vestergaard and Wade 2011, 1).

Moreover, some cases actually run counter to the general trend of slightly expanded decision-making power for the developing countries. Witness, for example, the venue shifting on the part of the major industrialized countries, which have recently shown preference for smaller, informal negotiating groups like the AFPAK Group and the Climate and Clean Air Coalition, as well as bilateralism (Skidmore 2012; WTO 2011). Not surprisingly, the key multilateral negotiations are increasingly stuttering. Just think of the Doha Round of multilateral trade negotiations or the global climate change conferences in Copenhagen, Cancun, and Durban.

However, on the part of both developing and industrialized countries, international cooperation in the form of cross-border policy harmonization appears to be on the rise. Global concerns are being endorsed at national level and taken into account in national policymaking. This is notably the case when such steps generate "immediate" national co-benefits, as they often do in the areas of climate change mitigation and energy security (for example, see REN21 2013), and when a market-based, private-good approach to meeting global concerns can be taken, promising new growth opportunities (ILO and OECD 2012; OECD 2012).

Thus, what we seem to be witnessing is a multiplication of venues, and with it, a growing de-concentration, as well as an informalization, of decision making on global issues. This includes the wielding of more responsibility and initiative by non-state actors and, frequently, their bypassing of the conventional organizations. Two main forces appear to be propelling this trend: first, the fact that development and national capacity-building have progressed in the South; and, second, the greater acceptance of public-private partnering. Indeed, the fundamentals of international relations have changed. The conventional pattern of state-based, highly centralized, hegemonic decision making is undergoing a gradual—vertical and horizontal—de-concentration.

To the extent that this change will happen ad hoc as well as form part of a deliberate strategy of vertical and horizontal subsidiarity, it could ultimately have important positive effects in affording different actor groups enhanced policy space. For the time being, however, the de-concentration processes seem to be happening in lieu of—and, perhaps, even as an escape from—multilateral agreement.

As regards the second dimension of global fairness—the pursuit of mutually-beneficial cooperation bargains—signs of positive-sum thinking and the development of win/win strategies are barely evident. The conventional powers, and most notably the United States, are no longer as willing to "foot the bill" for international cooperation; and the new, emerging powers are not yet prepared to step into the resulting void (Ikenberry 2008; Skidmore 2012). Moreover, this retreat from multilateralism means more unresolved challenges and, in turn, less evidence and fewer arguments with which policymakers can try to convince their electorates about the merits of international cooperation. This task is becoming especially difficult in many wealthy countries as the notion of "embedded liberalism" wanes and inequity rises (Stiglitz 2013; Ruggie 1997). In fact, some analysts (e.g. Bremmer 2012 and Rachman 2010) warn that we are heading not toward a positive-sum world, but away from it.

To summarize, the policy interdependence and cooperation that GPGs require are being recognized slowly and hesitantly.

2.3 Function 3: Facilitating Global-issue Management

The trends toward actor pluralism and the de-concentration of international cooperation are perhaps even more pronounced on the operational side of international cooperation than on its agenda-setting and decision-making side.

Most striking is the proliferation of single-issue delivery and financing mechanisms since the 1990s, such as the Global Alliance for Vaccines and Immunization (GAVI) and the Financial Action Task Force (Conceição 2006; Reisen 2010). An important driving force behind this trend has been the encouragement of a greater role for private-sector actors in international cooperation, including through new and innovative methods of tapping private finance and the creation of incentives for private business to engage in pro-poor production efforts. Another impetus for the rise in single-issue mechanisms has come from civil society and its strengthened international engagement. Lastly, a third propelling force has been the realization that some summation-type provision processes—for example, polio eradication or terrorism control—include "weak links" that require targeted support in order for the good to emerge (Kaul and Conceição 2006).

Also, while foreign aid initiatives have conventionally been based on bilateral, country-to-country relations, under conditions of openness and policy interdependence, greater emphasis is now being placed on "fighting" specific externalities like a particular type of disease or pollution in a targeted way.

Although these varieties of global-issue management are important and might contribute to a strengthened result-orientation, they concern only select sub-components of global public goods. To understand this point, one need only consider that while a new drought-resistant crop may be a critical input in enhanced food security, much more than this lone input will be required to achieve the overall goal.

Awareness of the importance of overseeing the provisioning of global public goods in a more holistic and consolidated way appears to be growing slowly. The UN Secretary-General has, for example, appointed a number of eminent personalities as his Special Representatives to issues of global concern, yet their role to-date mainly consists of sporadic advocacy.

Similarly, states are now appointing "issue ambassadors" as diplomats assigned not to countries but to topics like HIV/AIDS, climate change, energy, multilateral trade, or human rights. One outcome is that issue-specific transnational networks of government officials have become a reality (Slaughter 2004; Hale and Held 2011; Reinicke 1998). Examples include the Financial Stability Board and the International Association of Insurance Supervisors. However, national institutional arrangements that allow global issues to be addressed in a comprehensive manner are still scarce, both on the legislative and the executive side of policymaking.

For the most part then, issues like global energy security, financial stability, and global public health are still being approached in a highly fractured manner (as shown by Dubash and Florini 2011; Davies 2010; and Kickbusch and Gleicher 2013).

Therefore, it should not come as a surprise that despite countless and highly valuable practical-political initiatives at all levels, many of these goods remain in a state of under-provision. That this fact is being noticed is evident from the risk and disaster management initiatives that are being established in a number of issue areas, including the IAEA's Response System, the IMF's work on surveillance and national capacity building for managing spillovers, the UN's Global Platform for Disaster Risk Reduction, and the WHO's Global Alert and Response (GAR). And, as a Google search shows, risk management has become a thriving business area.

Interestingly, reactive crisis prevention and management meets with more attention and willingness to act than the proactive investment in effective and fair international cooperation necessary to resolve the lingering global issues. One reason might be that crisis management is often approached with a strong country-focus centered on "building national resilience." Actually resolving the pending issues would call for more multilateralism, specifically an anchoring agency or agent to push all concerned actors to go the extra mile to jump over their narrowly conceived individual or national interest hurdles and do what is required to actually get to the good. The fact that this is not happening at present might be partly rooted in the to-date faint recognition of the transnationalness of GPGs' provision path.

Problematically, in some cases we not only note an absence of the global-issue management discussed above, but also of any focus on the global public domain, as detailed next.

2.4 Evidence of Function 4: Fostering a Balanced and Coherent Global Public Domain

When the financial crisis erupted in 2008, the G-20 was established as the world's premier forum for international economic cooperation and tasked with warding off the risk of a global depression. The development of the G-20 has constituted a major step toward recognition of the global public domain and the phenomenon of global systemic risk. However, member states' resolve to cooperate in tackling the financial crisis has weakened over time. This conclusion can certainly be tempered to some extent, because when assessing the G-20's performance, one must bear in mind that what, "was done in 2008–2009 was by nature exceptional and the following steps were bound to be of lower intensity" (Pisani-Ferry 2012, 33). Also, as Kharas and Lombardi (2012) remind us, the G-20 is not an operational body itself. Rather it tries to help build global consensus and to provide the required political momentum to jolt others into action. With these mitigating factors in mind, the authors' view is that the G-20 appears—at least for the time being—to be, "the 'best available option' for global economic governance" (Kharas and Lombardi 2012, 16).

While this might be so, the fact is that several aspects one would expect a "premier forum of international cooperation" to address have yet to receive the Group's full attention.

For example, one would expect G-20 leaders to do more in terms of urging the key actors in the finance sector to move rapidly toward the construction of a crisis-proof international financial architecture. However, there are several unresolved issues preventing the emergence of that architecture, including global financial regulation, the provision of a mechanism for guaranteeing consistent macroeconomic policies among the major economies, and a true global reserve currency (Brown 2013; Griffith-Jones and Ocampo 2012).

Such pressure to act is perhaps even more important in the area of global warming. However, despite the rapid multiplication of warning calls from reports such as the one detailing why we must avoid a 4-degree global temperature rise (PIK and Climate Analytics 2012), decisive multilateral action on mitigating and adapting to climate change is still gridlocked, at least at the global level. Much the same holds regarding the broader issue of global inequality of opportunity (Stiglitz 2013) and the need for a new, more sustainable and inclusive growth and development paradigm, as shown by the 2012 Rio + 20 Conference (Hale and Held 2011; Khor 2012).

Even more "limited" issues remain unresolved, such as the continuing inconsistencies between the global intellectual property rights regime on the one hand, and on the other, goals like fostering the dissemination of clean technology and critical medical and pharmaceutical technologies (Abbott 2009; Brandi et al. 2010; Kickbusch and Gleicher 2013).

Visions of how the world could use its vast stock of knowledge, technology, and wealth to create a better life for all are more or less absent from the G-20's deliberations. These include the question of "missing" GPGs, for example, a true global reserve currency (Ocampo 2010) or a well-stocked global pool of essential health and environmental technologies. Also absent is a discussion of the desirable balance between public and private, and among national, regional, and global.

Today, it is mainly the Global Risk Forum of the World Economic Forum which looks at the global public domain in a comprehensive manner, and its findings underline the critical importance of doing so. As the Forum's reports on *Global Risks* (WEF 2011, 2012, 2013) show, the interplay and negative feedback loops between multiple stresses on today's economic, environmental, social, and political systems will create unprecedented challenges to global, regional, and national resilience.

Awareness of global systemic risks is growing, yet on the practical-political level, global surveillance systems and risk management remain fragmented, as Goldin and Vogel (2010) have found. Just as the transnational policy space comprising global issues is not yet fully recognized, the global public domain is yet to be discovered as a "territory" that requires governance. Policy studies and policymaking remain in large measure focused on the traditionally-cited territorial spaces: the national domain and the international domain (Shah 2012; Stone 2008).

2.5 A Summary of the Evidence

The evidence presented above does reveal pertinent policy initiatives, but there is not yet a coherent, effective approach to the provisioning of GPGs. Thus, while we can discern various and proliferating measures fitting the profile of the governance requirements identified in Section 1, most of these seem to be of an ad hoc, uncoordinated, and often experimental nature. Still, amongst the initiatives, three trends are becoming visible.

First, a de-concentration of international cooperation appears to be occurring. This involves vertical de-concentration processes, which are shifting the action away from the conventional multilateral agencies toward more regional and national-level interventions, and horizontal de-concentration processes. The latter are characterized by the growing involvement of non-state actors and thus, move us away from a mainly statist system of international cooperation.

Second, while these de-concentration processes augur well in terms of more open and participatory international cooperation, at present they often serve as incomplete substitutes rather than complements to central, world-level GPG provisioning (see Figure 2.2). This absence of world-level inputs is indicated by relevant actors' common non-recognition of the emerging global spaces of policy interdependence identified in Section 1, namely the global-issue space and the global public domain.[8] Effective leadership of the latter is urgently needed and it cannot be sufficiently or efficiently provided in a decentralized manner.

There can be no doubt that new policy approaches, instruments, and mechanisms are rapidly proliferating in many global-issue areas. Unfortunately, they often aim precisely at fostering the observed processes of de-concentration by encouraging public-private partnering and greater reliance on market-based mechanisms or the spread of new policy approaches and instruments to regional and national levels. In other words, they reinforce, rather than reduce, the disconnect between the globalness of the challenges we face and the fractured nature of the policy responses they receive.

Third, governments can often be counted among the more reluctant actors in the international cooperation realm. They appear especially reluctant when the purpose of international cooperation is to commit to global norms and standards that require adjustment on their part. Conversely, they are quite forthcoming in exploring new and innovative methods for public-private partnering, especially financing methods that might reduce the amount they would otherwise have to contribute to joint international endeavors. Governments are the actors that have often demonstrated a clear preference for subsidiarity. This is a welcome trend in many respects, as emphasized previously, but it is extremely difficult for many goods to actually emerge if the necessary international cooperation among states is lacking.

Thus, we are witnessing the difficult beginnings of interdependence governance in today's multi-polar world. In this world, individual nation states are operating under a precarious balance between state and non-state actors—a balance that is currently tipped in favor of the latter, notably the market actors among them. The provisioning of GPGs does occur, but mainly to the extent that it aligns with the interests of individual actors, both state and non-state types.

Importantly, though, in policy fields marked by interdependence, actors will not be able to successfully continue solitary pursuit of their individual interests, at least not in the medium to long-term future. And for that reason, we must consider potential steps to correct for the current failure of multilateral approaches.

Evidently, something more than the four governance functions discussed so far is required if we are to break this vicious circle of multilateral inaction. Section 3 explores what that something might be.

3 PROVIDING GLOBAL PUBLIC GOODS: BRINGING THE UNITED NATIONS BACK IN

Based on the foregoing discussion, it seems that two sets of reforms—both concerning the UN—are necessary to facilitate the provisioning of GPGs.

Regarding the first set of reforms, the role of states in international cooperation, specifically in the management of interdependence, requires a fresh look. While the greater involvement of non-state actors in international cooperation is to be welcomed and encouraged, it should not be seen as a substitute for active state engagement in global matters.

The problem here is that when added to the currently constrained engagement by states, the decentralized policy responses produced thus far by non-state actors, despite often being innovative and socially or globally-minded, simply do not sum up to a policymaking capacity sufficient to bring about effective resolution of contemporary global challenges. As indicated previously, one set of actors must be ready to counteract shortfalls in the provisioning of GPGs and take on the responsibility of ensuring that, when a global prisoner's dilemma situation arises, the world can break out of it in time to avoid the pending crisis. Which actor, aside from states working as "united nations," is positioned to become this critical "coordinator of last resort?"

This, however, begs another question: how can we strengthen states' motivation to cooperate? As this chapter implies, their motivation levels do not presently seem equal to the tasks at hand. In fact a reserve of cooperative sentiment will need to be generated because, as we have seen, several obstacles have rendered international negotiations more difficult, including the changed nature of many global challenges; the ongoing global power shifts, which have made it particularly difficult for states to agree on how to resolve those challenges by adding fuel to the sovereignty paradox; and a change in adjustment burdens, which in contrast to previous decades, now fall relatively heavily on the North, seemingly reducing industrialized nations' incentives to cooperate (witness the United States' recent reticence toward multilateralism or, viewed differently, its penchant for bilateralism). Though much ancillary work will need to be done to incentivize and maintain cooperation amidst these obstacles, the key goal must be the forging—in and through the United Nations—of global consensus on a sovereignty-compatible rationale for international cooperation. This aim is detailed in Section 1.1.

In the second set of reforms, it will be important to explicitly and systematically introduce interdependence management into the architecture of the UN system, including the associated Bretton Woods institutions—the IMF and the World Bank. This would imply adding to the country and regional focus of these entities the two new global spaces of policy interdependence identified during the discussion of Functions 3 and 4: the global-issue space and the global public domain.

Both sets of potential reforms are explained in more detail below.

3.1 Forging Global Consensus on a Sovereignty-compatible Rationale for International Cooperation

The way in which policymakers, scholars, journalists, and the public at large now speak about international cooperation shows that it is often perceived as running counter to the core principle on which the present world order rests: non-interference by external forces into states' internal affairs, or, put differently, into their national policymaking sovereignty.

At first sight, international cooperation appears to imply exactly that type of "interference." It requires the recognition of common interests and a bridging of the foreign/domestic divide. This suggests a blending of national and external policy concerns. To achieve that, the state would need to act—at least in fields of policy interdependence among countries—as an intermediary between national and global concerns. In many instances, states are already playing this role (see Kaul 2006). Yet they often do so reluctantly, because many perceive it—for understandable reasons—as entailing a loss or transfer of national policymaking sovereignty to international organizations and other globally engaged actors. After all, international cooperation has so far been, and in large measure still is, a "power play."

Accordingly, national-level policymakers frequently shy away from international cooperation even where it would constitute the better approach to meeting national interests. The reasoning underlying this "better approach" claim is that countries inherently lose policymaking space and options when, due to a lack of international cooperation on key challenges, they come under attack from forces such as financial crises, catastrophic storms or floods, terrorist actions, or new and resurgent communicable diseases that hold no respect for national borders.

In these cases, reluctance to engage in multilateral cooperation leads to the aforementioned "sovereignty paradox" (Kaul 2013): the harder governments try to hold onto a conventional, absolute notion of sovereignty in policy fields marked by interdependence, the more they fail to meet global challenges, and the consequences of each of these failures further undermine their policymaking autonomy and capacity.

In order to persuade policymakers and their constituencies to break free from this trap, we need to define and prove a sovereignty-compatible rationale for a more genuinely global approach to the GPG provisioning that will be required to meet these challenges. This will entail two main steps.

In the first one, the rationality and feasibility of state engagement in effective—and to that end, fair—international cooperation must be established, especially in policy areas involving interdependence challenges. This could be done, for example, by complementing global studies on the economics and politics of particular global issues, such as the Stern Review (Stern 2007), with more country- and region-specific analyses. In addition to issue-focused studies, others could be undertaken comparing the costs and benefits of inaction and action on global imbalances or examining incoherence between various global public goods, again in a disaggregated, context-specific way. The emphasis ought to be on demonstrating the possibility of constructing positive-sum cooperation bargains, i.e., bargains that would meet national, regional, and global interests in a mutually beneficial way.

In the second step, the compiled evidence could be utilized to help forge consensus on a notion of mutually respectful sovereignty (as suggested in Kaul 2013). This notion of sovereignty, based on states' acceptance of the rationality of cooperation in interdependent policy areas, would combine the pursuit of national and regional interests with respect for the sovereignty of other states, and therefore, with respect for environmental boundaries and other global systemic balances (De Brabandere 2013; Țuțuiana 2013).[9] Such consensus would reassure countries that their negotiating partners will come to the table with similar, positive-sum strategies.

In the field of international security we have long realized that collective defense of states' borders makes every state more secure than if they relied solely on their own defenses. A very similar argument can be made for the new types of security threats infringing on states' sovereignty (e.g. financial contagion or environmental degradation): their mitigation necessitates cooperation and the understanding of sovereignty as a good that, in such cases, is best provided and secured collectively (see Box 2.2 for additional details).

If framed in this way, sovereignty would "allow" policymakers to engage in global public policy without being concerned about betraying—or being perceived as betraying—the national interest. It would then be clear that sovereignty as such is not in question. To the contrary, the strategies for exercising national sovereignty would be adjusted to current policymaking realities, notably the challenge of interdependence, in order to safeguard it.

In other words, a sovereignty-compatible rationale for international cooperation would identify it as the preferred strategy for responding to interdependence challenges, because by cooperating on these challenges states: (1) foster policy efficiency and effectiveness, while maintaining their national policymaking capacity; and (2) show respect for the concerns of other states, reinforcing, with each application, the norm of mutually respectful sovereignty. Thus, if widely adopted, the norm of respectful sovereignty would protect countries against negative spill-ins from abroad, and thereby help safeguard their policymaking sovereignty.

There is, of course, a "but." The feasibility of this reform depends on global fairness: on constructing positive-sum bargains and on the net-benefits from international cooperation being shared regionally and nationally in order to secure broad-based, popular support for international cooperation.[10]

States have been granted their legal status as independent, sovereign nations by ratifying the UN Charter. Therefore, the UN is now the best positioned entity to consult on and foster world-wide agreement on the rethinking of which strategies need to be pursued in order to better combine openness and national policymaking sovereignty.

Box 2.2 Responsible Sovereignty—A Collective Approach to Safeguarding National Policymaking Capacity

International cooperation is often seen as undermining states' policymaking sovereignty. No doubt, it often does; and therefore, governments frequently shy away from a global, concerted policy response, even in issue areas that involve transnational challenges that no single nation can effectively and efficiently address alone. In the absence of a cooperative approach, global challenges will linger unresolved, potentially making all parties worse off.

When confronting challenges that entail policy interdependence, it is in the enlightened self-interest of all concerned states to offer fair and mutually beneficial cooperation. This requires mutual confidence and trust. Accordingly, there must be a shared commitment among states to act responsibly, both toward their own territories and constituencies—protecting against negative spill-ins from abroad—and toward other states, because non-cooperation could undermine welfare and well-being for all.

In other words, exercising responsible sovereignty means pursuing national interests in a way that is fully respectful of the sovereignty of other nations and, to that end, oriented toward the maintenance of global balances and planetary environmental boundaries.

Just as states' commitment to the norm of collective security strengthens the inviolability of national territorial borders, a commitment to exercising their policymaking sovereignty in a mutually respectful and responsible manner could, in areas of policy interdependence, be the best way to secure their national policymaking capacity.

Source: Kaul (2014)

Maybe the UN Secretary-General could be asked to establish a high-level panel of independent eminent personalities to assist member states in this endeavor? Such a panel's goal ought to be not only to strengthen states' willingness to cooperate, but also to address their willingness to assume more of a "global public actor" role by serving as a broker and intermediary among national, regional, and global concerns and exigencies—at home and abroad.

In sum, the reform steps proposed to strengthen states' willingness to cooperate fairly and effectively, and in a manner complementary to the work done by non-state actors, are the following:

- Reform Step 1: Introduce a notion of smart, responsible, and respectful national policymaking sovereignty; and establish the rationality and feasibility of state engagement in positive-sum international cooperation, specifically in policy areas characterized by interdependence challenges, through both global and country-level reports, and issue-focused cost/benefit analyses.

- Reform Step 2: Make use of the established evidence to foster agreement on this notion of sovereignty and, thereby, on an enhanced role for states internationally, i.e., an expectation that they function collectively as guardians of the global common good by taking on a role as intermediaries among national, regional, and global concerns (with the hope that this will lead to more balanced, fair, and sustainable growth and development).

As repeatedly emphasized, these reforms would apply mainly to policy fields marked by interdependence, i.e., to cases in which leaving countries to their own devices would be a recipe for collective disaster (Rodrik 2012). In many other respects, states would likely continue their rivalries. But, if they were to cooperate where cooperation is clearly the best strategy, inter-state rivalry and competition among market actors could become less ruinous, and perhaps even sustainability-enhancing.

3.2 Incorporating "Interdependence Management" into the Architecture of the UN System

As Weiss (2012, 19) notes, "[The UN] was not built to confront many of the challenges that face the world today." In fact, the UN has helped promote and bring to near completion the present world order based on individual sovereign states. Many aspects of the UN's structure and functioning are therefore based on country-centric considerations. These are complemented by organizational arrangements, such as the specialized agencies, that mainly follow economic-sector lines, e.g., agriculture, education, health, and industry. The UN regional commissions are organized along similar lines.

Indeed, more so than its actual focus and functioning, it is the near-universal country representation, i.e., its 193 member states, that makes the UN a world body. So far, the organization has not systematically adjusted its architecture to the present era of globalization, notably to the reality of border-transgressing, global challenges. No doubt, many UN entities do deal with a range of global issues. However, they tend to approach these issues from a country or regional perspective—not from the viewpoint of the global issue itself. What the various countries, non-state actors, or multilateral agencies are doing in response to a given issue is regularly examined, but other issues are rarely considered, such as what is required to ensure adequate provisioning of a GPG and how well state and non-state efforts meet those requirements.

Thus, if the UN is to help promote and operationalize a notion of smart sovereignty, it would be desirable to request the UN system agencies to expand their focus. The UN system ought to deal more explicitly and systematically with global concerns, including global-issue management, the fostering of a balanced and coherent structure of the global public domain, and the functioning of that domain.

In regards to global-issue management, this would imply exploration of whether the key global concerns have an institutional anchor within the system. This anchor could take the form of a unit or individuals charged with the responsibility for ascertaining that all required GPG inputs are being assembled, relevant incentives provided, financial resources mobilized, and results monitored.

Establishing global-issue anchor agencies or agents within the multilateral system might encourage the setting-up of institutional counterparts at the national and regional levels, which would, in turn, facilitate coordination and cooperation between these different levels of governance. In fact, from the viewpoint of ensuring policy commitment to international cooperation it would be best for policymaking to start from the domestic level in each country. National or regional cooperation requests and offers could then be channeled up into international negotiations and once agreed, travel back down to the lower levels for implementation. The creation of such multi-level, multilateral, global policy loops would go a long way towards fostering the integrated, transnational policy approach that the provisioning of many GPGs requires.

The role of the UN global-issue anchors in this process could be a light-footed one geared toward process facilitation, e.g., on the identification of potential shortfalls that can only be addressed by a coordinator of last resort, i.e., those tasks which other actors might not be able to undertake or complete sufficiently.

While global-issue management requires a vertical, subsidiarity-based policy approach, surveillance of and leadership for the global public domain requires primarily a horizontal, cross-issue approach. This approach allows the monitoring of conflicts and synergy between GPGs, and the detection of issue areas in which underprovision is worsening and assuming crisis-proportions, perhaps even threatening to transgress planetary boundaries and undermine the resources and policy options available to future generations.

In order for the UN system to perform this role in a more explicit and systematic manner, the UN Secretariat could be requested to establish a new unit: an observatory of global trends, challenges, and opportunities.

The analyses undertaken by this Observatory could be discussed at an annual conference of the heads of UN system entities and feed into the high-level debates of the UN legislative bodies, as well as into other global debates, including the annual G-20 leaders' summit, the World Economic Forum, and the World Social Forum. One could even establish a standing high-level body of independent, eminent personalities—a Global Stewardship Council. Such a body could lend additional political clout to the Observatory's studies and "nudge" governments into taking account of emerging risks and the requirements of longer-term sustainability. Measures such as these could help restore the UN's role as a leader in providing a global vision of world order fit for the present age of openness.

In sum, translating the notion of smart sovereignty into practical, political action would require institutional adjustments at all levels of governance. The UN could provide an important impetus to these reforms, if it were itself to undertake the following additional reform steps:

- Reform Step 3: Appoint, in key global-issue areas, a high-level issue manager charged with identifying missing or lagging inputs and proposing measures to incentivize concerned actors and foster a timely, effective, efficient, and equitable provisioning of the desired global-public policy outcome.
- Reform Step 4: Create, within the UN Secretariat, a new observatory of global risks and opportunities mandated to survey the global public domain to determine how well—and how equitably—it serves different groups of states, as well as different actor and population groups, including current and future generations.

Taken together, the proposed UN reform steps 1–4 could go a long way toward strengthening the four governance functions discussed in Sections 1 and 2 (and also summarized in Table 2.1).

Table 2.1 Meeting the governance requirements of GPGs–current impediments and longer-term corrective measures

GPG governance requirement	Current impediment	Longer-term corrective measure
Averting risk of dual actor failure	Adherence to the conventional notion of sovereignty and the resultant sovereignty paradox	Forging—in and through the UN – global consensus on a notion of responsible sovereignty
Promoting global fairness	Continuing power politics	Accepting policy interdependence and that it "pays" to engage in fair international cooperation
Facilitating global-issue management	The conventional foreign/domestic divide	Recognizing the provision path of GPGs as new, added policy spaces and introducing a global-issue focus into governance systems, nationally and internationally
Fostering a coherent, global public domain	A "silo approach" to GPG provisioning	Recognizing the the global public domain and establishing, within the UN, an independent Global Stewardship Council plus a UN Secretariat unit to serve as an observatory to assist in monitoring the structure and functioning of the global public domain

4 CONCLUSION

This chapter began by examining the governance requirements for an enhanced provisioning of global public goods (GPGs) under the current global policymaking realities (Section 1). It subsequently searched policy practice for signs that relevant initiatives are underway (Section 2). Finally, it discussed (in Section 3) some of the missing links that will likely have to be inserted if the word is to disentangle itself from the current web of global crises.

The analysis has shown that many relevant initiatives can be identified. However, they mainly occur to the extent and in a form that fits into conventional governance molds. Genuine interdependence management is still in short supply. As possible corrective steps, the chapter suggests two sets of measures: first, to utilize global experience to-date, as well as research and analyses on positive-sum potentialities, to forge global consensus on a sovereignty-compatible rationale for international cooperation in policy fields marked by interdependence; and, second, to introduce a focus on the "global" into the present system of international cooperation, complementing its conventional country and economic sector focus. The United Nations has an important role to play in both of these efforts—efforts that constitute important steps towards a new era of fair and effective multilateralism, enabling policymakers to catch up with globalization and foster more sustainable and inclusive growth and development.

NOTES

1. For additional details on the properties of public goods and global public goods, including the free-rider problem that plagues their provision, see Box 2.1, as well as the associated text throughout Section 1.
2. For reasons of brevity, the term "United Nations" (UN) is being used here to refer to the UN system as a whole, including specialized agencies and related organizations such as the International Monetary Fund, the World Bank, and the International Atomic Energy Agency.
3. The present paper draws on Kaul (2014).
4. The type of state failure identified here is not to be confounded with the types of government failure that public choice scholars tend to focus on, namely the self-interested behavior of politicians and bureaucrats. The state failure referred to here is systemically rooted in the fact that the present world order is composed of individual sovereign nation states.
5. The other new global space of policy interdependence—the global public domain—has been mentioned above, and is described in more detail in conjunction with Function 4.

6. As defined here, the term "global public domain" refers to a "stock variable," viz. the ensemble of natural and human-made GPGs, including intermediate GPGs like international organizations or norms and standards, as well as final GPGs like international financial stability, peace and security, biodiversity preservation, or disease control, i.e., goods that may actually contribute to our well-being, if well-provided, or subtract from it, if underprovided.

   Other authors (e.g. Ruggie 2004) have used the term to refer to a related "flow variable," viz. the process of multi-actor decision making on global issues, a dimension captured in this article under Function 2, i.e., the requirement of more open, participatory, and fair decision making—a requirement seen as resulting, in part, from the changed balance between state and non-state actors but also, and importantly, as shown in Figure 2.2, from the nature of the global challenges themselves—their transnationalness or, put differently, global publicness—and their actual provision status.
7. BRICS is a forum of leading emerging economies, including Brazil, Russia, India, China, and South Africa.
8. To reiterate the conceptualizations discussed in Section 1, global-issue spaces comprise the provision path of particular GPGs, which inherently criss-cross the traditional policy spaces defined by geographic criteria, economic sector, and actor group. Thus, the global-issue spaces overlay these established policy spaces. The global public domain, meanwhile, comprises the ensemble of the world-spanning effects of global public policy, primarily GPGs and the relationships between these goods.
9. This is because respect for the sovereignty of other states will necessarily entail respect for the environmental and systemic problems that are disproportionately affecting some states, e.g., the tiered impact of global warming on different states based on their geography.
10. Notions of responsible sovereignty have been under discussion for a number of years. For example, Deng et al. (1996, 6) referred to "sovereignty as responsibility," meaning that "national governments are duty bound to ensure minimum standards of security and social welfare for their citizens and be accountable both to the national body politic and the international community." The International Commission on Intervention and State Sovereignty carried this notion of sovereignty as responsibility one step further, suggesting that, "[s]tate sovereignty implies responsibility, and the primary responsibility for the protection of its people lies with the state itself," and that, "Where a population is suffering serious harm…, and the state in question is unwilling or unable to halt or avert it, the principle of non-intervention yields to the international responsibility to protect" (ICISS 2001, XI). This ICISS recommendation provided the basis for the emergence of the norm now known as "responsibility to protect" or R2P.

    In the late 1990s/early 2000s, a second strand of contributions to the discussion on responsible sovereignty emerged (see, among others, Kaul et al., 1999, 2013; Jones et al. 2009). These contributions linked the notion to global, transnational challenges, reminding all states of their responsibility to be accountable for cross-border externalities that emanate from their jurisdiction and could potentially harm other nations. This broadened notion of responsible sovereignty also covers challenges like consciousness-shocking human rights violations, because those could also spill across borders. They could generate streams of illegal migrants, lead to civil strife and conflict that might necessitate international peace-keeping missions, or lead to failed and failing states.

REFERENCES

Abbott, Frederick M. 2009. "Innovation and Technology Transfer to Address Climate Change: Lessons from the Debate on Intellectual Property and Health." Geneva: ICTSD (International Centre for Trade and Sustainable Development). Issue Paper No. 24.

Bandura, Romina. 2011. *Composite Indicators and Rankings: Inventory 2011*. Working Paper. Available at http://nebula.wsimg.com/beb0f5b0e9b6f0c298ae72e7519b22a4?AccessKeyId=EA00C1BFA208EDA3747F&disposition=0.

Barrett, Scott. 2007. *Why Cooperate? The Incentive to Supply Global Public Goods*. New York: Oxford University Press.

Brandi, Carla, Christine Ladenberger, and Anna Pegels. 2010. *Intellectual property rights as a challenge to providing global public goods—the case of public health, food security and climate stability*. Bonn: German Development Institute. Discussion Paper 17/2010.

Bremmer, Ian. 2012. *Every Nation For Itself; Winners and Losers in a G-Zero World*. London: Penguin.

Brown, Gordon. 2013. "National Drift or Global Mastery." *Project Syndicate*. http://www.project-syndicate.org/commentary/the-global-economy-s-nationalist-traps-by-gordon-brown.

Conceição, Pedro. 2006. "Accommodating New Actors and New Purposes in International Cooperation: The Growing Diversification of Financing Mechanisms." In *The New Public Finance: Responding to Global Challenges*, edited by Inge Kaul and Pedro Conceição, pp. 269–80. New York: Oxford University Press. DOI: 10.1093/acprof:oso/9780195179972.001.0001.

Davies, Howard. 2010. "Global financial regulation after the credit crisis." *Global Policy* 1 (2): pp. 185–90.

De Brabandere, Eric. 2013. "The Impact of 'Supranationalism' on State Sovereignty from the Perspective of the Legitimacy of International Organizations." In Duncan French (ed.) *Statehood and Self-Determination*. pp. 450–70. Cambridge: Cambridge University Press.

De Lombaerde, Philippe, Francis Baert, and Tânia Felício, eds. 2012. *The United Nations and the Regions; Third World Report on Regional Integration*. New York: Springer.

Deng, Francis M., Sadikiel Kimaro, Terrence Lyons, Donald Rothchild, and I. William Zartman. 1996. *Sovereignty as Responsibility: Conflict Management in Africa*. Washington, DC: The Brookings Institution.

Dubash, Navroz K., and Ann Florini. 2011. "Mapping Global Energy Governance." *Global Policy* 2, Special Issue "Global Energy Governance": pp. 6–18.

Finnemore, Martha, and Kathryn Sikkink. 1998. "International Norm Dynamics and Political Change." *International Organization* 52 (4, Autumn): pp. 887–917.

Goldin, Ian and Tiffany Vogel. 2010. Global Governance and Systemic Risk in the 21st Century: Lessons from the Financial Crisis. *Global Policy* 1 (1): pp. 4–14.

Granville, Brigitte, and Janet Dine, eds. 2013. *The Processes and Practices of Fair Trade: Trust, Ethics and Governance.* New York: Routledge.

Griffith-Jones, Stephany, and José Antonio Ocampo. 2012. "International Financial Architecture Seen through the Lens of the Crisis; Some Achievements and Numerous Challenges." In *Development Cooperation in Times of Crisis,* edited by José Antonio Alonso and José Antonio Ocampo, pp. 82–141. New York: Columbia University Press.

Hale, Thomas, and David Held, eds. 2011. *The Handbook of Transnational Governance: Institutions and Innovations.* Cambridge: Polity Press.

ICISS (International Commission on Intervention and State Sovereignty). 2001. *The Responsibility To Protect.* Ottawa: ICISS.

Ikenberry, John G. 2008. "America and the reform of global institutions." In *Can the World Be Governed? Possibilities for Effective Multilateralism,* edited by A.S. Alexandroff, pp. 110–38. Waterloo: Wilfrid Laurier University Press.

ILO (International Labour Organization) and OECD (Organization for Economic Co-operation and Development). 2012. *Sustainable development, green growth and quality employment; Realizing the potential for mutually reinforcing policies.* Background paper for the Meeting of G20 Labour and Employment Ministers, Guadalajara, May 17–18. Geneva: ILO and Paris: OECD.

IMF (International Monetary Fund). 2014. "IMF Executive Board Reports to the Board of Governors on the 2010 Reforms and the Fifteenth General Review of Quotas." Press Release No. 14/22, January 23. Washington, DC: IMF.

Jones, Bruce, Carlos Pasqual, and Stephen John Stedman. 2009. *Power and Responsibility; Building International Order in an Era of Transnational Threats.* Washington, DC: Brookings Press.

Kaldor, Mary, Sabine Selchow, and Henrietta L. Moore, eds. 2012. *Global Civil Society 2012: Ten Years of Critical Reflection.* Basingstoke: Palgrave Macmillan.

Kaul, Inge and Mendoza, Ronald. 2003. "Advancing the concept of global public goods." In, *Providing Global Public. Managing Globalization Goods,* edited by I. Kaul, P. Conceição, K. Le Goulven, and R. Mendoza. New York: Oxford University Press.

Kaul, Inge. 2006. "Blending External and Domestic Policy Demands: The Rise of the Intermediary State." In *The New Public Finance: Responding to Global Challenges,* edited by Inge Kaul and Pedro Conceição, pp. 73–108. New York: Oxford University Press. DOI: 10.1093/acprof:oso/9780195179972.001.0001.

Kaul, Inge. 2013. "Meeting Global Challenges; Assessing Governance Readiness, in Hertie School of Governance." *The Governance Report 2013,* pp. 33–58. Oxford: Oxford University Press.

Kaul, Inge, and Pedro Conceição, eds. 2006. *The New Public Finance: Responding to Global Challenges.* New York: Oxford University Press. DOI: 10.1093/acprof:oso/9780195179972.001.0001.

Keohane, Robert O. 2012. "Twenty Years of Institutional Liberalism." *International Relations* 26(2): pp. 125–38.

Kharas, Homi, and Domenico Lombardi. 2012. *The Group of Twenty: Origins, Prospects and Challenges for Global Governance*. Washington, DC: Brookings Institution.

Khor, Martin. 2012. "Rio+20 was not all in vain." *IDN-InDepth News* (July 9). http://www.indepthnews.info/index.php/global-issues/1039-rio20-was-not-all-in-vain.

Kickbusch, Ilona, and David Gleicher, eds. 2013. *Governance for Health in the 21st Century*. Copenhagen: World Health Organization Regional Office.

Ocampo, José Antonio. 2010. *Why Should the Global Reserve System Be Reformed?* Berlin and New York: FES (Friedrich Ebert Stiftung). FES Briefing Paper 1/2010.

OECD (Organization for Economic Cooperation and Development). 2012. "The jobs potential of a shift towards a low-carbon economy." Final Report for the European Commission, DG Employment. Paris: OECD.

Pisani-Ferry, Jean. 2012. "Macro-economic Coordination: What Has the G-20 Achieved?" In *Think Tank 20: New Challenges for the Global Economy, New Uncertainties for the G-20*, pp. 28–34. Washington, DC: Brookings Institution Press.

PIK and Climate Analytics [Potsdam Institute of Climate Impact Research, Climate Analytics]. 2012. *Turn Down The Heat: Why a 4°C Warmer World Must be Avoided*. Washington D.C: World Bank.

Rachman, Gideon. 2010. *Zero-Sum World; Politics, Power and Prosperity After the Crash*. London: Atlantic Books.

Reinicke, Wolfgang. 1998. *Global Public Policy; Governing without Government?* Washington, DC: Brookings Institution Press.

Reisen, Helmut. 2010. "The Multilateral Donor Non-System: Towards Accountability and Efficient Role Assignment." *Economics: The Open-Access, Open Assessment E-Journal* 4(5): pp. 1–22.

REN21. 2013. *Renewables 2011 Global Status Report*. Paris: REN21 Secretariat.

Rodrik, Dani. 2012. "Leaderless Global Governance." *Project Syndicate*. Available at http://www.project-syndicate.org, accessed 23/2/2013.

Ruggie, John Gerard. 1997. "Globalization and the Embedded Liberalism Compromise: The End of an Era?" Cologne: Max-Planck-Institute for the Study of Societies. Working Paper 97/1.

Ruggie, John Gerard. 2004. "Reconstituting the Global Public Domain; Issues, Actors, and Practices." Harvard: Corporate Social Responsibility Initiative, John F. Kennedy School of Government. Working Paper No.6.

Scholte, Jan Aart. 2010. "Civil Society in multi-level governance." In *Handbook on Multi-level Governance*, edited by Henrik Enderlein, Sonja Wälti, and Michael Zürn, pp. 383–96. Cheltenham, UK: Edward Elgar.

Sen, Amartya K. 2006. *Identity and Violence.: The Illusion of Destiny*. London: Penguin Group.

Shah, Nisha. 2012. "The Territorial Trap of the Territorial: Global Transformation and the Problem of the State's Two Territories." *International Political Sociology* 6: pp. 57–76.

Skidmore, David. 2012. "The Obama Presidency and US Foreign Policy: Where's the Multilateralism?" *International Studies Perspectives* 13: pp. 43–64.

Slaughter, Anne-Marie. 2004. *A New World Order*. Princeton: Princeton University Press.

Stern, Nicholas. 2007. *The Economics of Climate Change: The Stern Review*. Cambridge: Cambridge University Press.

Stone, Diane. 2008. "Global Public Policy, Transnational Policy Communities, and Their Networks." *The Policy Studies Journal* 36(1): pp. 19–38.

Ţuţuianu, Simona. 2013. *Towards Global Justice: Sovereignty in an Interdependent World*. The Hague: Asser.

UNDP (United Nations Development Program). 2013. *Human Development Report 2013—The Rise of the South—Human Progress in a Diverse World*. New York: UNDP.

Vestergaard, J., and Robert H. Wade. 2011. "The G20 has Served its Purpose and Should be Replaced." *Journal of Globalization and Development* 2(2): pp. 1–17.

WEF (World Economic Forum). 2011, 2012, 2013. *Global Risks*. Geneva: World Economic Forum.

Weiss, Thomas G. 2012. *What's Wrong with the United Nations and How to Fix it*. Cambridge, UK: Polity.

Willetts, Peter. 2011. *Non-Governmental Organizations in World Politics: The Construction of Global Governance*. New York: Routledge.

WTO (World Trade Organization). 2011. "World Trade Report 2011: The WTO and Preferential Trade Agreements: From Co-existence to Coherence." Geneva: WTO.

Further Reading

Elson, Anthony. 2012. "International Financial Architecture; A Report Card." *World Economics* 13 (2): pp. 155–70.

Galbraith, James K. 2012. *Inequality and Instability: A Case Study of the World Economy Just Before the Great Crisis*. New York: Oxford University Press.

Howse, Robert, and Ruti Teitel. 2010. "Beyond Compliance: Rethinking Why International Law Really Matters." *Global Policy* 1(2): pp. 127–36.

IMF (International Monetary Fund). 2013. *2013 Spillover Report*. Washington, DC: IMF.

Kaul, Inge. 2014. *Fostering Sustainable Human Development: Managing the Macrorisks of Vulnerability*. New York: UNDP Human Development Report Office. Occasional Paper.

Kaul, Inge. 2013. *Meeting Global Challenges: Assessing Governance Readiness. In Hertie School of Governance. The Governance Report 2013*. Oxford: Oxford University Press.

Kaul, Inge, Pedro Conceição, Katell Le Goulven, and Ronald U. Mendoza, eds. 2003. *Providing Global Public Goods; Managing Globalization*. New York: Oxford University Press.

Kaul, Inge, Isabelle Grunberg, and Marc A. Stern, eds. 1999. *Global Public Goods; International Cooperation in the 21st Century*. New York: Oxford University Press.

Mattoo, Aaditya, and Arvind Subramanian. 2013. *Greenprint: A New Approach to Cooperation on Climate Change*. Washington D.C: Center for Global Development.

Ocampo, José Antonio, Stephany Griffith-Jones, Akbar Noman et al., eds. 2012. "The Great Recession and the Developing World." In *Development Cooperation in Times of Crisis*, edited by José Antonio Alonso and and José Antonio Ocampo, pp. 17–81. New York: Columbia University Press.

Petersmann, Ernst-Ulrich. 2011. "International Economic Law, 'Public Reason', and Multilevel Governance of Interdependent Public Goods." *Journal of International Economic Law* 14(1): pp. 23–76.

Sandler, Todd. 2004. *Global Collective Action*. Cambridge: Cambridge University Press.

Severino, Jean-Michel, and Olivier Ray. 2010. *The End of ODA (II): The Birth of Hypercollective Action*. Washington DC: Center for Global Development.

Stiglitz, Joseph. 2013. *The Price of Inequality. How Today's Divided Society Endangers Our Future*. Norton: New York.

Weiss, Thomas G., and Ramesh Thakur. 2010. *Global Governance and the UN; An Unfinished Journey*. Bloomington and Indianapolis: Indiana University Press.

3

De-colonizing the 2030 Development Agenda

Moving Towards a Universal Partnership for Sustainable Development

Alicia Bárcena

The world is confronting epochal changes in this second decade of this millennium. Overlapping crises are striking simultaneously. These crises are not only of a financial or economic nature, but are also social, political, and environmental. Financial globalization in a de-regulated world has created a jobless generation within a context of greater inequality, particularly in developed countries. As shown by Piketty, inequality has maintained its trend, has continued to grow in the aftermath of the global financial crisis, and is a worldwide phenomenon. In the case of the United States, the income share of the richest (top 1% income) reached 22.5 percent of total income in 2012, representing the highest concentration of wealth in over eight decades. Some OECD countries show a similar distributive pattern (Alvaredo et al. 2013).

In emerging economies, demographic trends show that rising population and incomes per capita will increase the demand for food—even as nearly 1 billion people, most in Africa, already suffer chronic hunger. Inequality manifests itself in a variety of forms in developing countries including in income, education, health, and access to technology. Globally, environmental integrity and earth dynamics are reaching threatening boundaries. Anthropogenic interference is affecting crucial cycles such as water, nitrogen, and carbon, and, in particular, the climate system, as recently reported by the Intergovernmental Panel on Climate Change (IPCC, 2013). Overall, there is the crisis of the fossil-energy-intensive industrial model. The accumulation of such crises has created a high level of volatility and uncertainty and a greater concentration of wealth and income in few hands.

In this context, during 2014 and 2015, the world designed and agreed upon the development agenda for the next 15 years. This process within the UN system was underpinned by a transition from an international community that gave priority mainly to fulfilling the Millennium Development Goals (MDGs), which were based on what rich countries pledged they would do for poor countries to overcome extreme poverty and attain their basic needs, to a new global deal that took the shape of the 2030 Agenda for Sustainable Development with renewed partnerships for development. This renewed Agenda contains a set of universal Sustainable Development Goals (SDGs) embracing economic development, environmental sustainability, and social inclusion that applies to developed and developing countries alike (United Nations 2012a).

In the discussions and negotiations on the new agenda, there was a broad understanding among Member States that completing the unfinished business of the Millennium Development Goals—particularly with regard to the eradication of poverty, inequality, and other important social objectives—must figure centrally in the SDG framework. The outcome document of the United Nations Conference on Sustainable Development (Rio+20), entitled "The future we want," states clearly the importance of sustainable development, without losing focus on the commitment of eradicating poverty by 2030 and achieving the MDGs (United Nations 2012a). The SDGs are aspirational, global in nature, and universally applicable to all countries (United Nations 2012a, para. 247). It also takes into account the Principles of the Rio Declaration on Environment and Development, including the principle of common but differentiated responsibilities. At the sixty-seventh session of the General Assembly, Member States established an Open-ended Working Group on the Sustainable Development Goals, comprising 30 representatives from the five United Nations regional groups, to prepare a proposal for SDGs to be submitted to the General Assembly at its sixty-eighth session (United Nations 2011, 2013c). The Open Working Group conducted 13 sessions between March 2013 and July 2014 in a singularly open and substantive process, which included a wide variety of stakeholders and voices. The international community sought coherence among the dimensions of sustainable development by linking issues in new ways and trying to break down the traditional sectoral silos. By the end of 2014, governments had agreed on negotiating modalities and, most importantly, produced a document with proposed goals and targets together with some suggested corresponding means of implementation (financing and technology, for example). In September 2015, Member States of the United Nations agreed on a set of 17 indivisible Sustainable Development Goals that are "action-oriented, concise, measurable, and easy to communicate, limited in number, aspirational, global in nature, and universally applicable to all countries" (United Nations 2012a, para. 247). The deliberations that led to those

Goals took into account all the principles of the Rio Declaration on Environment and Development, including the principle of common but differentiated responsibilities, as set out in principle 7 and in paragraph 15 of "The future we want."

A key input for the inter governmental process was the establishment in 2012, by the Secretary General of the United Nations, of a High-Level Panel of Eminent Persons on the Post-2015 Development Agenda to advise on the global development framework beyond 2015. The report of this panel was released in May 2013 and presented concrete recommendations to eradicate extreme poverty by 2030 and to move towards the SDGs. It called upon the international community to support a new global deal. It proposed five key ideas to drive the 2030 Agenda for Sustainable Development:[1]

- Leave no one behind
- Put sustainable development at the core
- Transform economies for jobs and inclusive growth
- Build peace and effective, open, and accountable institutions for all
- Forge a new global partnership

In his report to the Member States, entitled "A life of dignity for all," the Secretary-General set these elements as the basis of the Agenda and placed equality at the center with a rights-based approach (United Nations 2013a). The report outlines a number of key elements of the emerging vision of the new agenda, which include economic transformations–in ECLAC's terms structural progressive change–backed by the new technological paradigm. It entails at least three means of implementation: first, the promotion of fair trade and on narrowing financial asymmetries; second, the creation of decent jobs for all based on the principle of full employment; and third, full participation and inclusion by leaving no one behind or at the margin of the decision-making processes. The dramatic technological, economic, and social changes that this will entail would involve the international community, including the United Nations System, Bretton Woods institutions, global and regional international financial institutions, the private sector, and civil society. However, the main questions still remain: How ready is the world to re-organize human activity to work towards shared prosperity and improvement of the well-being of this and future generations within the planet's ecological boundaries? How ready is society for the dramatic technological and societal change that will be needed in all countries, and not only in developing countries? Will the principle of "common but differentiated responsibilities" remain as the main basis for negotiation and implementation, or will the pragmatic approach of the trade agreements of "leveling the playing field" prevail? Is the international community ready to de-colonize the development agenda and avoid conditional and detrimental donor-recipient relations?

1 PARALLEL TRACKS DURING THE 1990S: THE NORMATIVE DECADE OF THE UNITED NATIONS VS. TRADE AND FINANCIAL LIBERALIZATION

The decade of the 1990s was the normative and policy-setting decade of humanity in terms of sustainable development. The major world conferences held in those ten years resulted in the Millennium Declaration in 2000. After the Declaration, a set of non-binding goals supported by voluntary financing mechanisms was presented and launched. Called the Millennium Development Goals (MDGs), these goals tried to encapsulate the priorities of the fight against poverty in different parts of the world.

As it did 20 years ago, the international community continues to debate these global topics, trying to find common solutions in different forums, without connecting or integrating economics with social sciences, environmental sciences, or policies. Yet any viable approach must result from the real integration of economic development, environmental sustainability, and social inclusion. The correct path for countries, institutions, and society to tackle these global challenges in times of remarkable technological advancements remains open for discussion.

The twentieth century, some claim, did not end in 2000, but rather with the fall of the Berlin Wall in 1989. This is partly true when considering how much has changed since this historic milestone and the extent to which the global political and economic architecture has been redesigned.

This was the background for the preparations leading up to the Earth Summit in 1992, which adopted a set of principles and modalities of debate that have prevailed until now (United Nations 2012c). The Earth Summit led to the adoption of unprecedented political agreements enshrined in the 27 principles of the Rio Declaration on Environment and Development, Agenda 21, the United Nations Framework Convention on Climate Change, the Convention on Biological Diversity, and the United Nations Convention to Combat Desertification in Those Countries Experiencing Serious Drought and/or Desertification, particularly in Africa.

This meeting marked a milestone in the United Nations development pillar, but paradoxically far-reaching changes were also taking place in the economy and within societies, ushered in by a new production paradigm based on consumerism, progressive globalization of markets and communications, trade openness, and financial and labor market deregulation.

Since the fall of the Berlin Wall, the world has moved along two parallel tracks. The first was that of the Washington Consensus, characterized by the emergence of a new emphasis within the production paradigm based on the sovereignty of the consumer and new and unprecedented levels of consumerism (see Table 3.1 for a summary of the events that marked this "first track" and a brief characterization). At the same time that consumption was elevated

Table 3.1 First global track: Washington Consensus

Year/Selected events	Implications
1989: Fall of the Berlin Wall	Rise to pre-eminence of liberal democracy as dominant economic and political system worldwide Reduced role for the State in particular with regard to production activities
1986–1994: Uruguay Round of the General Agreement on Tariffs and Trade (GATT) negotiations (outside the UN system)	Trade liberalization. Reduction in tariff and non-tariff barriers
1995: World Trade Organization (WTO) succeeds GATT	Consolidation of trade liberalization (globalization) Dominance of transnational enterprises and global value chains
1997: Liberalization of telecommunications and financial services	The liberalization of trade is accompanied by the liberalization of finance (globalization) Finance takes precedence over production
2001: Doha Round of trade negotiations: agriculture and services, Trade-Related Aspects of Intellectual Property Rights (TRIPS)	Re-consideration of the free market paradigm

at the core, governments pursued the progressive liberalization of trade through the reduction of tariff and non-tariff barriers and a renewed impetus in formalizing free trade reciprocity, first through their participation in the Uruguay Round of trade negotiations (1986–1994) and then in the World Trade Organization (WTO) since 1995.

Free trade, which initially covered commodities, was extended to include services in an agreement signed by several countries to liberalize telecommunications and services in 1997. These initiatives were often reinforced by the signature of bilateral free trade agreements, which in some cases included labor and environmental negotiations.

Trade liberalization has been pursued hand in hand with domestic and external financial liberalization facilitated by the rapid improvement in technology and communications. Financial liberalization not only removed restrictions on banking and financial activities, it also involved a process of outright deregulation in some cases. Rather than promoting investment and productive development, financial liberalization opened the way for an era of unbridled capitalism based on values on paper, rather than solid and sound production potential.

Financial deregulation has produced greater economic and social instability, as it has rendered countries more prone to financial crisis. Excessive market orientation as well as outright financial liberalization has led to greater levels of inequality and income and wealth concentration. Inequality occurs at two levels: between developing and developed regions *and* within countries. Over-reliance and complacency with regard to market mechanisms has contributed to rising food and energy prices, as well as aggravating food and energy price volatility.

A third important element of the Washington Consensus was the reduction in government involvement in economic and productive activities, in line with the argument that government involvement crowds out private initiative. Furthermore the Washington Consensus viewed government failures as more damaging to allocation and production than market failures. As a result the Washington Consensus narrowed significantly the policy space for government intervention.

In practice, the Washington Consensus went beyond stabilization policies; to place crucial emphasis on structural reforms. These reforms encompassed deregulation and liberalization in goods and services markets, including the financial and labor markets.

The Washington Consensus took hold of the Bretton Woods institutions, including the International Monetary Fund (IMF) and the World Bank. In spite of the fact that the multilateral system created in Bretton Woods (New Hampshire, July 1944) was established in part to promote social and economic development, policies became subsumed under the Washington Consensus mantra: "stabilize, privatize, and deregulate." The implementation of the Washington Consensus, throughout the countries of the "periphery" (developing countries) during this decade, undermined public policy in social spheres and weakened strategic productive sectors at the national level.

The second track, parallel to that of the Washington Consensus, was marked by the world conferences within the United Nations system that became the universal multilateral forum to define the "development decade or normative decade" (see Table 3.2). The objective of many of these conferences was to place economic, social, and environmental concerns and policies on an equal footing. This broader set of objectives also demanded the expansion of policy space, such that the agencies in charge of global architecture and national governments had the appropriate tools to ensure stability and development.

During these years, discussions were held on the meaning, content, and direction of development, touching on imperatives relating to sustainable development, children, women and gender equality, population, social development, human settlements, urban development, education, and financing for development.

These multilateral processes stressed the need to create an environment conducive to economic and social development and improved welfare, through the creation of global public goods. Rather than focusing on stabilization, privatization, and liberalization, they focused on the eradication of poverty, the achievement of sustainable growth, and the creation of an

Table 3.2 Second global track: The normative path: sustainable development and the Millennium Development Goals

Year/Selected events	Implications
1985: Conference of Plenipotentiaries on the Protection of the Ozone Layer	Framework established for the international efforts to protect the ozone layer
1990: World Summit for Children	Adoption of the Declaration on the Survival, Protection and Development of Children and Plan of Action for implementing the World Declaration in the 1990s
1990: World Conference on Education for All	Adoption of the World Declaration on Education for All. Education is a fundamental human right. Countries must improve education standards to meet basic education needs by providing universal primary education and taking steps to reduce illiteracy by the end of the decade
1992: International Conference on Nutrition	Adoption of the World Declaration on Nutrition, 1992. Ensure that freedom from hunger becomes a reality
1992: United Nations Conference on Environment and Development	Drafting of Agenda 21 to address the pressing problems of today. Agenda 21 aims at preparing the world for the challenges of the next century and reflects a global consensus and political commitment at the highest level on development and environment cooperation. The summit produced the United Nations Framework Convention on Climate Change (1992) to prevent dangerous interference with the climate due to greenhouse gas emissions; the Convention on Biological Diversity (1992), to mitigate the current mass extinction of species, and the Convention to Combat Desertification to halt the advance of desertification worldwide and particularly in Africa (1994)
1993: World Conference on Human Rights	Adoption of the Vienna Declaration and Programme of Action, 1993. Political, economic, social, and cultural rights are indivisible
1994: International Conference on Population and Development	Adoption of the Cairo Programme of Action. Focusing on the eradication of poverty, stabilizing population growth, greater focus on the equality and empowerment of women
1995: World Summit for Social Development	Adoption of the Copenhagen Declaration on Social Development, and the Programme of Action of the World Summit for Social Development. Key objectives of development should include eradication of poverty, full employment, and social integration

1995: Fourth World Conference on Women	Adoption of the Beijing Declaration and Platform for Action. Advancement in the goals of equality, development, and peace for all women
1995: Kyoto Protocol	The Kyoto Protocol sets binding targets for 37 industrialized countries on reducing greenhouse gas emissions
1996: United Nations Conference on Human Settlements (HABITAT II)	Adoption of the United Nations Declaration on Cities and Other Human Settlements in the New Millennium in which governments reaffirmed their commitments concerning "adequate shelter for all, sustainable human settlements, enablement and participation, gender equality, financing shelter and human settlements, international cooperation, and assessing progress"
1997: Earth Summit+5	Reaffirmed the importance of Agenda 21. Led to the adoption of General Assembly resolution A/RES/S-19/2 entitled "Programme for the Further Implementation of Agenda 21"
2000: Millennium Summit	United Nations Millennium Declaration. The Declaration addresses different issues of importance to the United Nations including basic development rights, peace, security, disarmament, democracy, and governance. Adoption of the MDGs
2002: World Summit on Sustainable Development (Johannesburg)	Adoption of the Johannesburg Declaration which stressed the need "to advance and strengthen the interdependent and mutually reinforcing pillars of sustainable development—economic development, social development and environmental protection—at the local, national, regional and global levels"
2012: United Nations Conference on Sustainable Development (Rio+20)	The Conference focused on the green economy in the context of sustainable development and poverty eradication; and the institutional framework for sustainable development. Seven areas for priority attention were highlighted; decent jobs, energy, sustainable cities, food security and sustainable agriculture, water, oceans, and disaster readiness. The outcome document entitled "The future we want" was endorsed by the General Assembly
2013: Sixty-eighth session of the General Assembly. Inaugural meeting of the High-level Political Forum on Sustainable Development (held under the auspices of the General Assembly).	The outcome of the inaugural meeting of the High-level Political Forum on Sustainable Development emphasizes the need to accelerate on MDGs and reach an agreement on a strong Agenda 2030
2015: United Nations Sustainable Development Summit	Adoption of the 2030 Agenda for Sustainable Development, which includes the 17 SDGs

inclusive and equitable global economic system as fundamental priorities of the development agenda.

Some of the world conferences, such as the International Conference on Financing for Development/IFCD (held in Monterrey in 2002) and the first phase of the World Summit on the Information Society (held in Geneva in 2003) were relevant to both tracks.

The ICFD (Monterrey Conference) highlighted the fundamental role of national policies and development strategies in achieving sustainable development. However, the Conference proceedings also underscored that national efforts should be complemented and sustained by supportive global and regional programs along with institutions designed to expand development opportunities, while recognizing the specificities of domestic conditions.

As emphasized in the Monterrey Consensus, this endeavor required improvement in the strength, coherence, and consistency of the global and regional financial systems. An efficient international financial system was thus understood as a fundamental pillar of an international policy agenda in the pursuit of sustainable development and a fair and equitable trading system.

These multilateral processes culminated in the Millennium Summit (2000) where heads of state and government agreed on basic development principles and benchmarks based on the previous processes, which were adopted and successively embraced by future sustainable development summits (Johannesburg in 2002 and Rio+20 in 2012).

The MDGs and the targets that were used to monitor progress were mostly designed and selected centrally by United Nations experts on the basis of the accords and treaties agreed upon during the 1990s, with little participation by Member States. This will be further analyzed in Section 2.

These two parallel tracks with contradictory principles, embodied on the one hand in the Washington Consensus (promoted by the Bretton Woods institutions, including the World Trade Organization) and on the other in the Millennium Declaration (under the aegis of the United Nations), prevented the formation of the kind of broad-based approach to governance founded on universality, that was needed to confront the social and economic challenges of development which came to head in the first global economic crisis of the twenty-first century. Rather, a form of elite multilateralism emerged to coordinate responses to globalization, particularly after the 2008 crisis. These parallel tracks represented two very different development views: the first reliant on a trickle-down effect; and the second set on increasing the number of countries that participate in international decision making as a starting point (Ocampo 2013b).

This elite multilateralism, as defined by Ocampo, is based on the fact that the global architecture and its development agenda were established by global institutions, but through the dictates of small developed country groupings such as G-7, G-8, and G-20. Countries included in these small developed country groupings have the greatest participation, voting, and decision-making power in international organizations. As a result, developing countries' regional bodies and authorities play only a minor role in the implementation of the global development agenda. This has limited the space for global coordination and reduced the scope for the provision of global public goods from the perspective of developing countries. This was based on the assumption that the existing governance structure could be overhauled, but must be adapted.

Those are our two parallel worlds. The contradictions between the Washington Consensus and the view of inclusive development propounded at the United Nations conferences were brought to light in the follow-up to the United Nations Conference on Environment and Development (held in Rio de Janeiro in 1992). Comparative indicators reveal that two decades of reiterated commitments by the international community without financial support and without the effective transfer of technology agreed upon in Rio de Janeiro, have not been sufficient to eradicate poverty, hunger, inequality, and environmental degradation. In addition, Principle 7 of the Rio Declaration relating to common but differentiated responsibilities was watered down internationally within the framework of trade negotiations that advocated leveling the playing field as a baseline for all parties. The common but differentiated responsibilities principle was the most controversial aspect of the negotiations on the 2030 Agenda for Sustainable Development and the intention of some parties was to apply it only to non-binding, environmental agreements.[2]

2 ASSESSING PROGRESS AND LOOKING AHEAD: THE SCALE OF THE GLOBAL DEVELOPMENT CHALLENGES IS DIFFICULT TO ANTICIPATE

The sub-prime mortgage crisis that broke out in 2007–2008 in the United States and the subsequent Eurozone crisis have had a significant economic, social, and political impact. These crises fuelled serious debate on the direction and rationale for accumulating economic wealth, the rules governing the global economic system, the role of public policy, and the inability of global institutions to confront and respond to, or even possibly prevent, systemic problems. Moreover, these crises struck at a time when strong doubts were being raised about the social and economic benefits of democracy, world economic integration, and the uneven advances of regional integration.

The enduring crises have severely tested the entire Bretton Woods institutional response and the economic model of private, deregulated growth and the trickle-down process that forms its foundation. The rise to preeminence of emerging market economies has cast doubt on the developed countries' political and economic influence in world affairs.

The growing importance, share, and participation of emerging market economies in world affairs are visible in several respects. Emerging market economies are home to over one half of the world's population. They also account for roughly one half of the world's GDP (when measured in purchasing power parity terms) and are on their way to overtaking developed economies in the next decade. By 2017, 54% of the world's GDP will originate in emerging market economies (ECLAC 2013). In social terms, emerging market economies account for the bulk of an expanding middle class with greater spending power.

The technological revolution has not only spearheaded globalization through lower costs and faster communication speeds, it has also facilitated a greater sense of participation of the world's population in the globalization process. Finally, the environmental challenge calls for changes to daily habits and production matrices to ensure a sustainable growth and development path, especially for developed countries and the high-income segments of developing countries. Developed countries must lead the way in making these changes before emerging market economies will place a similar level of importance on making the adaptations required to mitigate environmental negative impacts.

In short, the world has changed drastically. A hundred years ago, the struggle of the working class proletariat was the focus of concern. Today, discontent arises from the situation of those who are living in precarious conditions, those living without formal jobs, and those who are dissatisfied with the existing development model. This is the reality of our society today: discontent has shifted from the working class to the vulnerable middle class.

Twenty years after the United Nations Conference on Environment and Development (Rio de Janeiro, 1992), the world community is more acutely aware of the discontent among the middle classes but is in a weaker and more worrying position to address it, facing additional political challenges. Development, as we have experienced it, has reached a breaking point.

It is true that the Washington Consensus era witnessed an improvement in macroeconomic stability, with better fiscal accounts and less inflation. However, many countries experienced higher levels of social and economic inequality.

The case of Latin America and the Caribbean illustrates the failures of the Washington Consensus to promote growth, stability, social inclusion, and equality. Over the past three decades, the performance of the Latin America and Caribbean region has been characterized by an increasing degree of volatility in terms of output and investment behavior. Following the debt crisis of the 1980s, per capita growth did not exceed 1.5% on average in the 1990s. The growth rate was one of the lowest since the 1960s. This meager rate of growth was accompanied by rising inequality and social exclusion. Furthermore, the region was unable to improve productivity and overcome structural heterogeneity, thus hampering social and economic development.The structural reforms promoted by the Washington Consensus weakened public institutions, deteriorating the capacity of governments to provide public goods, to implement production and industrial policies, and to make strategic plans more generally. Furthermore, the track record of the UN after 20 years presents mixed results.

The 2030 Agenda for Sustainable Development sought to build on the MDGs. Introduced in 2000 as a package of priorities with a set of eight goals with measurable targets, including the timeframes and expected outcomes, the MDGs promoted awareness and commitment at the national level, but were mainly targeted at poor countries, with the exception of Goal 8.[3] The MDGs became a sort of a comparable report card with incentives to improve performance. Unquestionably the MDGs represented a historic and relatively effective process for evaluating progress towards the eradication of extreme poverty and hunger, the reduction of maternal and infant mortality, and the attainment of basic needs, such as access to drinking water and sanitation. However, they represented a reductive and poorly integrated approach to development, progress, and well-being, lacking an emphasis on closing equality gaps, addressing social exclusion, and halting environmental degradation. Closing said gaps entails profound structural changes, particularly in developing countries that need technology, greater productivity, capital, jobs, and, most of all, more redistributive policies to close the asymmetries between the rich and the poor, between transnational corporations and small and medium-sized companies, and between men and women.

If progress is assessed using 1990 as the baseline and up to 2015, it is true that important strides have been made in combating poverty; however, at least 1 billion people still live in extreme poverty. In relation to the other MDGs, great advances were achieved in infant mortality, primary education, HIV-AIDS, prevention of malaria and tuberculosis, and access to drinking water. Much less progress was seen on maternal mortality and environmental sustainability. Also, many key issues were not covered by the MDGs, such as access to energy, biodiversity, employment, inequality, and social inclusion.

Most of all, the MDGs ended up being a prescriptive agenda for developing countries rather than a global road map for development. As Ocampo pointed out, the MDGs captured only a small segment of the "internationally agreed development goals" and ignored key economic and social issues, with great shortcomings related to the rule of law, productivity, and environmental sustainability (Ocampo 2013b, p. 3). Developed countries failed to meet their commitments, particularly with the agreed levels of official development assistance, nor with the transfer of resources. In fact, they maintained the distorted donor-recipient inertia.

As stated above, the MDGs were a set of clear, measurable objectives that were easy to document and had high political visibility, which served for advocacy mainly related to poverty, hunger, and gender equity. Another positive element was the increased participation of private foundations. However, the process of defining the 2030 Agenda for Sustainable Development took a bottom-up approach, seeking to re-orient cooperation and de-colonize the relationship between developed and developing countries. Implementation of the 2030 Agenda includes reforming the global architecture and re-directing global governance to achieve sustainable and welfare-enhancing inclusive growth paths based on policy coherence at the international, regional, and national levels. It entails the need to recognize that development and equality are fundamental, and must acknowledge that development and market-oriented policies are not mutually exclusive.

3 RIO + 20: IN PURSUIT OF A SINGLE DEVELOPMENT VISION

The United Nations Conference on Sustainable Development (Rio+20) presented the opportunity to redefine the development agenda. The conference's two main themes were (i) a green economy in the context of sustainable development and poverty eradication, and (ii) the institutional framework for sustainable development.

The outcome document of the conference, entitled "The future we want," highlighted that countries need to change their development patterns and promote sustained, inclusive, and equitable economic growth, create greater opportunities for all, reduce inequalities, raise basic standards of living, foster equitable social development and inclusion, and promote integrated and sustainable management of natural resources and ecosystems that supports, inter alia, economic, social, and human development while facilitating ecosystem conservation, regeneration and restoration, and resilience in the face of new and emerging challenges.

Rio+20 led two crucial processes under the responsibility of the General Assembly in its sixty-seventh and sixty-eighth sessions (2013 and 2014). The first process, which started in 2013 and concluded in 2014, aimed to define a common vision and agreement on a set of goals that are scaled-up (from a poverty focus to a development focus) and universal (valid for developed and developing countries). These goals, which have now been adopted as the Sustainable Development Goals (SDGs), build on the experience of the MDGs in that they are quantifiable and simple to understand and communicate. They define the concept of sustainability, mark a way forward, and are not sector-specific in nature. In their pursuit, the present route of development is steered towards a more balanced interaction among economic, social, and environmental global public goods.

The second process related to the challenge of global governance in ensuring the protection and provision of shared commons and global public goods. "The future we want" proposed the creation of a High-level Political Forum on Sustainable Development[4] to coordinate and foster global coherence from countries and international agencies and organizations for sustainable development (United Nations 2012a, para. 84). A decision was thus taken to conduct an in-depth revision of global governance under the extended United Nations (United Nations proper plus Bretton Woods institutions) and non-United Nations organizations, such as the WTO.

The meetings of the High-level Political Forum on Sustainable Development are held under the auspices of the General Assembly, at the level of heads of state and government,[5] and under the auspices of the Economic and Social Council. Implementation would cascade down to the rest of the extended United Nations through their governing councils, in order to establish priorities and coherence. A monitoring mechanism would be set up to ensure that decisions are taken on a scientific basis and, in the meantime, relevant ministries would be responsible for follow-up, leading to the integration of policies and priorities at the national and global levels.

The global reform of the governance for sustainable development that emerged from Rio+20 and the ongoing negotiations that followed reflected the growing importance of the regional perspective. "The future we want" and the General Assembly sessions (2012 and 2013) recognized the need to have a bottom-up process that acknowledges the importance of the regional dimension.[6] The High-level Political Forum will meet every four years[7] at the heads of state level, and be informed by a global report on the progress of sustainable development with input from the regional commissions and with the support of the United Nations agencies that operate in each region.[8] Also, it was decided that the countries will have a yearly regional meeting at the ministerial level to assess their progress on sustainable development.[9]

In the global public goods discussion there are some evident tensions. The first tension is conceptual. One standpoint envisions global public goods as having the transformative potential to bring about a shift towards a new, more sustainable development paradigm. In this paradigm, simple yet overarching goods entail substantive change in development, such as (a) the pursuit of healthy and secure lives; (b) quality of energy and universal access to it; and (c) eliminating all forms of exclusion or discrimination, whether social, economic, or environmental. The competing vision prioritizes addressing negative traits of current trends as insufficiencies or side effects. These "side effects," including extreme poverty, loss of biodiversity, gender inequality, and even climate change, fall mostly under sectoral approaches and under the purview of social or environmental ministries.

A second tension is more practical and relates to the mandates or interests of specific international agencies or clusters of countries, whose priorities include aid, money flows, and institutional relevance. The definition and hierarchy of SDG related global public goods have profound implications for these flows, which guarantees a bumpy road ahead.

The United Nations system embodies the two tensions described above. Within the United Nations programs, agencies, and treaties are an archipelago of independent entities with equal rank. The international system's rules of representation elevate to the same standing levels and areas of governments that are in fact very different. In the governing bodies and programs, country representatives speak in the name of their country with the same hierarchy among all those bodies and programs, and there is no overarching decision mechanism in the system other than the rule of consensus.

Combined, these two elements (governance and the need for specific direction that results in new global public goods) can result mostly in paralysis as different visions among countries and present mandates among international bodies limit effective action to protect the global commons.

Traditionally, international and regional public goods included peace, trade rules, economic stability, and public health (for instance, the control of pandemics). Countries have now expanded the definition of global commons and public goods to cover dimensions such as climate security linked to global warming, public health, and chemical safety (linked to clean environments), the ozone layer (linked to emissions of industrial pollutants into the global atmosphere), healthy oceans (linked to land-based pollution and overfishing), the survival of biodiversity (linked to land-use change), and the stability of the planetary nitrogen cycle, among others. Even public goods previously regarded as regional, as identified earlier, have been gradually ascended to a global scale due to the increase in travel, trade, and communications.

Can countries cooperate internationally without coercion from a third party, as individuals do under certain circumstances? Will they be able to monitor and sanction problems associated with free-riding? In a globalizing world, the effects of endangering the planet's life-support systems of transboundary nature, resulting in a growing need for international collective action, are well beyond the traditional notion of interdependence.

The concept of global public goods should considerably influence the implementation of formulation of the 2030 Agenda. Regional and global public goods comprise not only those goods that have the technical attributes that economists define as intrinsic to public goods (non-rival and non-excludable), but also goods of social value and universal access—that is, those goods and services that should be guaranteed to all citizens of a society, regardless of their economic conditions and ability to pay. In this regard regional and public goods should also encompass forms of cooperation among nations that level the playing field.[10]

However, international cooperation faces two crucial problems: the piecemeal approach of the international agenda, and the weak institutional mechanisms for decision making, prioritization, follow-up, accountability and enforceability of international commitments.

Questions regarding funding to provide global public goods also remain unanswered. Some fear that dwindling available funds will be taken from international aid, while others propose global funding mechanisms, in the form of progressive taxes or controls on tax avoidance, for example, as efficient and universal means of distribution.

4 THE IMPORTANCE OF REGIONAL ACTION FOR SUSTAINABLE DEVELOPMENT

Sustainable development will require considerable collective action. However, multilateral development agreements on objectives and targets need to be de-colonized in the sense that they should be universal in nature. It will no longer be acceptable for the developing world to adopt prescriptive agendas based on asymmetric economic and trade relations. Regional and sub-regional institutions are best placed to ensure the inclusion and protection of weaker players, for example, least developed countries and small island developing states (SIDS). The provision of public goods, such as financial security, can also be facilitated through a network of regional institutions.

Regional dialogues and agreements can play an important role in helping to improve developing countries' maneuvering capacity through the greater policy space. The need for more and better public policies has been reinforced by the experience of the global economic crisis (2007–2008). The global crisis showed that governments in emerging regions, such as Latin America and Asia-Pacific, have limited space to participate globally in the mitigation of the effects of financial crises. These regions, however, are building resilience at the regional level with initiatives such as the Chiang-Mai Initiative or the proposal emerging from the Union of South-American Nations (UNASUR) allowing governments to draw resources from the stock of reserves accumulated in the pre-crisis period or establish anticyclical economic mechanisms for the future. However, rather than promoting the growth and development of countries, the flow of reserves accumulated by developing economies found its way back to the markets of developed economies. Thus developing countries and particularly emerging economies still need to seek a way to broaden their policy space without compromising development.

To move ahead, Latin America, for example, must reverse the trend towards an economy reliant once again on primary exports, as is especially the case in South America. High commodity prices, while generating substantial profits, also impact the production network by concentrating production in the primary sector and causing the currency to appreciate. It must be considered how best to administer the financial resources obtained through commodity exports and how to invest in the creation of physical and technological capital and in the improvement of human capital.

In addition, Latin America should strengthen joint political action and take advantage of its international position, along with other emerging countries. In doing so, it should bear in mind the shift in power from the North Atlantic to the Pacific and the increase in South-South economic and trade interactions, which have been overtaking North-North trade. This structural change dates back to 1985.

Yet the major obstacles to sustainable development in the developing countries remain basically the same: short-term economic decisions prevail in spite of the environmental and social costs. In the case of Latin America, international financial and trade asymmetries are exacerbated by the new and more compelling demands of a changing and uncertain context. These demands are wide and varied. They involve the eradication of poverty and elimination of social and economic inequalities. They also include halting the destruction of ecosystems that serve as a habitat for the region's rich biodiversity and as a source of livelihood for local populations. Furthermore these demands include achieving a level of local development (rural and urban) that meets the human security and economic needs of citizens. Finally, at the institutional level, institutional development must be consolidated to ensure the continued improvement of policies in different spheres of development and prevent backsliding in relation to achieved progress in adverse situations by promoting the full participation of all actors.

The unsustainable use of natural endowments is inextricably bound with the regulation of economic activity. This relationship is attributed to the failure to address the causes and effects of climate change, the protection of biological diversity, the reduction of emissions of ozone-depleting gases, desertification, land degradation and drought, the use of water resources, and environmental management of toxic chemicals. All these issues come from a combination of market and government failures.

Climate change is expected to have a significant impact on fragile ecosystems (in particular mangroves, glaciers, and coral reefs), productive sectors (agriculture and infrastructure), and human welfare (water scarcity, communicable diseases such as dengue and malaria, and extreme temperatures). These concerns impose increasing economic costs on Latin America and the Caribbean. As a share of GDP, these costs are estimated to be higher than in developed countries and over 1% of GDP annually in most areas.[11]

Further, climate change has increased the severity and frequency of extreme weather events and heightened their impact. Economic, structural, ecological, and human losses as a result of extreme weather can potentially delay an already fraught development process in Central America and the Caribbean. Countries with small and vulnerable economies, such as SIDS, not only suffer more severe economic losses, but also their low resilience to loss can cause major setbacks in their economic development.

Global warming and climate change pose, like the other global commons, a global collective-action problem. Conventional collective-action theory predicts that a problem will not be solved unless an external authority determines appropriate actions to be taken, monitors behavior, and imposes sanctions. In a global context, this authority is inevitably designed and established by governments themselves. However, despite numerous debates on the matter, that global authority has not yet been created by nations and no effective global treaty for collective action has yet been achieved.

However, progress made by multiple units at diverse scales can cumulatively make a difference. Ostrom (2010) argues that instead of focusing only on global efforts (which are indeed important and part of a long-term solution), it may be better to simultaneously encourage polycentric efforts to reduce the risks associated with the emission of greenhouse gases.

Polycentric approaches facilitate achieving benefits at multiple scales, as well as experimentation and learning from experience with diverse policies.

> Polycentric connotes many centers of decision-making that are formally independent of each other. To the extent that they take each other into account in competitive relationships, enter into various contractual and cooperative undertakings or have recourse to central mechanisms to resolve conflicts, the various political jurisdictions in a metropolitan area may function in a coherent manner with consistent and predictable patterns of interacting behavior. To the extent that this is so, they may be said to function as a 'system' (Ostrom 2010, 552).

Why is this polycentric approach relevant to the analysis of global public goods? It supports the idea that while large-scale units are part of effective governance, small and medium-scale units are also necessary components. An important lesson is that pursuing a single governance unit to solve global collective action problems can be seriously rethought. This logic gives regional organizations more intellectual space to deal with such issues. If conditional cooperation must still face important hurdles at the global level, the regional level might be able to achieve cooperation through local discussions and meetings that build on some of the necessary design rules for collective action to prosper, such as small, more homogenous groups and self-designed rules. These regional processes can bring minds together in a framework of important similarities on context and information. The regional level can make data available to countries on a vast number of issues. Their collective perspective, including on the unrecognized costs of individual, family, and business activities, could potentially lead to a change in the preferences of individuals involved and the expected behavior of others.

According to Ostrom (2010), when individuals are well informed about the problem they face and who else is involved, they can build settings that allow trust and reciprocity to emerge, flow, and be sustained over time. Costly positive actions can be taken without waiting for an external (in this case, global) authority to impose rules, monitor compliance, and hand down penalties.

Legitimate economic competition in the globalized economy[12] and further integration in trade and infrastructure require policy harmonization in order to simultaneously meet the economic, environmental, and social aims. Environmental performance and economic competition must be achieved and protected in a synergistic manner. Latin America has achieved a level of maturity which can enable it to propose and manage its own change (a rule-setting process) and build its own regional agenda, including its ad hoc institutions for the provision of regional and global public goods.

Individual countries will find it difficult to change their economic or regulatory policies without considering the repercussions for regional and global competitiveness. For example, eliminating the present structure of fossil fuel subsidies or the externalities of private mobility in isolation may prove more difficult than in coordination with neighboring economies. The region will reap the benefits of collective action, in the form of perceived shared responsibility, followed by culturally acceptable monitoring and enforcement mechanisms that allow countries to exchange experiences, adjust progress, share information, and pursue the necessary change to contribute to regional level. That also helps harmonize the respective contributions to regional public goods.

Similar processes are gaining momentum in other regions, where countries in the Global South are finding a new strength and autonomy that promise the emergence of polycentric contributions to the provision of environmental global public goods through better management of the global commons.

There are some relevant and interesting examples of the emergence of such polycentric contributions to public goods from the regions. First, the decades-long effort to produce comparable statistics on the economic, social, and environmental spheres for the Latin American region as a whole has been successful, bringing in more countries to populate comparable sets of data year after year. Producing regional and national data as a high-quality, reliable public good is an ongoing achievement.

More recently the region has created a policy dialogue space to discuss connectivity and the introduction of broadband access in cities or countries as a common resource pool, or public good. The region is highly dependent on a single connecting cable for its global and regional Internet access and modern communications, and the digital divide calls for expedited access to broadband that is not dependent on personal income.

On the basis of national experiences and the progress in the Aarhus Convention, Latin America and the Caribbean decided at the Rio+20 conference to take a step towards providing better access to environmental information as a public good by negotiating a regional treaty to harmonize policies relative to Principle 10 of the Rio Declaration (1992) on the rights of access to information, participation, and justice in environmental matters. To date, 20 countries are involved in this initiative to level the field up in these matters and to provide another regional public good.

In the same vein, the region has developed a database on past and projected economic and physical impacts of climate change both inland and in coastal areas. Climate change negotiators meet to discuss the market mechanisms to protect forests from depletion (known as Reducing Emissions from Deforestation and Forest Degradation [REDD]). Negotiators have re-established a regional platform for discussing progress towards agreement under the United Nations Framework Convention on Climate Change. This informal mechanism played a key role for the region and particularly vis-à-vis the Paris Agreement reached at COP 21 in December 2015.

There have been efforts in the past to better manage some natural assets with a sub-regional scope such as the Amazon rainforest and the endangered vicuña in the high Andes. There have also been attempts to create economic stability and openness in the economy as a regional public good with varied results. Some progress has been made on trade, despite structural limitations due to the low diversification of the region's economies, on infrastructure integration, though with a strong bias still towards carbon-intensive modes of transport and on stabilizing short-term balance-of-payment fluctuations through a regional monetary stabilization fund,[13] and even the creation of a fully-owned regional development finance institution.[14] Within this context, mention should be made of the success of regional development banking institutions such as the Latin American Development Bank (formerly the Andean Development Corporation) (Ocampo 2013a). The region has also taken a stronger collective stance in the protection of democracy against threats such as coups, and has used the regional fora to incentivize the return to normality.

The array of regional public goods could multiply if the regional groups such as the Community of Latin American and Caribbean States (CELAC) set in motion similar policy coordination mechanisms for other shared resources of regional and global concern. Such policy coordination could address areas including intraregional and international trade, low-carbon infrastructure, shared research and development initiatives, peer reviews of policies, biodiversity and the sustainable use of oceans, quality urban development, and the management of and infrastructure for hazardous wastes.

A universal development agenda that takes into account the needs of both developed and developing countries requires strong linkages between global and regional public goods. One example of the complementarities between the two types of public good is seen in Latin America's regional financial architecture that plays a crucial role as a buffer stock for financial instability. The regional financial architecture complements the multilateral institutions that provide financial public goods.

Another example is the Latin American Investment Facility. This facility uses the limited funds contributed by the European Commission to attract sizeable loans from the European Investment Bank, the Inter-American Development Bank, and bilateral sources. It therefore involves not only official development assistance (ODA), but also cooperation in a broader sense: the initial funding provided by the European Commission is leveraged and ends up generating considerable volumes of financing, which is in turn channeled into energy infrastructure and other projects of greater scope than could otherwise be attempted.

The region now faces "graduation" from ODA, as many of its countries are reclassified into the middle-income country category. As bilateral cooperation is dwindling, regional approaches to policy development are becoming more prevalent in line with the countries' own drive for higher levels of policy integration. The present difficulties associated with coordination through global processes and conventions and current institutional arrangements call for a stronger regional effort to find sustainable mechanisms for prosperity, higher levels of equality, and better ways of harmonizing our economies within the constraints of the planet and shared regional resources.

5 DE-COLONIZING THE 2030 SUSTAINABLE DEVELOPMENT AGENDA

The adoption of a global compact that reflects clear solidarity with future generations, who will be living in a more uncertain world and with a more acute scarcity of natural resources, requires a different approach to global governance. It means calling for the signing of international trade, environmental, and social agreements, and ensuring that the burden of the higher costs for this change does not fall on the poor or the most vulnerable countries. It means re-thinking the development paradigm in terms of more sustainable patterns of production and consumption, particularly in developed countries in a context of shared prosperity. This proposal must be expressed in a renewed partnership for sustainable development that reconciles the commitment of the economy in relation to the environment and the eradication of poverty and inequality.

There is an urgent need for a more representative, politically legitimate leadership to strengthen the United Nations development pillar. One of the future requirements of global governance is the creation of more comprehensive and inclusive bodies for coordinating and implementing the global development agenda. Thus, just as the G-20 has a central role in global financial governance, steps must be taken in the multilateral sphere to create a similar mechanism to enhance governance of development.

Global governance must be universal and inclusive, and reflect the interests, needs, and objectives of the international community as a whole. We need global institutions that will bring together the action of organizations and agencies in the global and regional intergovernmental system to support the implementation of the 2030 Agenda for Sustainable Development.

This will mean harmonizing the different international agreements and treaties. These new global institutions call for greater coherence between the negotiations and commitments adopted at different international forums, whether they relate to trade, climate, the environment, social issues, or finances. They also call for an equitable distribution of scientific and technological advances, as well as financing and institutions based on multilateralism. The process of adopting these changes must be different and shorter, with well-defined goals, and with an accountability framework that is also inclusive, sustainable, and efficient.

It is essential to support the multilateral architecture for development of the United Nations by strengthening and reinforcing the role of the Economic and Social Council (ECOSOC) so that it can function with similar procedures as the Security Council. The Security Council has neither the means nor the mandate to analyze climate change or the food crisis. For this reason, the creation of the High-Level Political Forum on Sustainable Development (which meets under the auspices of ECOSOC and the General Assembly) should become the venue where these issues are discussed. Kwame Sundaram (2011), a prominent Malaysian economist who served as the United Nations Assistant Secretary-General for Economic Development in the United Nations Department of Economic and Social Affairs from 2005 to 2012, presented several issues related to United Nations Reform that emerged from the Stiglitz Commission (formally the Commission of Experts on Reforms of the International Monetary and Financial System) established by the President of the General Assembly in 2009 (Sundaram 2011). Those recommendations included the creation of the global economic coordination council that would meet at the level of Heads of State (as does the current G-20) and would enjoy the formal support of a subset of existing United Nations system entities.[15]

The High-Level Political Forum should converge into a security economic council with a membership that could represent all the regional groups and have sufficient power to make decisions. This council could serve as the forum for deliberations on financial, economic, energy, social, or food crises, and for discussing security issues such as climate change. While human security is indeed at stake, the issues are structural in nature and above all relate to development.

Implementing the 2030 Agenda will require the active participation of multilateral organizations such as the World Bank, the IMF, and the WTO. The major groups and other stakeholders representing civil society should be fully involved in the follow-up with more power in the accountability framework. Last but not least, the private sector, both transnational and national should play a key role particularly in fostering low-carbon infrastructure and green technologies.

Lastly, there is a need to strengthen regional integration. It is now generally acknowledged that no single model or solution applies equally well to all countries. Different approaches are needed for confronting different problems. What unites Latin America and the Caribbean, however, is the value attached to democracy and the desire to seek areas of political convergence regarding integration and development which is coming to fruition. For example, Latin America and the Caribbean has forged new approaches and more pragmatic modalities for strengthening intraregional trade and developing value chains based on intermediate goods, not just on competition for marketing end products. As more national entities join global markets, it is vital to empower multilateral and cooperation bodies to address the threats and uncertainties in a more coordinated way.

The Latin American and Caribbean region has made major strides in setting up mechanisms for regional and subregional deliberation and cooperation. These include the Central American Integration System (SICA), the Southern Common Market (MERCOSUR), the Andean Community, the Bolivarian Alliance for the Peoples of Our America (ALBA), the Caribbean Community (CARICOM), the Union of South American Nations (UNASUR), and the Community of Latin American and Caribbean States (CELAC). Even though some of these integration processes currently face severe constraints and limitations, they could contribute to building consensus on issues such as the easing of intellectual property rights; joint technological innovation projects; lower-carbon infrastructure; regulatory frameworks in the fiscal sphere; mechanisms for deepening intraregional trade; and the foundations for a new financial architecture, including a cooperation platform and a forum for the full participation of all stakeholders.

The consensus being reached in Latin American and the Caribbean encompasses economic, social, and environmental issues and is grounded in the following considerations[16]:

1. It was not possible for all countries to close the remaining gaps in order to meet the MDGs before 2015.
2. Addressing new challenges as well as old ones calls for a new development model based on a structural change for equality and environmental sustainability.

3. Policy and institutions matter. The shift towards sustainable development requires appropriate regulation, enforcement, funding, and natural-resource governance. New political coalitions are necessary to reach long-term accords among the State, the private sector, and civil society.
4. A wider variety of ways to measure progress is needed to complement GDP and thus better inform decision making for sustainable development. This will require new multidimensional indicators.
5. The capacity for global governance in relation to sustainable development must be built. Priority should be given to consistent global policies on sustainable development, fair trade, technology transfer, international finance reform, and new funding mechanisms, in addition to promoting South-South cooperation and enhancing mechanisms for social participation.
6. The SDGs were designed to move towards more *resilient, self-sufficient, secure, and balanced* economies and will require a *global financing and technology transfer covenant.*

From this starting point the aim is to pursue for more equitable global governance between developing and developed countries, including least developed countries (LDCs), middle income countries (MICs), and small island developing States (SIDS). These considerations will help build political consensus and create means of implementation to ensure shared prosperity for all.

An essential point for the future regional agenda must be financing for development. Once again, we need to devise innovative mechanisms for development, such as the tax on speculative income. This could be a significant source of additional, innovative financing, which should be separate, additional, and apart from the developed countries' commitment to devote 0.7% of their gross national income to official development assistance as agreed upon in Rio de Janeiro, Monterrey, Johannesburg, Addis Ababa, New York, and Paris.

However, the implementation of the above proposals is subject to certain conditions. First, policy must play a role in guaranteeing the effective provision of public goods. By "public," we mean collective, or that which belongs to society as a whole, not that which is the domain of the government. It is not that the State is the owner of the public goods, but rather that society generates public goods with the participation of the private and corporate sectors and that the principles of corporate social responsibility are applied to all forms of investment. Levels of expectations for well-being have risen along with a higher demand for more and better public goods. This change is grounded in better-quality, rights-based, and universal state/public policies on social protection, health, education, and employment.

Second, institutions must be set up to deliver high-level multilateral intergovernmental dialogue with full legitimacy and power. Thus, the regulatory bureaucracy must have technical capacity and there must be sufficient social empowerment to face up to the tremendous power of the major corporations. The democratic order must be such that the course of development can translate the will of the majority and allow for the participation of all stakeholders.

Third, democracies must be deeper, more participatory, and more transparent, since under the democratic system, it is the citizens who decide what type of society they want to construct. Principle 10 of the Rio Declaration on Environment and Development must be fully implemented. This principle is more relevant today than ever, since it provides a clear and pioneering vision with regard to transparency, participation, environmental justice, and access to information as the basis for deepening democracy and doing away with global asymmetries.

Lastly, the proposal of a new global agreement for sustainable development must address in depth four structural trends, which imply a genuine change of era (ECLAC, 2010b).

1. Climate change: Climate change is closely linked to the long history of industrialization and the production patterns it ushered in, which generate high levels of carbon emissions and consumption of fossil fuels. Moreover, this trend is linked to the specific way in which human beings interact with nature in order to ensure their collective reproduction. Climate change imposes limits, forces us to change the production paradigm and consumption patterns, places intergenerational solidarity at the heart of the agenda for equality, and even challenges our relationship with the world. In other words, each individual's future is inextricably tied to the future of all. Now more than ever before, with the threat of global warming looming before us, the destruction of the environment, and a crisis in energy sources, our interdependence cannot be ignored. Alternative ways must be worked out and constraints faced, specifically by the Latin American region in its shift towards economies based on lower carbon emissions and options of reduced use of fossil fuels must be examined. In Latin America and the Caribbean, climate change can turn into a new restriction on economic growth or, if approached in a timely and integrated way, an opportunity. Retrofitting for climate change could lead to renewal and improvement of infrastructure, the advancement of production processes, the creation of more efficient and less pollutant transport modes, and the promotion of a gradual change towards a pattern of development with a lower carbon footprint. This move can have a significant impact from the point of view of equality and convergence of production, insofar as it entails the provision of

enhanced public services that are fundamental for the well-being of the least privileged strata of society. The United Nations Economic Commission for Latin America and the Caribbean (ECLAC) is working to build up evidence of the shift toward greater equality, and, indeed, the preliminary findings of economic studies are already highly conclusive in this regard. In fact, the evidence shows that the impact of global warming will be much harsher in the developing countries and for the weakest social groups. We must promote the transition to a lower carbon economy.

2. Technological change and what is often referred to as social networks, the information society, or the knowledge society: Innovations in information and communication technologies are shaping a very different society that will bring about changes in economic and production patterns, ways of working and organizing, communications systems, learning and information processes, social linkages, forms of government and ways of exercising democracy, and controlling society. The network system leans towards deregulation and self-regulation. The problem arises when this ethos is projected onto areas of global life in which deregulation has proved harmful and dangerous, as in finance, arms trafficking, liberalization of labor markets, and environmental management. For this very reason, the network system itself must put in place a mechanism for strengthening the regulation of those spheres of global life that, precisely because of this lack of control, generate global economic, production, environmental, and security crises. Here, for example, we have pointed to the importance of regulating the financial system and labor institutions.
3. Demographic transition: Changing demographics will bring about a shift in the relative weight of different age groups of the population over the coming decades. The decline in the child population, coupled with an aging population, is just beginning. Attention has been drawn to the demographic dividend, which Latin America and the Caribbean will enjoy, albeit with major differences between countries. This region will see a disproportionately large working-age population compared to the age-dependent population. This dividend must be harnessed in the coming decades, since the expected shift towards an aging population will alter the relationship between the economically active population and the dependent population, and high levels of productivity will be needed to generate the necessary resources to cover health care and social security requirements. Finally, the demographic transition shifts the equation of state, market, and family in reference to meeting well-being and capacity-building needs. As the proportions of the different age groups change, the way these three agents interact to provide

services, monetary outlays, and support networks must be reassessed. Transfers and care services are a strategic part of this interaction.

4. Cultural change: Greater global interconnections create greater awareness of the diversity of values, beliefs, and tastes, but they also generate instances of deep-seated cultural and religious intolerance, some of which crystallize into virulent forms that pose fresh threats to world security. After the fall of the Berlin Wall, the collective notion of democracy as part of global cultural heritage spread, but ethnic conflicts revived the ghosts of collective violence. The spread of consumerism and financing have given the market a pivotal role in defining meanings, identities, and symbols. For many, the globalization of communications and information, together with the mass use of information and communications technologies, has shifted references in space and time, as well as portrayals and visions of the world, at the same time as it raises questions about the pace and depth of changes in preferences, life plans, and norms of coexistence. The consolidation of religious identities is progressing side by side with the secularization typical of modernity. The foundations of ethnocentrism and patriarchy are increasingly being shaken by indigenous and women's movements. Cultural change is challenging the ways in which society is organized. For example, any policy on youth must take into account the very radical cultural changes that young people are experiencing. Gender and cultural values are increasingly recognized as cutting across all policies for equality and the balance between equal opportunities and respect for differences is a delicate one. Equality, which ECLAC has adopted as its core value, is the cornerstone of political action because it enshrines a universal aspiration that is capable of absorbing and reconciling the rapid cultural changes taking place worldwide.

6 WHY EQUALITY SHOULD BE THE BASIS FOR A NEW VISION ON SUSTAINABLE DEVELOPMENT

There is broad agreement that the fulfilment of MDGs is necessary but not sufficient. All countries agree that greater efforts should be made to close the remaining gaps by 2015. However, the 2030 Development Agenda and the 17 SDGs aim at closing structural gaps and disparities (income inequality, productivity, lack of infrastructure, connectivity, financial exclusion, among others). This clearly calls for a new development model based on a progressive structural change for equality and environmental sustainability (ECLAC 2012a).

Second, the 2030 Development Agenda has moved from national targets oriented around developing countries to universal objectives, with equality at the center as an ethical principle and ultimate goal of development. The concept of equality has been broadened to encompass autonomy, recognition, and dignity. This means that all individuals are recognized as equal in civil and political rights. This is termed equality with a rights-based approach. This concept goes beyond distributive fairness in terms of income, assets, and resources. It considers other dimensions: capabilities, social protection, and broad access to public goods, respect, and dignity. It connects identity and discrimination, gender and generation, ethnic and generation.

This approach requires a new development paradigm: growth for equality and equality as a driver of growth. It requires a new set of public policies and new multidimensional measures for inclusion. A focus on inclusion—closing gaps on productivity, capabilities (education), and employment (including job segmentation and informality)—can target the main causes of inequality.

Reducing inequality requires a new equilibrium among state-market-society, which should be specific to each country. No one size fits all. The central objective is for the State to recover the capacity to ensure redistributive policies and ensure public access to financing, technology, and innovation. This is not the role of the market; it never was and never will be.

Public policies should reinforce the synergies between equality and inclusion. Equality shall be placed as the main objective and inclusion as the process for its achievement.

The 17 sustainable development goals focus on the following dimensions:

1. Social inclusion should be oriented towards the progressive compliance and fulfilment of rights to attain critical aspirations of society: safety, health, and a prosperous society within the planetary boundaries.
2. Economic inclusion should focus on closing structural gaps such as productivity and technology to achieve income and functional distribution, full employment opportunities, and universal social protection.
3. Environmental inclusion should enhance re-distribution of rents and productive gains from extraction of natural resources, quality of life for all, and access to global public goods.

Citizens are claiming their right to take part in decision making on issues that concern them and are calling for the urgent redefinition of the state-market-society equation: a market that is dynamic and innovative and that can respond to the interests of the society, an inclusive and innovative society, and a more modern, streamlined State that guarantees well-being and the sustainability of development.

The onus is on this generation to take up the challenge of this era and to assume responsibilities. Today, after decades of dismantling, States and governments are ill-prepared to regulate the economy, lead technological change, guarantee well-being, close production and social gaps, and advance in the area of environmental sustainability. The challenge is to restore to the State and the public sector to their rightful role in shaping the future and strengthening social covenants and public-private partnerships.

There is an urgent need to move forward more rapidly and decisively, to redirect the approach to development and bring about the more far-reaching structural changes that are needed following the collapse of the self-regulating market model. In doing so, countries must be mindful of their regional identity.

The redefinition of a development agenda based on the perspective of the South with sustainability as the conceptual basis and with equality at the center is required. The present moment demands an agenda that is more balanced and takes into account the interests of the developing countries above those of the developed countries. We need an agenda that is universal in nature and not solely prescriptive for the developing countries like the MDGs were.

However, the global financial crisis (2007–2009) has demonstrated that there is an imperative to act much more efficiently and consistently through collective action to confront the challenges of a more uncertain, volatile, and changing environment.

The new development paradigm must reinforce the multilateral space as a community of interests to ensure the provision of global public goods; the objective is to achieve political agreements and a universal compact for sustainable development with equality at its core. Enhancing a culture of collective action requires an awakening of democracy across the planet, by affording a voice to the most diverse range of actors possible, and ensuring the inclusion of sectors that are not present among the major groups, namely indigenous peoples and Afro-descendent communities.

Finally, the 2030 Agenda will require the gradual convergence between MDGs and SDGs to achieve coherence, consistency, and universality of purpose. The 2030 Agenda was developed through participatory, bottom-up processes at the national, regional, and global levels, with the involvement of civil society, academia, and other institutions. This practice should be preserved all through its implementation. A multidimensional approach to the measurement of sustainability is moving beyond GDP. Feasible indicators are currently being designed by the member states through their national statistics offices with the support of the United Nations Statistical Commission and important participation of regional statistical entities aimed to ensure that diversity among regions is properly reflected together with a robust assessment of data and capacity gaps. In relation to means of implementation, the Addis Ababa Action Agenda (AAAA) is an important step that needs to be complemented with a real global governance on financing for development to include tax avoidance, fiscal coordination, credit, investment, and innovation in addition to official development assistance. In terms of technology transfer and innovation, a Technology Facilitation Mechanism was launched though the AAAA,[17] but a more committed effort is needed from developed countries to contribute seriously to the process of appropriation of environmentally sound technology.

In synthesis, in addition to national efforts it will be indispensable to address global governance in at least three dimensions: financial, environmental, and technological with equality in the horizon.

NOTES

1. See High-Level Panel of Eminent Persons on the Post-2015 Development Agenda (2013).
2. Such as the implementation of carbon footprints in trade, regardless of origins, or the attempt at the fifteen session of the Conference of the Parties to the UNFCCC (COP 15) in Copenhagen in 2009 to compel developing countries into mitigation commitments like those for developed countries in the Kyoto Protocol.
3. Goal 8 called for actions from developed countries through official development assistance (up to 0.7% of GDP), better trading conditions, including elimination of subsidies and transfer of technology.
4. United Nations 2012b, entitled "Format and organizational aspects of the high-level political forum on sustainable development," anticipates that the High-level Forum could be a reformed Economic and Social Council: paragraph 3: "Also decides that the meetings of the forum will be convened under the auspices of the General Assembly and of the Economic and Social Council; [...]."
5. See United Nations 2012b, paragraph 6: "Also decides that the meetings of the forum under the auspices of the General Assembly: (a) Shall be convened at the level of Heads of State and Government; (b) Shall be convened every four years by the President of the Assembly for a period of two days, at the beginning of the session of the Assembly, as well as on other occasions, on an exceptional basis, upon a decision by the Assembly; (c) Shall be chaired by the President of the Assembly; (d) Shall result in a concise negotiated political declaration to be submitted for the consideration of the Assembly."
6. See United Nations 2012b, paragraph 13: "Acknowledges the importance of the regional dimension of sustainable development, and invites the United Nations regional commissions to contribute to the work of the forum, including through annual regional meetings, with the involvement of other relevant regional entities, major groups and other relevant stakeholders, as appropriate."
7. It is important to note that the High Level Political Forum met exceptionally in September 2013 under the auspices of the General Assembly, which confirmed global readiness to implement the vision of Rio+20 and place poverty eradication and sustainable development at the core of the post-2015 development agenda. In July 2014, the second meeting of the High-level Political Forum took place under the auspices of the ECOSOC and was attended by the representatives of 193 Member States, intergovernmental organizations, and other entities and representatives of

the UN system, as well as representatives of Major Groups and other stakeholders. The second meeting concluded with the adoption of a Ministerial Declaration that called, among other things, for the urgent implementation of all commitments under the global partnership for development, in order to overcome gaps identified in the MDGs Gap Task Force reports.

8. United Nations 2012b, paragraph 20: "Decides that the forum shall strengthen the science-policy interface by examining documentation, bringing together dispersed information and assessments, including in the form of a global sustainable development report [...]."
9. United Nations 2012b, paragraph 7: "Further decides that the meetings of the forum under the auspices of the Economic and Social Council: (f) shall benefit from regional preparatory processes".
10. See Chapter 1 in this volume by J. A. Ocampo.
11. As documented in the national and sub-regional studies on the economic impact of climate change conducted by ECLAC. See ECLAC (2009a, 79; 2009b, ch.4; 2010a, 93–4; 2012b, 147–9; 2014, 20). See also Vergara et al. 2013, 33.
12. As opposed to what is known in structuralist literature as *spurious competition,* based on the creation of negative externalities, social or environmental.
13. The Latin American Reserve Fund (*Fondo Latinoamericano de Reservas*).
14. The Bank of the South (*Banco del Sur*).
15. See Chapter 1 in this volume by J. A. Ocampo.
16. As expressed in the Conference on Sustainable Development in Latin America and the Caribbean: follow-up to the United Nations development agenda beyond 2015 and to Rio+20, held in Bogota, from 7 to 9 March 2013.
17. See United Nations 2015, para. 123.

REFERENCES

Alvaredo, F., A.B. Atkinson, T. Piketty, and E. Saez. 2013. "The Top 1 Percent in International and Historical Perspective." *Journal of Economic Perspectives* 27(3): pp. 3–20.

ECLAC. 2009a. "La Economía del Cambio Climático en Chile: Síntesis." *CEPAL* LC/W.472. http://www.cepal.org/publicaciones/xml/8/37858/W288.pdf.

ECLAC. 2009b. "Economics of Climate Change in Latin America and the Caribbean: Summary 2009." *CEPAL* LC/G. 2425. http://www.cepal.org/publicaciones/xml/3/38133/02_Economics_of_Climate_Change_-_Summary_2009.pdf.

ECLAC. 2010a. "Economics of Climate Change in Central America: Summary 2010." *CEPAL* LC/MEX/L.978. http://www.cepal.org/publicaciones/xml/9/41809/ECCA-SUMMARY-102911peq.pdf.

ECLAC. 2010b. "Time for Equality: Closing Gaps, Opening Trails." *CEPAL* LC/G.2432 (SES.33/3). http://www.cepal.org/publicaciones/xml/1/39711/100604_2010-115-SES-33-3-Time_for_equality_doc_completo.pdf.

ECLAC. 2012a. "Structural Change for Equality: An Integrated Approach to Development." *CEPAL* LC/G.2524 (SES.34/3). http://www.cepal.org/publicaciones/xml/0/48140/2012-SES-34-Structural_Change.pdf.

ECLAC. 2012b. "La economía del cambio climático en Ecuador." *CEPAL* LC/W.560. http://www.cepal.org/publicaciones/xml/9/51439/CambioclimaticoEcuador.pdf.

ECLAC. 2013. "Political and Economic Perspectives on Latin America." *Latin American and Investment Forum*. London.

ECLAC. 2014. "La economía del cambio climático en la Argentina: Primera aproximación." *CEPAL* LC/MEX/L.978. http://www.cepal.org/publicaciones/xml/8/52168/CambioClimaticoArgentinaWEB.pdf.

High-Level Panel of Eminent Persons on the Post-2015 Development Agenda. 2013. *A New Global Partnership: Eradicate Poverty and Transform Economies through Sustainable Development*. New York: United Nations.

IPCC (Intergovernmental Panel on Climate Change). 2013. *Climate Change 2013. The Physical Science Basis*. Cambridge University Press: New York.

Ocampo, J. A. 2013a. *The History and Challenges of Latin American Development*. ECLAC: Santiago.

Ocampo, J. A. 2013b. *The Post-2015 UN Development Agenda*. Future United Nations Development System. CUNY Graduate Center. Briefing 11.

Ostrom, E. 2010. "Polycentric systems for coping with collective action and global environmental change." *Global Environmental Change* 20(4).

Sundaram, Jomo K. 2011. "Multilateralism: the United Nations and Global Governance." In *The United Nations in Global Governance: A Latin American and Caribbean Perspective*, edited by ECLAC and the Ministry of Foreign Affairs of Chile. Santiago: ECLAC.

United Nations. 2011. General Assembly Resolution A/RES/66/203.

United Nations. 2012a. *The future we want*. General Assembly resolution A/RES/66/288.

United Nations. 2012b. General Assembly Resolution A/RES/67/290.

United Nations. 2012c. *Sustainable Development 20 Years on from the Earth Summit: Progress, gaps and strategic guidelines for Latin America and the Caribbean*. Santiago: United Nations.

United Nations. 2013a. *A life of dignity for all: accelerating progress towards the Millennium Development Goals and advancing the United Nations development agenda beyond 2015*. Report of the Secretary-General (A/68/202). New York.

United Nations. 2013b. General Assembly Resolution A/67/L.48/Rev.1.

United Nations. 2013c. General Assembly Decision 67/555.

United Nations. 2015. Addis Ababa Action Agenda (A/RES/69/313).

Vergara, W., A.R. Rios, P. Gutman, L.M. Galindo, P. Isbell, P.H. Suding, and J.L. Samaniego. 2013. *The Climate and Development Challenge for Latin America and the Caribbean. Options for climate-resilient, low-carbon development*. Washington DC: Interamerican Development Bank. http://publications.iadb.org/bitstream/handle/11319/456/The%20Climate%20and%20Development%20Challenge%20fpr%20Latin%20America%20and%20the%20Caribbean.%20Options%20for%20climate-resilient%2c%20low-carbon%20development.pdf?sequence=1.

Part II

The Development Dimensions of Global Governance

4

Beyond Aid

Reshaping the Development Cooperation System

José Antonio Alonso

The adoption of the new 2030 Agenda for Sustainable Development when the Millennium Development Goals (MDGs) era has come to an end will have wide-ranging implications for the development cooperation system. Through the list of Sustainable Development Goals (SDGs) the international community has defined an agenda vastly more ambitious than the MDGs. While eradicating extreme poverty will remain the primary objective, new fields and more ambitious objectives will also be part of the new agenda. The document finally agreed in September 2015 confirms this idea and shows that the agenda as a whole will be made up of three large components: i) the work required to make MDGs mandate a reality, particularly in the social fields; ii) commitments for supporting countries' transition toward strategies for an inclusive and sustainable development; and iii) tackling some systemic issues, including a better provision of crucial regional and global public goods.

Given its enlargement, the 2030 sustainable development agenda will require the support of a renewed global partnership for development to mobilize unprecedented resources and political engagement. Both private and public financing from domestic and international sources will be necessary, and both need to be effectively exploited. But the role of development cooperation, financial and otherwise, will remain critical because of its unique characteristics. Official development assistance (ODA) and other ODA-like flows will still be important components of the international financing for development, particularly for the poorest countries. But if ODA wants to be effective, it should be redefined in the broader context of the development cooperation system (ODA and beyond ODA flows) and taking into account the dramatic changes that have happened recently in the international landscape.

It is true that over the last decade the international community has already taken some steps forward in reforming the international aid policy, in order to improve its levels of effectiveness and widen its inclusiveness. It is not the first time donors have proposed such objectives. The Development Assistance Committee (DAC) defined guidelines to improve aid implementation and effectiveness in 1979 and adopted some new guiding principles for aid coordination emphasizing the central role of recipient countries in 1986 (Fürher 1996). However, in the 2000s these efforts acquired a new momentum. The 2005 Paris Declaration, the subsequent Accra Agenda for Action in 2008, and the Busan Partnership for Effective Development Cooperation in 2011, are the main exponents of those efforts. Essentially, that agenda was oriented toward reducing the transaction costs of aid (harmonization among donors and alignment with recipients' procedures) and to re-balancing the relationship between developing countries and donors (ownership, transparency, and mutual accountability). The extent to which these purposes have been achieved is, nevertheless, limited (OECD 2011). Besides that, new institutional mechanisms for a more inclusive coordination among donors and partners, such as the UN Development Cooperation Forum and Global Partnership for Effective Development Cooperation, were created.

In the same period, donors drove a significant increase in aid resources. This process began in the late 1990s, when donors broke from a previous decade of stagnant aid. The upward trend of aid was maintained, with some minor setbacks, throughout the 2000s. The effects of the "great recession" made themselves felt during 2011–2012, when the volume of ODA decreased 6 percent accumulated in real terms. However, in 2013, aid showed an unexpected turnabout, mainly caused by the expansionist behavior of a few larger bilateral development providers that pushed aggregated flows to a historical peak. However, it is not expected that this upward trend will be maintained in the next few years, bearing in mind that donors' spending plans anticipate a stagnation of aid between 2014 and 2016 (OECD 2014).

If aid increased in the period, international private flows did so at a much faster rate. Accompanying the processes of capital account deregulation, there was an unprecedented expansion of international private financial flows. Some of these flows were oriented to developing countries, particularly those with emerging markets. As a consequence, the share of aid in the international financing of developing countries as a whole decreased significantly. This fact led some analysts (perhaps prematurely) to consider aid as a negligible financial source in the future development agenda.

As part of the Paris Declaration agenda, donors have tended to reduce the number of countries in which they operate, choosing to assist mainly those with the lowest level of development. As a result, during the past decade, least developed countries (LDCs) and low-income countries (LICs), particularly in Sub-Saharan Africa, have become more important aid recipients,[1] while middle-income countries (MICs) have significantly reduced their weight in ODA allocation.

Such a swing in aid allocation could seem appropriate to the economic progress that some MICs achieved over the last decade in a process that turned some MICs into the new poles of world economic dynamism.[2] This shift in the drivers of global growth is a new reason for some sectors considering aid as an irrelevant factor in future development, as the process of convergence is supposed to reach almost all developing countries. However, it would be a mistake to think that the features of a small group of successful cases can be generalized to all MICs. Several MICs are suffering severe bottlenecks related to their process of change, along with other structural weaknesses that put their possibilities for further development at risk. Even if the focus on LICs is maintained, development cooperation can make a difference by helping some MICs to overcome their structural vulnerabilities.

This last statement becomes even more appropriate if we take into account the changes that have occurred in the geographical patterns of global poverty. In the last fifteen years, there has been both a perceptible reduction in global extreme poverty and a dramatic shift in the location of the poor: according to current data, MICs now host the bulk of the globe's people living in poverty (Sumner 2010, 2012). Both changes suggest that eradicating absolute poverty is now more affordable than before, since the number of people living in poverty has been reduced and the countries in which they are living are richer. But that task could likely turn very difficult if some MICs are left to tackle this poverty alone. International support is required, especially in MICs with severe vulnerabilities, limited scope for redistribution, or a particularly large impoverished population.

As part of their new international role, an increasing number of MICs have begun to pursue their own international development policies through South-South cooperation. These emerging (or re-emerging) donors have not only enlarged the resource pool for international aid but have strengthened the bargaining power of recipient countries. Besides that, new providers of development cooperation place traditional DAC members under competitive pressure, applying new (less intrusive and more resolute) styles of relationships among countries while giving greater attention to areas that traditional donors had largely ignored in previous decades, such as infrastructure or productive capability.

Together with the emergence of new official donors, other actors are increasingly involved in the development cooperation system, expanding the number and diversity of development cooperation providers. A portion of these new actors comes from the private sector. As part of this process, new instruments and ways of managing development interventions have emerged, some of them operating outside the strict borders of ODA, making today's global aid architecture more complex and fragmented than ever before. The emergence of these new actors has challenged previous rules and governance mechanisms of the development cooperation system.

In sum, in the last two decades, the development cooperation system has been subject to several changes that have affected aid doctrine, the spectrum of actors involved, and the range of instruments put into play. But if the cooperation system has changed, international reality has evolved even more quickly and intensively. We are now facing a more heterogeneous, complex, and multi-polar world, with new powers coming from developing regions being called on to take on a more prominent role in the international arena. This is a world likely to see fewer absolutely-poor but more relatively-poor, in which national inequalities will become more challenging; a world in which developmental results will be more connected with the provision of global and regional public goods, particularly those related to environmental issues; and a world in which global responsibilities and voices must be better distributed. These changes will affect the aid system in ways that we can hardly predict.

This chapter aims to contribute to the discussion regarding the effects that these changes could have on the international cooperation system. The chapter is structured as follows: Section 1 is dedicated to analyzing the evolution of aid over last decade; Section 2 looks at the main changes in the international order and their implications for the international cooperation system; Section 3 focuses on some important issues that international cooperation policy needs to face in this new environment; Section 4 is an observation of some areas in which international cooperative action from the South is crucial; Section 5 focuses on the governance of the cooperation system; finally, some conclusive remarks are presented in Section 6.

1 EVOLUTION OF AID

1.1 Aid: Resistance to Growth

Development aid has historically behaved as a financial flow with rather limited dynamism. Between 1960 and 2013, the volume of aid (at constant prices) has multiplied by 3.5, going from $38 billion to $137 billion (at 2011 prices). In the same period the number of donor members of the DAC increased from 8 to 28 (plus EU), and the aggregated GNI of this group of countries multiplied by more than 4.5.[3]

The modest growth in the volume of aid has been paralleled by a falling trend in the ratio of ODA as a percentage of the GNI of the DAC donors. For the last two decades, that coefficient has remained below 0.33 percent (see Figure 4.1). Indeed, despite repeated commitments, only five donors in 2013 were meeting the agreed-upon goal of dedicating 0.7 percent of their GNI to ODA, while the average ratio for the group was less than half that coefficient (at 0.3 percent in 2013).[4]

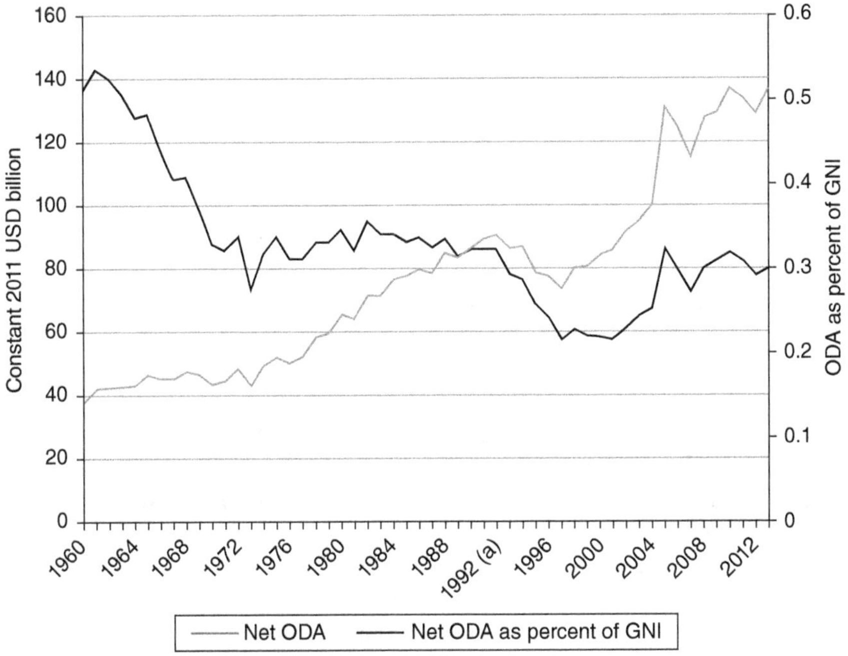

Figure 4.1 Net official development assistance, 1960–2013
Source: DAC (OECD) Last updated: 16-Aug-2013

In spite of its tradition of stagnation, ODA during the 2000s saw a sustained upward trend: it went from \$84 billion in 2000 to \$137 billion in 2013 at constant 2011 prices. In other words, aid increased by 63 percent during the period. The ratio of ODA over GDP followed the same trajectory, going from 0.22 percent in 2000 to 0.30 percent in 2013 (with 0.32 percent in 2010).

Some massive debt relief operations (Nigeria) and reconstruction programs (Iraq and Afghanistan) have had their impact on ODA figures in the period from 2000–2013. However the upward trend of aid resources was also encouraged by the "spirit of mission" that the Millennium Declaration and Monterrey Consensus motivated among donors. The enlargement of the DAC membership during this time, with six new members (Czech Republic, Iceland, Rep. of Korea, Poland, Slovak Republic, and Slovenia), also contributed to maintaining aggregate figures of ODA.

Accompanying this process, there was a significant shift in the geographical allocation of aid. Two tendencies were exhibited by donors during this period: i) a process of geographical concentration of partners; and ii) a more selective focus on targeting resources to the poorest groups of countries. More precisely, LDCs and LICs witnessed an increase in their shares of aid from about 37.9 in 2000–01 to 52.8 percent in 2010–11 (see Table 4.1). Conversely, in the same period the share of MICs declined from 62.1 to 47.2 percent of total allocated aid. It is worth mentioning that in the last two years (2011/2012) the share of

Table 4.1 Distribution of aid (%)

	2000/01	2010/11
LDCs	35.0	49.0
LICs	2.9	3.8
LMICs	39.0	33.8
UMICs	23.1	13.4

Source: DAC (OECD)

ODA to LDCs has reduced, in part as a consequence of the more important role that concessional loans have acquired within the ODA.

1.2 Public and Private Funds

In contrast to the limited dynamism of aid is the expansion in private financial flows to developing countries (see Figure 4.2). ODA grew at a slower rate than that of workers' remittances, direct investment, and other private flows. As a consequence, there has been a notable shift in the structure of international financing of developing countries, with private finance growing at the expense of public funding. In this context, it is not surprising that some sectors have questioned the importance of aid in the future development agenda. It would seem as if ODA had been condemned to become increasingly irrelevant in a world of deregulated financial flows.

However, such a conclusion could present a new version of the fallacy of composition. The contribution of aid to total sources of international financing is indeed irrelevant in the case of the upper middle-income countries (UMICs), but more significant in the case of the lower middle-income countries (LMICs), while it is by far the greatest source of international funding in the case of the LICs and the LDCs (see Figure 4.3). In fact, ODA still represents over 70 percent of total external finance in LDCs, despite some progress in increased availability of private funds.

Moreover, for many countries, the most important aspect of aid is not so much the volume of resources it brings, but its role as an incentive to promote changes, or as a means for leveraging additional resources and technological capacities (Kharas et al. 2011; Alonso 2014). From this perspective, aid should continue to play an important role in the future agenda of development.

1.3 The Current Crisis and New Financial Mechanisms

The current crisis affected aid with some delay: from 2008–2010 rates kept positive, but in 2011 and 2012 aid in real terms fell by 2.7 and 3.6 percent, respectively. However, in 2013 ODA did an unexpected turnaround and grew

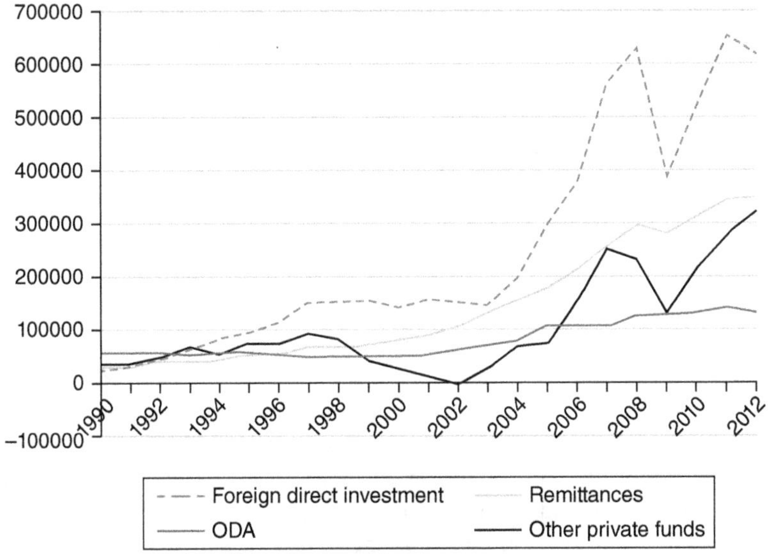

Figure 4.2 Finance sources to developing countries (US$ million)

Source: World Development Indicators (World Bank)

Note: Other private funds: Portfolio equity, net inflows, and Net flows on external debt, long-term

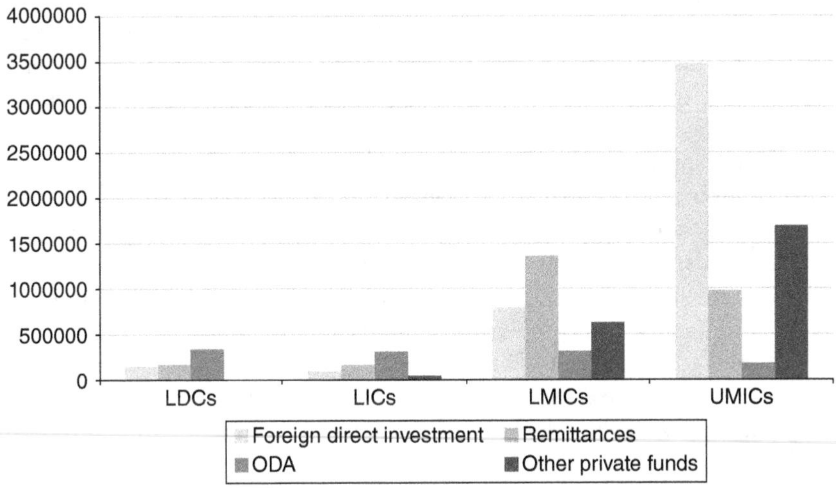

Figure 4.3 Financial sources for development by income groups (US$ million 2003–2012, accumulated)

Source: World Development Indicators (World Bank)

Note: Other private funds: Portfolio equity, net inflows, and Net flows on external debt, long-term

6 percent in real terms, putting the aggregated figure close to that of 2010 (close to US$135 billion). This increase in aid was pushed by a small group of larger donors (particularly, Japan and the United Kingdom) and was compatible with decreasing rates in 11 of the 28 bilateral member of DAC. In fact, a new stagnation of ODA is expected in the next few years, as donors' forward spending plans suggest (OECD 2014). With continuing tight budgets in OECD countries, it will be very difficult for donors to return to the previous upward trend in aid. This is why several commentators have proposed the need to search for new sources of financing that are subject to a lower degree of discretionary decisions by donor governments.

A strong new argument has recently supported the same idea: the need to look for new resources to finance international public goods, which have been poorly provided for in the past. Some of these international public goods are intimately related to the development agenda, but cannot be financed through ODA. For instance, according to the OECD, $320 billion a year is needed to pay for mitigation of and adaptation to climate change, on top of $130 billion of development aid—and climate change is just one of many international public goods under consideration.[5]

Proposals in this field are very diverse. Many of them fall under the category of "innovative financing" (even though some are very old). The Leading Group on Innovative Financing for Development[6] described this category as comprising all mechanisms for raising funds for development that are complementary to ODA and are predictable, stable, and closely linked to the idea of global public goods. DESA (2012), in a less normative way, considers innovative finance to be all mechanisms that share three basic characteristics: a) official sector involvement, including the use of public resources; b) international cooperation and cross-border transfer of resources to developing countries; c) innovation, in the sense that mechanisms are used in a new context or incorporate innovative features in the way resources are collected or managed. However, this definition is broad and makes it difficult to offer a single characterization of innovative finances since it includes mechanisms that are very differently conceived.

In a summary presentation, the category could be divided into six basic groups (see Table 4.2): i) proposals aimed at gathering resources (both public and private) to focus on a defined priority (vertical funds); ii) proposals to allow for an anticipated use of resources through the securitization of future aid funds (for example, the International Finance Facility for Immunization [IFFIm]); iii) initiatives aimed at encouraging voluntary private contribution to actions with social or environmental interest (for example, corporate social responsibility); iv) proposals aimed at encouraging better use of private resources which have a potential development effect (for example, remittances); v) new aid mechanisms for strengthening the capacity to leverage new resources for aid (for example, guarantees and other financial instruments); and vi) new taxes on negative international externalities (for example, the financial transaction tax).[7]

Table 4.2 Innovative finance for development mechanisms

	Characteristics	Examples
Traditional	-Public resources -Private resources	-ODA from developed and emerging sovereign donors -Private contributions to development cooperation system
Innovative	New institution for frontloading resources	-International Financial Facility (IFF for Immunization) -Advance Market Commitments
	New ways to put together public and private funds for specific goals	-Global Fund -GAVI
	New mechanisms for voluntary contribution	-Global or national lotteries -Digital Solidarity Social Fund -REED
	New incentives for a better use of private resources	-Corporate Social Responsibility -Support to some uses of remittances -Clean Development Mechanisms -Carbon Funds
	New ways of leverage	-Public-private partnership in infrastructure investment -Development Finance Institutions (investment, debt, and guaranties)
	New levies	-Airline ticket taxes -Tobin tax -Financial transactions tax -Carbon emission tax

Some of these mechanisms are already in use (such as, the IFFIm global partnership or the taxes on airline tickets); others are being used at the national level without any link with international agreements (carbon emissions taxes); and finally others are still being debated (the tax on financial transactions). The ability of most of these modalities to mobilize resources is somewhat limited and, in many cases, there is no guarantee that collected resources are additional to ODA. Of all the mechanisms mentioned, those that have the greatest ability to mobilize resources are those associated with new global taxes, whether on financial transactions, on carbon emissions, or on the use of associated fuels. However, these mechanisms have so far gained limited political support.

2 NEW TRENDS IN THE INTERNATIONAL SYSTEM

During the last two decades the aid system has changed, but the world has also evolved more rapidly and more profoundly. Four changes seem to be especially important.

2.1 Increasing Heterogeneity in the Developing World

Development theory was born in the 1950s, based on the conviction that developing countries constituted a socially specific reality, relatively homogeneous and different from that of industrialized countries (the principle of "difference" mentioned by Corbridge [2007]). International aid was built on the same assumption, implying the existence of a sharp North-South divide. Now the reality is very different: the heterogeneity among developing countries has increased, with economies located along a more continuous scale of levels of development. As Hirschman (1981, 20) put it more than three decades ago, "[T]he concept of a united body of analysis and policy recommendations for all underdeveloped countries...became in a sense a victim of the very success of development and of its unevenness."

Figure 4.4 illustrates the aforementioned tendency. The level of heterogeneity among countries is measured by the coefficient of variation of the countries' per capita GDP (converted in PPP) for the period 1950–2008. Heterogeneity in the world economy and, particularly, among developing countries increased after the 1980s.

Figure 4.5 offers another way to illustrate the same process. In this case, four density functions of the countries' GDP per capita (in PPP) are presented with data from 1960, 1970, 1990, and 2008. The level of dispersion in the lower tail of the distribution (the left hand side of the graph, corresponding to the bulk of developing countries) increases over time. In fact, currently most countries

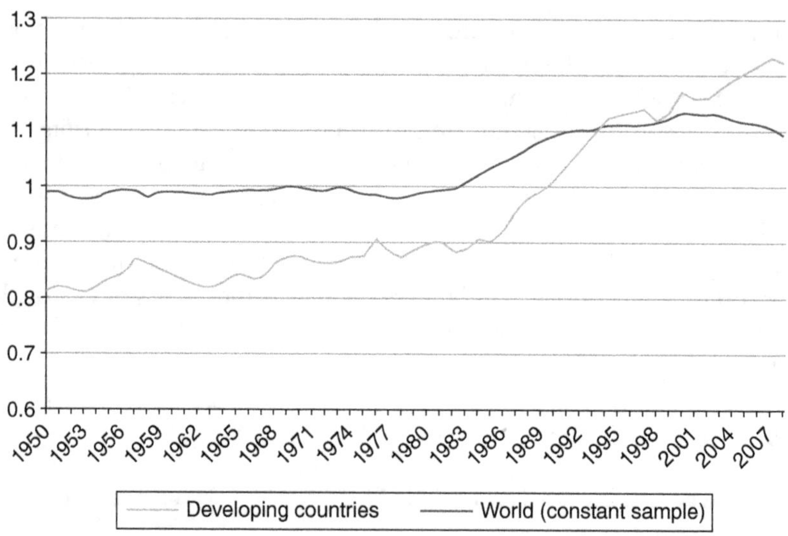

Figure 4.4 Heterogeneity (coefficient of variation among GDP pc PPP)

Source: Maddison (http://www.ggdc.net/MADDISON/oriindex.htlm)

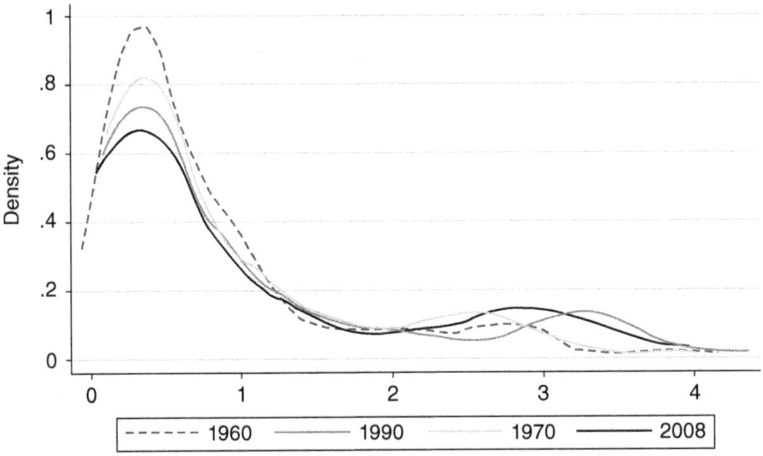

Figure 4.5 Standardized distribution of GDP pc (PPP)
Source: Maddison (http:www.ggdc.net/MADDISON/oriindex.htlm)

and the majority of the population of the developing world are located in the heterogeneous middle-income category. The need to respond to this growing heterogeneity is a challenge for the development cooperation system.

2.2 The New Patterns of Global Poverty

The estimates of the evolution of poverty over the last two decades reveal two important features. Firstly, there has been a significant decrease in the number of people who live on less than $1.25 a day (and the same could be said for people under $2 a day). However, the intensity of this reduction is subject to debate: a moderate estimate puts the rate of poverty in 2010 at 21 percent (around 1.3 billion people) (Ravallion 2012; Chen and Ravallion 2012), while the more optimistic estimate reduces that rate to 15.8 percent (878 million) (Chandy and Gertz 2011; Kharas and Rogerson 2012) (see Table 4.3). In accordance with these estimates, in 2015 the rate of poverty is expected to be between 16.3 percent and 9.9 percent of the total world population, respectively. Bearing in mind that in 1990 (baseline year for the MDGs) poverty affected to 43 percent of world's population, we can understand the significance of the progress made up to now, even if most of the population lifted above the poverty line continue to suffer from economic insecurity (in the $2–$10 range).

While absolute poverty has been reduced, the number of relatively poor people has hardly changed in the last 20 years. Ravaillon and Chen (2011) presented a measure of "weakly relative" poverty in which the poverty line rises with the national mean of income per capita above some critical value, interpretable as the

Table 4.3 Global poverty in 2015 (two forecasts)

	Chandy and Gertz (2011)		Ravallion (2012)	
	Million	%	Million	%
East Asia	53.4	2.7	159.3	7.7
Europe and Central Asia	4.3	0.9	1.4	0.3
Latin America and Caribbean	27.3	4.5	33.6	5.5
Middle East and North Africa	5.4	1.9	9.7	2.7
South Asia	145.2	8.7	418.7	23.9
Sub-Saharan Africa	349.2	39.3	397.2	41.2
World	585.5	9.9	1,019.9	16.3

Table 4.4 Distribution of global poverty ($1.25 per day), 1990 vs. 2007

	Non-adjusted base years				Adjusted base years			
	1990		2007		1990		2007	
	Millions	%	Millions	%	Millions	%	Millions	%
LICs	1,596.1	94.5	305.3	24.1	1,632.5	93.1	342.7	29.1
MICs	93.2	5.5	960.4	75.9	121.4	6.9	836.0	70.9
Total	1,689.3	100	1,265.7	100	1,753.9	100	1,187.7	100
China and India	1,137.9	67.4	673.0	53.2	1,123.6	64.1	561.3	47.6
MICs minus China and India	–		287.4	22.7			274.6	23.3
LICs minus China and India	458.2	27.1			509.0	29.0		

Source: Sumner (2012)

minimum cost of social inclusion.[8] In their estimates, weakly relative poverty affected 2.4 billion in 1990, but that amount increased to near 2.7 billion in 2008. In relative terms, the ratio goes from 65 percent in 1990 to 47 percent in 2008. In sum, we are living in a world with fewer absolutely poor people, but with a stagnant number of relatively poor (Chen and Ravaillon 2012).

The second feature refers to the location of global poverty: in this case, all estimates confirm that poverty is no longer concentrated in LICs. More precisely, as many as 1 billion people living in poverty lived in MICs, with the remaining third (close to 300 million) living in LICs (Sumner 2010 and 2012). This pattern is entirely new: in 1990, 94.5 percent of people living in poverty lived in LICs and only 5.5 percent were located in MICs (see Table 4.4). Although this shift in the geography of poverty might be the result of the graduation to MIC status of a small number of populous countries (particularly China, Indonesia, India, Nigeria, and Pakistan), it defines a new reality that forecasts show will be sustained in the near future. Edward and

Sumner (2014) estimate across a range of growth and inequality assumptions that even in 2030 MICs could continue to account for between a third and a half of global $1.25 and $2 poverty, or even more (up to two-thirds) if inequality trends continue on their current trajectory.

In sum, we live in a world with less absolute poverty, but not less relative poverty, in which, according to the data, global poverty is not merely, or even predominantly, an issue for low-income countries. The bulk of people living in poverty now live (and are likely to continue living for a decade to come) in MICs. Both facts drive us to believe that the eradication of absolute poverty is now more feasible than before. Achieving that objective will require active redistributive policies not only among countries, but also within the affected countries.

2.3 A Multi-polar World

Development aid was born into a bipolar world (that of the 'cold war') characterized by the presence of two blocs in conflict—a struggle that permeated all international relationships. Today, that international reality has vanished. Instead, a more complex and multi-polar world is emerging. New global powers from the developing world are being added to traditional powers, and these new powers are highly dynamic. As a consequence, a new world order with a more competed and diffuse distribution of economic power seems to be taking shape, with new actors (different from States, such as global civil society or multinational companies) operating in the international arena.

Data confirm the aforementioned change. Emerging and developing countries contributed more than 52 percent of global GDP (in PPP) in 2010, with China, India, Indonesia, Brazil, and the Russia Federation representing 32 percent of the total (these proportions would be 34 percent and 18 percent, respectively, in current dollars). Furthermore, emerging and developing countries' share of international trade flows has risen steadily, from 26 percent in 1995 to an estimated 42 percent in 2010 (World Bank 2011). Much of this rise in trade has been promoted by a previously unheard-of expansion in transactions between developing countries. Besides that, emerging and developing countries hold 75 percent of all official foreign exchange reserves, and sovereign wealth funds and other pools of capital in developing countries have become important sources of international investment. In sum, there has been an undeniable change in the distribution of economic power at global level.

The World Bank (2011) confirms the aforementioned change through two "polarity indexes" that measure a country's contribution both to global economic growth (simple index) and to growth and other transactions—trade, finance, and technology—(multidimensional index). The results are clear: the indexes of traditional growth poles (the U.S., Japan, and the Eurozone) are stagnant or decreasing, while those of key emerging countries (China, India, Brazil, Korea, Turkey, or the Russian Federation) are rising.

There is another significant consequence of this process. Some economies have become important poles of growth in their regional areas, and the economic dynamism of the surrounding countries is highly conditioned by the growth of these key poles. In all developing regions (save Eastern Africa) there are one or two emerging economies whose weight in regional growth is at 40 percent or greater (see Table 4.5).

This broad evolution underway in the global economy will probably endure for at least the next two decades. In fact, Subramanian (2011) estimates that emerging and developing countries' share in global GDP (PPP) will climb to 67 percent in 2030, with China and India contributing 23 percent and

Table 4.5 New regional powers

	Number of countries	Percentage in regional population (%)	Percentage in regional GDP (PPP)	Weight in regional growth
Latin America and Caribbean				
Brazil		33	32.3	33
Mexico		19.2	23.5	14.7
Total	*33*	*52.3*	*55.8*	*47.7*
North Africa				
Egypt				
Total	*5*	*40.9*	*42.6*	*44.9*
Western Africa				
Nigeria		45.8	53.8	60.2
Total	*23*	*45.8*	*53.8*	*60.2*
Eastern Africa				
	11			
Southern Africa				
South Africa		30.3	66.9	55.9
Total	*14*	*30.3*	*66.9*	*55.9*
Western Asia				
Iran		35.6	32.2	32.9
Total	*13*	*35.6*	*32.2*	*32.9*
Southern Asia				
India		74.9	82.5	85.4
Total	*8*	*74.9*	*82.5*	*85.4*
Eastern Asia				
China		62.7	55.7	77.5
Indonesia		10.7	5.2	4.9
Total	*17*	*73.4*	*61.1*	*82.4*
Central Europe				
Russian Federation		40.4	52.9	50.8
Turkey		20.9	24.9	22
Total	*12*	*61.3*	*77.9*	*72.8*

Source: Author estimates based on the World Bank data.

10 percent, respectively, to total GDP (these proportions would be 53 percent, 16 percent, and 6 percent in current dollars).

As the world becomes ever more heterogeneous, with a new group of developing countries taking a more prominent role in the international realm, countries' commitments and efforts should adapt to a new distribution of wealth and capacities. The simplistic split between "developed" and "developing" countries should be replaced with a more complex and gradual distribution of responsibilities at the international level, including those linked to the development cooperation system.

2.4 International Public Goods

The globalization process now underway has tended to accentuate all types of interdependencies among countries, and as a consequence, the scope of international public goods arising from these interdependencies has widened. These goods are characterized by strong externalities, meaning that, once provided, their benefits are available to everyone in an unlimited way (the same could be said of "public bads"). The characteristics of public goods dictate that the market is incapable of ensuring their efficient provision and that some form of collective action is required. In the international sphere, the response must be carried out through diverse coordination and voluntary cooperation formulas among the relevant players. The multilateral system is the most appropriate framework to promote and articulate such cooperative action, even if its institutions should be seriously reformed.

A strong relationship exists between international public goods (IPGs) and the development agendas (Kaul et al. 1999, 2003; Sandler 2004). A new vaccine against malaria, the fight against climate change, or the improving of global financial stability (all of them IPGs) has more developmental impact than several aid interventions. Even so, these two agendas should not be seen as identical, but rather as complementary for two reasons. Firstly, they rest on different theoretical foundations; aid mainly refers to the realm of distribution, while IPGs refer to the field of economic allocation (market failures). Secondly, and more importantly, there is a difference in the preferential beneficiaries of each policy. In the case of aid, developing countries (particularly the poorest) are the main beneficiaries, while in the case of IPGs, all countries may benefit (although not necessarily to the same extent). In spite of these differences, sometimes it is difficult to establish where the development agenda stops and the IPG agenda starts. This suggests the need for an increasingly integrated perspective for both agendas, and the quest for new financing sources to support the IPG agenda. In any case, for IPGs provision, new rules and financial mechanisms—beyond ODA—will be required.

3 FROM ODA TO GLOBAL DEVELOPMENT POLICY: SOME ISSUES

3.1 Redistribution and Incentives

The need to respond to the aforementioned changes in the international landscape constitutes a challenge for the international cooperation system. More precisely, the cooperation system is facing two extreme options. One of them would be to maintain an integral perspective referred to all developing countries' progress, working through a differentiated agenda in accordance with the heterogeneous conditions of each country, based on the principle of common but differentiated responsibilities, including the contribution of partners from the South, the opening to new actors and instruments beyond ODA, and the ambition of interconnecting the agendas of development and IPGs. The alternative option would be to preserve aid as a focused policy, specialized in fighting extreme poverty almost exclusively in the poorest countries (and perhaps in fragile States), based mainly on ODA (perhaps with the contribution of some public-private partnerships) and centrally resting on the action of traditional donors and those emerging donors that are willing to share DAC rules.

There are reasons one might support the second option. Since aid resources are scarce, they should be focused only on the more needful countries (the "bottom billion" popularized by Collier [2007]). This might avoid excessive dispersion of objectives or a wasting of resources on countries with sufficient capacities to address their own problems.

However, such an approach has some questionable aspects. Firstly, it promotes an excessively narrow vision of the development agenda. Along with fighting poverty, other objectives need consideration if a fairer distribution of global development opportunities is to be pursued. Secondly, the approach overestimates the capacities of MICs to overcome their own problems, neglecting the fact that some of these countries suffer severe vulnerabilities that may require international support. Thirdly, it does not take into account that international aid, in addition to promoting redistributive action (facing needs of the poorest), must also define a framework of incentives able to maximize the developmental efforts of all countries involved.

Once these three aspects are assumed, international development cooperation can be understood as a comprehensive, complex, and differentiated policy, in accordance with the multiple objectives that it has to promote and the variety of countries where it should be allocated.

In a general perspective, development cooperation operates on two intertwined spheres: global redistribution and incentives for development. Both goals can be compatible, but they are clearly distinct. In comparative terms, the first role is more relevant in the case of poorer countries, where the transfer of aid resources covers a major share of the recipient's social expenses. The second role is the most prominent in the case of countries with a higher level of development, where aid is a relatively minor source of financing. In both cases, the role that international cooperation may play in modifying the framework of incentives in which agents operate in recipient countries should be emphasized.

The last argument is more appropriate if we take into account that aid is a decidedly sub-optimal option for world redistribution. Aid rests on a decentralized system, with voluntary international transfers and ample room for countries' free-rider behavior. This system is more effective than a decentralized scheme based only on national redistribution (without international transfers), but it is less effective than a centralized scheme based on a world income tax and rules that maximize a border-neutral social welfare function. In fact, empirical evidence suggests that aid produces only a minuscule effect on world redistribution (Kopczuk et al. 2005). In this context of low static redistributive effects, it is important to maximize the dynamic redistributive effects of aid (related to the incentives that aid promotes). In other words, the main contribution of aid would not be measured in what it could directly finance, but in the kinds of incentives to social and economic change that it might promote (Kharas et al. 2011; Alonso, 2014). Aid may also play this role in MICs, even if resources are proportionally minor.

The aforementioned objective may appear incompatible with plotting a sharp line between countries in relation to their GDP per capita both for country eligibility and aid allocation. Nothing automatically happens when a country crosses a line in per capita income that is somewhat arbitrary (Alonso et al. 2014b). A better system would be one that replaces graduation with gradualness, modulating aid intensity (and its content) to the abilities and needs of the recipient. This involves paying more attention to poorer countries, but it does not excuse donors from granting development cooperation to the most vulnerable middle-income countries. The developing world is more heterogeneous than before, and the cooperation system should be ready to tackle such diversity.

3.2 Poor People or Poor Countries?

The high levels of poverty found in MICs have motivated some analysts to inquire whether international community attention should be focused on people living in poverty, wherever they live, rather than on poor countries (Kanbur and Sumner 2012). If the amount of people living in poverty is our paramount concern, then MICs should become the main aid recipients. However, such an approach is defective, as international aid necessarily needs to consider a recipient country's capacities for tackling its own problems.

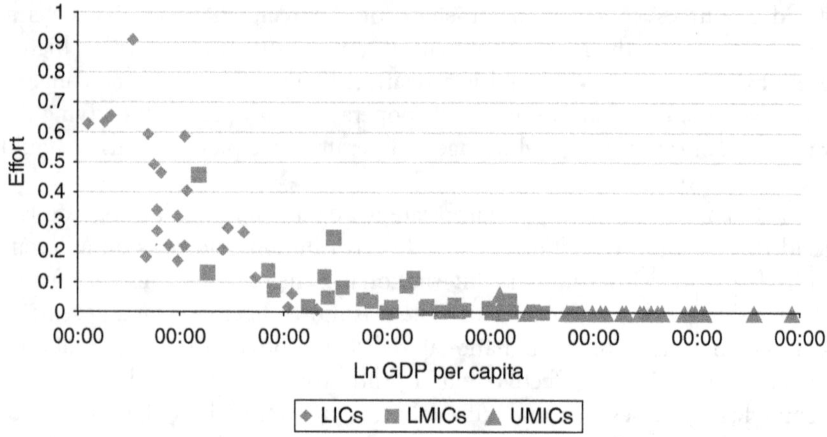

Figure 4.6 Transfer effort from fifth quintile ($2 poverty line)
Source: Author estimates based the World Bank data

Aid is meant to complement and encourage a recipient country's development capacities, not to substitute them.

If this principle is accepted, the relevant issue in aid allocation is not so much the number of people living in poverty in a given country, but rather the country's constraints for eliminating poverty by itself. Those restrictions are mainly linked with the fiscal space that the country has for funding redistributive policies against inequality and poverty. In order to obtain a notional measurement of this variable, we might estimate the transfer of income that the fifth quintile (the richest) would have to commit to in order that all people living in poverty be raised above the poverty line. As fiscal efforts usually rest on this fifth quintile, that ratio could be understood as an approach to the redistributive effort, through the taxation system, required for eliminating poverty (being the ratio dependent on the national GDP per capita, the level of inequality, the percentage of people living in poverty, and the poverty gap).

The estimates confirm that, to a large extent, LICs need to make a greater effort in order to eliminate poverty than MICs (see Figure 4.6). Therefore, as long as international aid aims to eradicate poverty, resources should be focused mainly on LICs (including LDCs). However, there is a group of MICs (mainly LMICs) that would also require high redistributive efforts.[9] Leaving these countries to their own capacities is likely to prolong the problem. In such cases, international cooperation could make a difference.

In sum, in spite of the new geography of global poverty, international aid should maintain its focus on LICs. Some MICs possess enough fiscal space to eradicate poverty by themselves through sound growth and redistributive policies. In these cases, aid should not be a substitute for these policies. However, it is equally true that some MICs lack the fiscal space for such a redistributive effort. In these cases, international aid might be needed to complement the national resources against poverty.

3.3 Focused or Wide-scope Policy?

In order to maximize developmental incentives, international cooperation has to support developing countries' efforts to overcome their structural vulnerabilities and to assure their social and economic achievements against shocks and possible relapses. The role of international cooperation in tackling these problems in LICs is well known, but it is less defined in the case of MICs.

MICs form a vast heterogeneous group, which contains countries of greatly differing size, development potential, vulnerabilities, and social achievements. As a result, there is no point in adopting a one-size-fits-all approach. That said, some useful observations can be made about the main challenges faced by countries in the transition from very poor to somewhat better off, specifically on the features and effects of an intermediate level of development. In that sense, MICs are usually affected not so much by absolute shortages but by asymmetries and bottlenecks in their process of development. These bottlenecks have a similar effect to "poverty traps," insofar as they drive countries to fall into a low-level equilibrium that ends up blocking or delaying growth. These situations are currently known as "MIC traps" (Aiyar et al. 2013; Agenor and Canuto 2012; Fallon et al. 2001; Alonso 2007). The effects of these traps could be illustrated with historical experience: there are numerous MICs that have experienced—in some cases repeatedly—episodes of accelerated growth, but only a few countries managed to sustain convergence paths towards the leaders' GDP per capita (Hausmann et al. 2004).

A simple way to illustrate this problem is by classifying countries in accordance with their GDP per capita (in PPP) relative to that of the United States in 1960 and 2008. Several cells are identified with countries that have experienced different paths of growth (see Figure 4.7). For example, cell 3 includes countries that were relatively rich in the past and that remain rich today (for example, the United Kingdom, France, or Germany); cell 1 includes those countries that were LICs in the past and that remain LICs now (some countries from Sub-Saharan Africa that seem to be caught in a poverty trap); cell 5 includes a small group of successful countries that were MICs in the past and are now HICs (among them Spain, Korea, Taiwan, and Ireland); cell 4 contains the few countries that managed to move from LIC to MIC status (among them Botswana or Mauricio); and finally, cell 2 groups those countries that were historically MICs and that remain MICs. These countries have not been able to maintain a sustained process of convergence to HIC status, and some in this group seem to be caught in MIC traps.

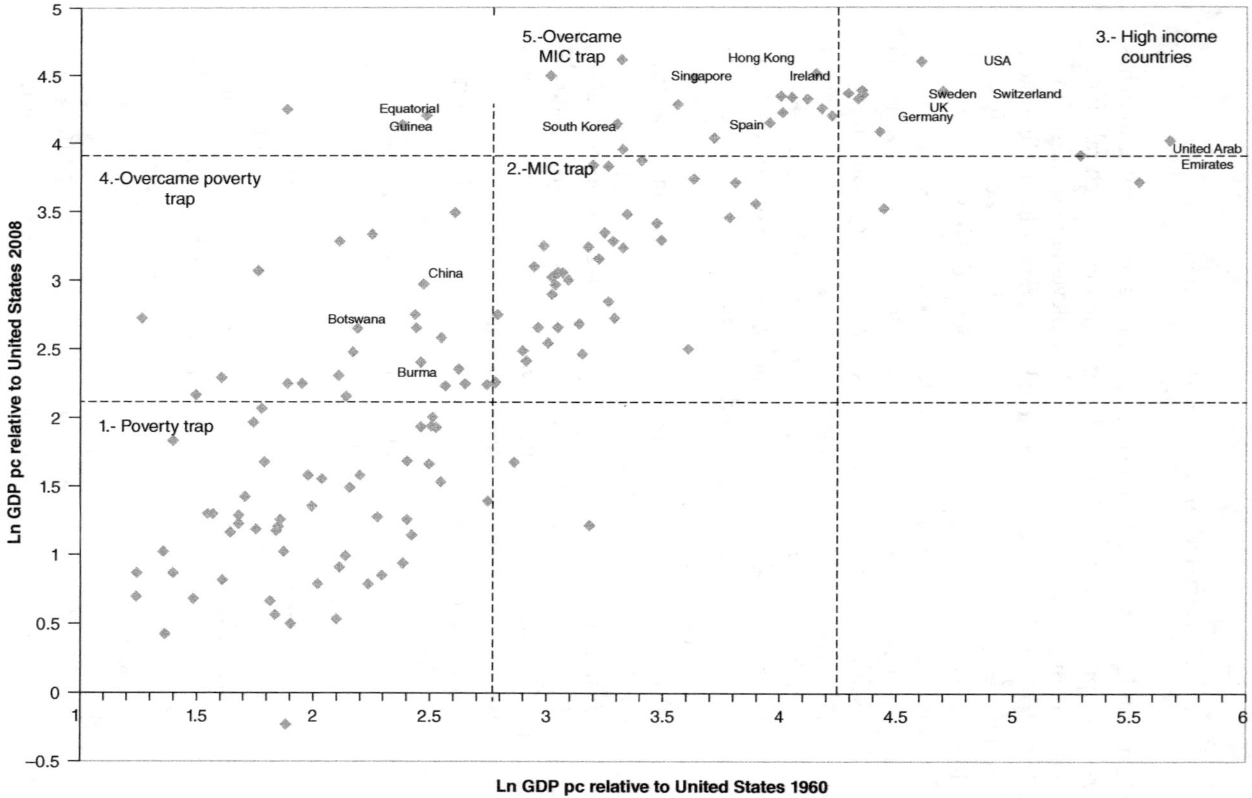

Figure 4.7 MIC traps (countries' GDP pc relative to the United States, 1960 and 2008)

Source: Author estimates based on the Maddison data

In spite of individual particularities, the traps that affect MICs are mainly located within three large dimensions of the development process: governance, financial and macroeconomic stability, and productive and technological change. Let me briefly present these three traps.

- The *"governance trap"*: As countries progress, they require more complex institutions to manage the problems of coordination that emerge in a more developed economy and to respond to a more demanding society in terms of governance conditions. In other words, the development process requires a path of institutional change. However, these two processes do not necessarily evolve at the same pace, with institutions more subject to inertia. This problem affects MICs especially, because these countries undergo a more intense process of economic and social transformation. Sometimes, the problem lies not only in the weakness and limited efficiency of institutions, but also in their reduced credibility. Such a situation is driven by, among other factors, the extraordinary levels of inequality that characterize some MICs. This acute inequality, deep-rooted in time, in a context of reduced social mobility, becomes a corrosive element of institutional legitimacy (Alonso and Garcimartín 2013). As a consequence, countries are less capable of providing public goods, managing distribution conflicts, facing external shocks, or addressing market failures.
- The *"financial trap"*: this trap refers to the difficulties these countries have in achieving a stable integration into international financial markets, and at the same time maintaining enough space for counter-cyclical macroeconomic policies. This difficulty is associated with the effects that international financial markets have on countries with a high tendency toward indebtedness in foreign currencies, limited fiscal space, and notably narrow national capital markets. With high debt ratios over GDP, and liabilities in foreign currencies (and, at times, in limited term bonds), countries will be subject to the influence of the "animal spirit" of international investors. The international financial environment accentuates the pro-cyclical tone of economic policy, which relaxes during times of abundance, when there is an influx of capital, and contracts when capital leaves the country. This factor has been aggravated as a result of the financial liberalization processes: as international experience shows, deregulated financial flows can produce important macroeconomic disruption, particularly in these kinds of countries (Ocampo 2011; Ocampo and Griffith-Jones 2007).
- The *"structural change trap"*: this trap refers to the difficulties experienced by MICs in sustaining a process of technical and productive change as they rise up the income ladder. Traditionally, the productive specialization of these countries has been based on sectors which are resource- and unskilled-labour-intensive. As long as productive costs increase with the

level of development, they need to move towards more dynamic and technological-intensive sectors. Necessary to achieving this end would be a combination of investment in physical and human capital, continuous promotion of technological capacities, creation of efficient infrastructures, and enhancement of a sound climate of competition in the markets. Fostering so complex a process with a weak institutional framework in a context of financial restrictions is no easy task.

The requirements of environmental sustainability have added new demands to the productive transformation process of MICs. These countries are forced to review their energy model and their technological-productive patterns, if they want their rate of growth, which may be intense, not to result in costly environmental damages.

In the aforementioned traps, the role of development cooperation is rather limited but not irrelevant (Alonso et al. 2014b). The effects of aid could be significant in dealing with problems related to social fragmentation, inequalities, fragile civil society, or institutional weaknesses; meanwhile, effects would likely be smaller, though perceptible, in the case of promoting innovation, change in energy patterns, or technology transfer; and the impact of aid would probably be very minor, if any, in promoting a wider fiscal space for countercyclical macroeconomic policies or financial stability. As a consequence, aid will be effective in MICs only if it is highly selective, identifying the most relevant problems in each case. Development organizations will have to customize their approaches and assistance more carefully to suit specific country context in MICs.

There are three other considerations in relation to cooperation with MICs: i) Given its limited weight on the GDP of the recipients, the effectiveness of aid will depend crucially on its leverage: that is, international cooperation will be much more important as a catalytic factor than as a financial source; ii) Given the areas in which international cooperation should work in MICs, it is just as important to provide ODA as it is to offer other elements of international cooperation beyond ODA, including blended and other market-like instruments of funding; and iii) Finally, the development cooperation effectiveness will depend on some policy changes oriented to improve policy coherence at national and international levels and to set an enabling international environment with fairer global rules and more representative structures of governance.

3.4 New Actors, New Instruments

Since the 1990s, the number and diversity of the aid providers has increased rapidly. As a consequence of this process, today the global aid architecture is more complex and fragmented than before—with costs in terms of aid effectiveness insofar as the level of coordination among the actors is very low.

However, from another perspective, the process has also a positive face: beyond the resources that they provide, the presence of these new actors enriches the aid system, incorporating new cultures, criteria, and procedures. For example, some emerging countries are less intrusive and demanding than traditional donors usually are, and the private sector is more concerned by the effectiveness of aid, searching for clearer results from their activities. Both could have positive effects on the development cooperation policy.

In addition to DAC official donors and civil society, three new actors have emerged with special force in the last decade. Firstly, an increasing number of emerging donors are providing resources through South-South cooperation (see later). Secondly, the private sector, directly or through its foundations, is increasingly supporting international aid programs besides promoting other activities such as philanthropy or social impact investment that have positive developmental effects without necessarily being ODA. Finally, as a consequence of the partnership between official and private providers, new mechanisms of funding have been created, particularly in fields such as health or climate.

With these new actors, the development cooperation system has also increased the range of its available instruments. Most of these new instruments are connected with private sector involvement in development activities. This is the case, for example, with social impact investment and corporate responsibility policies. In addition to these private sector instruments, over the last two decades, donors have used new financial instruments (including equity investment, loans, and guarantees) to promote the private sector in partner countries. Additionally, other new instruments were created to promote capacities in areas where aid had not focused previously, such as the Aid-for-Trade Initiative (AFT) promoted by the WTO to assist developing countries to better integrate into the multilateral system, or new mechanisms in the environmental area, particularly in relation to adaptation activities against climate change.

The composition of resources shows, albeit in an incomplete way, the increasingly complex structure of the development cooperation system. According to a recent estimation, in 2000, the sum of contributions by these new actors and mechanisms (emerging donors, private sources, and public-private partnerships), grouped under the label "non-traditional development assistance" (NTDA), was in the most modest estimation about \$5.3 billion (near 8 percent of total development assistance). That amount rose to \$53.3 billion by 2009 (30.7 percent of total development assistance) (Greenhill et al. 2013) (see Table 4.6).[10] This is only the tip of the iceberg, because part of the developmental activities and resources of these new actors are not well reported.

As a consequence of these changes, the complexity of the cooperation system has become higher, making it more difficult to preserve the levels of coherence of the system as a whole. As a consequence, overlap and contradictory efforts

Table 4.6 Traditional and non-traditional development assistance (2009)

Component	$ billion	%
Traditional development assistance	120	69.2
Philanthropic assistance and private giving	25.3	14.6
Oficial assistance from emerging donors	11.5	6.6
Social impact investment	1.6	0.9
Climate finance	11.1	6.4
Global health funds	3.8	2.2
Total	173.3	100

Source: Greenhill et al. (2013)

are possible. However, it is worth mentioning that the opinions of developing countries regarding these trends tend to be more positive than negative (Greenhill et al. 2013). The benefits of greater choice, due to a wider range of providers, seem to outweigh the potential costs of fragmentation or lack of coordination. The Paris Agenda has tried to encourage donors to reach more coordination, harmonization, and division of labor. But this approach faces an important problem: since more and more development actors are not official and operate in a field wider than ODA, the need for greater coordination is not merely a DAC issue.

4 A NEW SHAPE FOR THE PRINCIPLE OF COMMON BUT DIFFERENTIATED RESPONSIBILITIES

Development cooperation should be oriented not only to support developing countries' efforts for overcoming their specific development structural constraints, but also to encourage those countries to more actively take part in the international development agenda. This purpose manifests across various dimensions, but two seem especially relevant: developing countries' South-South cooperation and their contribution to the IPG agenda.

4.1 South-South Cooperation

South-South cooperation (SSC) has acquired increasing notoriety over the last decade. The exact volume of this kind of cooperation is not known, as deficient registration systems in the countries involved contribute to the lack of information in this area. In any case, according to the DAC, development cooperation by 28 non-DAC countries reached close to $23 billion (more than 15 percent of total ODA) in 2013, with Saudi Arabia ($5.6 billion), United Arab Emirates ($5.4 billion), Turkey ($3.3 billion), and China ($3 billion)

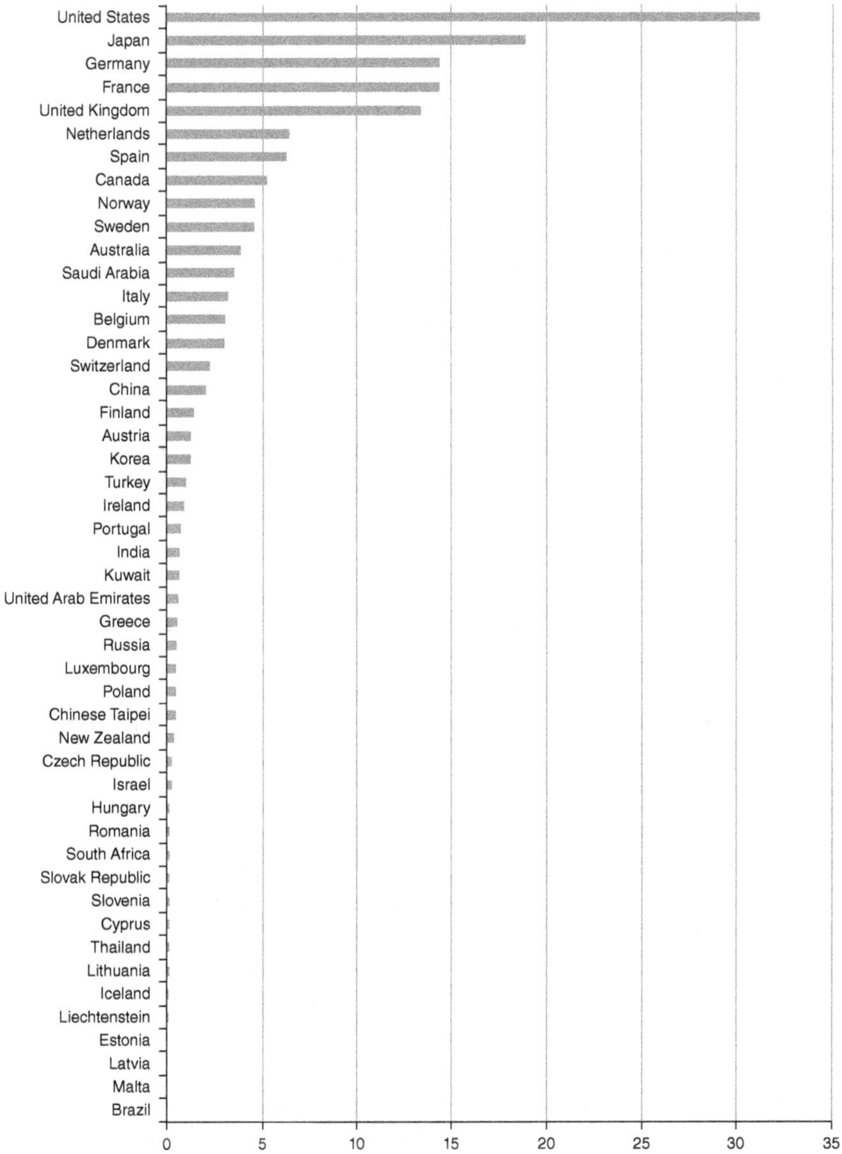

Figure 4.8 ODA from traditional and emerging donors (% of total, 2010)
Source: DAC (OECD)

being the most important contributors.[11] In fact, data for 2010 show that some emerging donors have climbed to prominent positions in the countries' ranking by resources mobilized as ODA (Figure 4.8). That said, these estimates do not include all new donors, suggesting that the total figures must exceed those mentioned.

There are very different models currently in action under the single label of SSC. In an attempt to simplify the diversity, we can distinguish five different groups[12]:

1. A group of new EU members that are setting their development cooperation policy as a part of their adaptation process to EU rules and policies. In this company we find Hungary, Romania, Bulgaria, Cyprus, Malta, and the Baltic countries. Most of these countries had previous experience in development cooperation within the Eastern Bloc during the Cold War, and most were recipients of official aid during their transition to market economies in the 1990s. The volume of their cooperation is still limited and is channeled mainly via multi-lateral systems (particularly through their contributions to the European Commission). Their bilateral cooperation is chiefly oriented toward neighboring countries and tends to be based on aid tied to purchases of national goods and services. Most of these countries share the DAC values and some are likely future members of the DAC (this was the case of Poland, the Slovak Republic, the Czech Republic, and Slovenia).
2. Emerging donors that are non-EU OECD members. Most of these countries could accept most of the DAC values and some probably aspire to DAC membership. In this group we could include Israel, Turkey, Chile, and Mexico, and, perhaps, in the near future, Colombia and Uruguay. Cooperation is mainly provided via bilateral channels, based on sharing experiences and technical assistance and focused on neighboring countries.
3. The Arab countries, a group comprising Saudi Arabia, Kuwait, Qatar, and the United Arab Emirates. This group is characterized by long-term involvement in international development cooperation. These countries focus their aid on other Arab countries and some African countries with large Muslim populations. Their aid, based on grants and loans, is not tied and is channeled mainly through bilateral mechanisms.
4. A heterogeneous group of countries that, at least rhetorically, defend the notion that SSC is inspired by different principles from those of North-South cooperation (based on the Bandung Conference Declaration of 1955 and the 1978 Buenos Aires Plan of Action). In this heterogeneous group we find Brazil, Venezuela, Cuba, Argentina, India, Indonesia, South Africa, Egypt, Malaysia, and Thailand. Their cooperation is mainly bilateral, composed of technical assistance, and based on the exchange of experience and technical skills among partners. Some of them (Venezuela and Brazil, for example) also extend loans.
5. Finally, China could be called a special case, not only because of the high dynamism of its aid, but also because Chinese aid is implemented through a complex mix of instruments. Cooperation is based on the

> declared principles of equality, mutual benefits, and respect of non-interference in other countries' national affairs. The definition of Chinese cooperation is broad, including support to investment abroad, trade preferences, debt cancellation, loans with no or low interest, scholarships to students from developing countries, and grants. Turnkey projects are also important in Chinese aid.

Beyond its diversity, SSC incorporates important new elements into the aid system. On the one hand, because this aid is more horizontal, it has greater potential for promoting a proper feeling of ownership on the part of the recipient. Secondly, SSC allows developing countries to learn from the experience of other countries that have faced the same problems in similar contexts. In several cases, this technical assistance is more appropriate and cheaper than that offered by traditional donors. Thirdly, SSC is more prone to reciprocity and tends to generate a "double dividend" with benefits for recipient and donor alike, supporting the development of technical and institutional capabilities in both. Fourthly, the presence of new (and not so new) non-DAC donors creates more donor competition, which may enlarge recipients' room for maneuver (Kragelund 2008; Zimmermann and Smith 2011). And, finally, SSC contributes to spreading a sense of shared responsibility—not only from traditional donors—in the task of addressing the existing international inequalities.

Obviously, SSC also has flaws that need to be overcome. Among them, its lack of transparency and accountability at the national and international levels and its limited efforts to open cooperation policies to other actors different from official ones (to civil society, for example) could be underlined.

The emergence of SSC has put the traditional conceptions and structures of governance of the international aid system under pressure (Park 2011). For example, some of the Paris agreements, such as the untying of aid, go against the very advantages that new development partners can bring to the aid system—namely, the provision of their own development experience in a direct and rapid way. In the same vein, the Paris Declaration's emphasis on harmonization tends to favor the approaches of the larger and more powerful donors, while it limits the scope for alternative approaches that new donors can put into practice. Therefore, in order to foster a more inclusive system, it would be necessary to review previous consensuses and to admit more flexible agreements on managing cooperation that involves these new players without renouncing to the experience accumulated by traditional donors.

4.2 Global and Regional Public Goods

Global welfare depends, to a large extent, on the appropriate provision of a set of crucial global and regional public goods. However, the provision of these goods is not free of costs, making it difficult for some developing countries to assume their contribution. In these cases there will be a tendency for countries to adopt "free-rider" behavior. In order to overcome such opportunistic conduct, the international community needs to define the right incentives and measures to compensate the costs, encouraging developing countries (particularly those with higher levels of development) to assume a more committed role in the provision of IPGs.

Developing countries (and particularly MICs) play a crucial role in providing diverse types of IPGs, especially those of an environmental nature. For example, MICs are responsible for 54 percent of the CO_2 emissions in the world, and this percentage is on the increase. Clearly, it will be difficult to establish a framework aimed at limiting these emissions without the effective backing of MICs. At the same time, among MICs are those countries that could be more affected by a sub-provision of IPGs. For example, a large group of MICs (among them islands and coastal countries in the Pacific and Caribbean) could be seriously affected by the effects of climate change—13 of the 15 countries most exposed to natural risks are MICs (World Risk Report 2012). Both aspects underline the crucial role that developing countries—particularly MICs—should play in the IPGs agenda.

5 NEW GOVERNANCE

Governance of the development cooperation system has long rested mainly on the DAC, a specialized committee of the OECD currently composed of 28 bilateral donors plus the EU. It is symptomatic that the same donors who defend the ownership principle for recipient countries have located the cooperation system's governance in a select body composed exclusively of traditional donors.

In terms of effectiveness, the DAC's score has been acceptable. During the last five decades, the DAC has played an important role in setting concepts, defining rules, registering ODA, and promoting a process of improvements to aid policies and practices. Within that process, the DAC's commitment to the systematic registration of ODA figures under common criteria has been particularly important, along with the process of recurrent donor country evaluations conducted through peer reviews. But if the DAC scores well in effectiveness, the same cannot be said in terms of representativeness: its membership does not reflect the plurality of actors currently operating within the development cooperation system.

Changes in the cooperation system suggest that a more inclusive forum of governance should be sought, in which all countries and actors could be represented (Barder et al. 2012). There is ample scope for better collective action and more effective networking among the actors in terms of information sharing (transparency, predictability), promotion of better behavior (accountability), learning from results (effectiveness), and identifying and addressing gaps and challenges (Killen and Rogerson 2010).

A first possible alternative along this line is the Development Cooperation Forum of the United Nations Economic and Social Council (UNDFC), where traditional donors, new donors, and recipient countries are represented. This alternative suitably fulfills the representative criterion being a good place for debating policies, but its record in terms of effectiveness is very low. In fact, until now, UNDFC has hardly played an operative role in setting rules, improving cooperation practices, or coordinating countries' policies.

Meanwhile, another alternative has emerged from the post-Busan dynamics: the Global Partnership for Effective Development Cooperation (GPEDC), created as a ministerial forum for dialogue and decision-making with a Steering Committee to support the ministerial platform. The Steering Committee is supported by the OECD and UNDP and includes all key stakeholders, both public and private. This alternative supposes an improvement in inclusiveness in relation to DAC, but it may encounter problems in terms of formal representativeness and new donors and actors' effective involvement. It is understandable that many non-OECD countries, enjoying their growing influence in international affairs, tag onto OECD-conceived projects.

Neither of these alternatives is totally satisfactory, but both mean an improvement in relation to the DAC. For this reason, probably the best option should be to support both initiatives and try to interlink their respective work processes. Clearly, the UNDCF is in better condition to offer the required legitimacy to build an open and inclusive platform of governance for the development cooperation system. At the same time, it would be necessary to back regional platforms of dialogue, coordination, sharing experiences, and monitoring among emerging donors. Probably, it is at regional level where more sound advances can be achieved in this area.

Besides the institutional architecture of the cooperation system, it is also important to define its perimeter. The presence of new donors, actors, and instruments, some of them operating outside ODA, obliges the international community to review the concepts, measures, and reporting systems. The DAC has begun a process of both reviewing ODA measurement and setting a complementary and wider concept of "total official support for sustainable development" (TOSSD). In the first case, the main purposes are to define ODA in a more precise way, counting grant equivalent in concessional credits (instead of the total face value) and removing "in-donor" costs. In the second case, the objective is to capture flows (not necessarily based on direct budgetary efforts) that are relevant for development and are mobilized with the help of official interventions.[13]

Even if this effort is well oriented, it does not give a satisfactory answer to the current panorama of international development policy, as long as more and more actors operate outside the intergovernment sphere and their means are not always financial in nature. Therefore, we should move from ODA to a broader concept able to hold the ample array of agents (public and private) and instruments (financial and non-financial) oriented towards deliberately supporting developing country efforts to build inclusive and sustainable development strategies. Alonso and Glennie (2015) suggest turning to the concept of *development cooperation*: a concept that is broader than those (such as ODA or TOSSD) limited to official financial means of development support, but narrower than that of "financing for development" that include private for-profit transactions (such as FDI or trade). In an effort to delimit the concept, they suggest including under the label of development cooperation all international interventions and activities (public and private) specifically intended to support development through actions that would not be promoted (or at least not in the same way) by the market alone, discriminate in favor of developing countries, in order to widen their opportunities of progress, and are based on cooperative relationships that try to enhance developing country ownership. Whatever the opinion about this proposal is, we are obliged to conceptualize the new reality that is coming in the development field.

6 CONCLUDING REMARKS

The analysis carried out in Sections 1–5 confirms that the international development aid system is undergoing a period of change. The current state of affairs is very different from what it was 60 years ago, when the aid system began. A careful consideration of the likely future evolution of the aid system is therefore necessary, particularly if we consider the challenges imposed by a highly integrated but notably unequal world, with new global powers emerging from an increasingly heterogeneous developing world, and with a global population that has reached 7 billion and is now facing serious environmental problems. It is impossible to predict whether the international aid system will be capable of adapting to these emerging trends, or whether it will become increasingly irrelevant.

In any case, one can foresee two extreme scenarios for the future. The first scenario could be the result of a progressive loss of drive for the aid-reform agenda and the relegation of ODA to a minor role in the ranking of donor interests. The severe effects of the current economic crisis on many OECD countries could lead to a new phase of "donor fatigue." The limited achievements of the Paris Agenda could meanwhile lead to revisionist attitudes already observable in some donors, aiming to return to more traditional formulas for managing aid. In this scenario, the Paris Agenda might not be abandoned completely, but efforts would be focused on reducing its degree of complexity. In that case, it is likely that aid would maintain its traditional agenda, without embracing new elements related to the provision of IPGs, perhaps with the exception of some environmental issues. In keeping with the general approach of this scenario, the governance of the aid system would continue to function around the OECD's DAC, with this institution being progressively enlarged so long as new OECD members take part. The OECD would maintain its control over the GPEDC and this platform would be a secondary forum for building wider consensus.

One can imagine a more radical scenario of change. Under this scenario, the aim would be to define a new global approach to development policy that overcomes the traditional separation between donors and recipients on which the aid system has been based (Alonso et al. 2014a). The goal would be to establish a new framework of development cooperation based on the principle of common but differentiated responsibilities. This scenario would entail the promotion of a more wide-ranging agenda based around three major tasks: (i) guaranteeing the provision of universal minimum social standards for the world population; (ii) providing international public goods; and (iii) correcting international inequalities and promoting convergence among countries (see Chapter 1 in this book). Problems associated with global rules (in trade, investment, technology, etc.) would also enter into this sphere, to ensure a better distribution of development opportunities, including penalties for practices that hinder that objective (illicit financial flows, tax heavens, etc.). The new system described here would also have a more open, wider acceptance of potential players, in order to incorporate not just new official donors but also private players implicated in the work. As a consequence of all these changes, a new structure of governance would be required in order to ensure that donor and recipient countries, public and private partners are all represented. Neither the UNDCF nor the GPEDC seems to represent a good alternative without deep transformations, although UNDCF has the advantage of its higher legitimacy in origin and representativeness.

It is likely that reality will drive the future cooperation system to an intermediate point between the two scenarios drawn up here. The closer the system comes to the second scenario, the more opportunities the system will have for responding to the new international landscape.

NOTES

1. It is worth mentioning that this increase in ODA to poorest income groups was significantly concentrated in a small number of countries. For example, only four countries (Afghanistan, Democratic Republic of Congo, Ethiopia, and Sudan) received more than a half of the increase in ODA to LDCs.

2. A tendency analyzed by the World Bank (2011), Spence (2011), and Subramanian (2011), among others.
3. We will follow the concept of ODA as defined by the DAC (OECD). Although the presence of some of its components (such as debt forgiveness) is debatable, the official figures will be used here.
4. In 2013, the Netherlands was replaced by United Kingdom in this select club. The other members are Norway, Sweden, Luxembourg, and Denmark.
5. See Greenhill and Ali (2013) for an estimate of the additional funds required for financing the post-2015 development agenda.
6. See http://www.leadinggroup.org.
7. Alternative classifications can be found in Sandor et al. (2009) or Girishankar (2009).
8. Traditionally, relative poverty is measured as a constant proportion of the median (or average) income per capita. In this case, if all incomes were to increase by the same proportion, then the measure of relative poverty would be unchanged. In fact, relative poverty appears as a measure of inequality. In the case of the Chen and Ravallion (2011) proposal (inspired by Atkinson and Bourguignon 2001), distribution-neutral growth will reduce the incidence of weakly relative poverty.
9. With a slightly different approach, Ravallion (2009) arrives at similar results.
10. The World Bank (2013) offers another measure of this process. In 2012, ODA from OECD donors mobilized US$128 billion, South-South cooperation US$19 billion, Other Official Flows US$79 billion, and Private Aid US$60 billion.
11. It includes what DAC defines as ODA-like flows. See http://www.oecd.org/dac/stats/statisticsonresourceflowstodevelopingcountries.htm.
12. Other classifications can be found in Kragelund (2008), Walz and Ramachandran (2011), or Zimmermann and Smith (2011).
13. See http://www.oecd.org/dac/financing-development.htm.

REFERENCES

Agenor, Pierre-Richard, and Otaviano Canuto. 2012. "Middle-income growth traps." *World Bank Policy Research Working Paper* No. 6210, September 2012.

Aiyar, Shekhar, Romain Duval, Damien Puy, Yiqun Wu, and Longmei Zhang. 2013. "Growth Slowdowns and the Middle-Income Trap." *IMF Working Paper* No. 13/71, March 2013.

Alonso, José Antonio (dir). 2007. *Cooperation with middle-income countries*. Madrid: Editorial Complutense.

Alonso, José Antonio. 2014. "Cooperation with middle income countries: and incentive-based approach." *AECID Working Papers* 3, (April). http://www.aecid.es/Centro-Documentacion/Documentos/Eficacia%20y%20calidad/DT03%20AECID_CooperationMiddleIncomeCountries_030414-final.pdf.

Alonso, José Antonio, and Carlos Garcimartín. 2013. "The Determinants of Institutional Quality. More on the Debate." *Journal of International Development* 25: pp. 206–26.

Alonso, José Antonio and Jonathan Glennie (2015): "What is development cooperation?", *2016 Development Cooperation Forum Policy Briefs*, nº 1, February, ECOSOC, http://www.un.org/en/ecosoc/newfunct/pdf15/2016_dcf_policy_brief_no.1.pdf.

Alonso, José Antonio, Jonathan Glennie, and Andy Sumner. 2014b. "Recipients and Contributors: Middle Income Countries and the Future of Development Cooperation." *DESA Working Paper* No. 135, July 2014.

Atkinson, Anthony B., and François Bourguignon. 2001. "Poverty and inclusion from a World Perspective." In *Governance, Equity and Global Markets*, edited by Joseph Stiglitz and Pierre-Alain. Muet, Oxford: Oxford University Press.

Barder, Owen, Mikaela Gavas, Simon Maxwell, and Deborah Johnson. 2012. "Governance of the Aid System and the Role of the European Union." In *Development Cooperation in Times of Crisis*, edited by José Antonio Alonso and José Antonio Ocampo. New York: Columbia University Press.

Chandy, Laurence, and Geoffrey Gertz. 2011. "Poverty in numbers: The changing state of global poverty from 2005 to 2015." Global Economy and Development at Brookings, *Policy Brief* 2011/01.

Chen, Shaohua, and Martin Ravallion. 2012. "More relatively-poor people in a less absolutely-poor world." *World Bank Policy Research Working Paper* No. 6114, July, 2012.

Collier, Paul. 2007. *The Bottom Billion. Why the poorest countries are failing and what can be done about it.* Oxford: Oxford University Press.

Corbridge, Stuart. 2007. "The (im)possibility of development studies." *Economy and Society* 36 (2): pp. 179–211.

DESA. 2012. *World Economic and Social Survey 2012. In Search of New Development Finance.* New York: United Nations.

Edward, Peter, and Andy Sumner. 2014. "Estimating the scale and geography of global poverty now and in the future: How much difference do method and assumptions make?" *World Development* 58 (issue C): pp. 67–82.

Fallon, Peter, Vivian Hon, Qureshi Zia, and Dilip Ratha. 2001. "Middle-Income countries: developmental challenges and growing global role." *World Bank Policy Research Working Paper* No. 2657, August 2001.

Fürher, Helmut. 1996. "The story of official development assistance: A history of the Development Assistance Committee and the Development Cooperation Directorate in dates, names and figures." *OECD/GD* 94 (67).

Girishankar, Navin. 2009. "Innovative Development Finance: From Financial Sources to Financial Solutions." *World Bank Policy Research Working Paper* No. 5111, November 2009.

Greenhill, Romilly, and Ahmed Ali. 2013. "Paying for progress: How will emerging post-2015 goals be financed in the new aid landscape?" *ODI Working Paper* 366.

Greenhill, Romili, Annalisa Prizzon, and Andrew Rogerson. 2013. "The age of choice: developing countries in the new aid landscape." *ODI Working Paper* 364.

Hausmann, Ricardo, Lant Pritchett, and Dani Rodrik. 2004. "Growth accelerations," NBER Working Paper No. 10566, June 2004.

Hirschman, Albert O. 1981. *Essays in Trespassing. Economics to Politics and Beyond*, Cambridge, Cambridge University Press.

Kanbur, Ravi, and Andy Sumner. 2012. "Poor countries or poor people? Development assistance and the new geography of global poverty." *Journal of International Development,* 24 (6): pp. 686–95.

Kaul, Inge, Pedro Conceiçao, Katell LeGoulven, and Ronald U. Mendoza (eds). 2003. *Providing Global Public Goods: Managing Globalization.* New York: Oxford University Press.

Kaul, Inge, Isabelle Grunberg, and Marc A. Stern (eds). 1999. *Global Public Goods: International Cooperation in the 21st Century.* New York: Oxford University Press.

Kharas, Homi, Koji Makino, and Woojin Jung (eds). 2011. *Catalyzing Development. A New Vision For Aid.* Washington: Brookings Institution Press.

Kharas, Homi, and Andrew Rogerson. 2012. *Horizon 2025: Creative destruction in the aid industry.* London: ODI.

Killen, Brenda, and Andrew Rogerson. 2010. "Global governance for international development: Who's in charge?" *OECD Development Brief* 2.

Kopczuk, Wojciech, Joel Slemrod, and Shlomo Yitzhaki. 2005. "The limitations of decentralized world redistribution: An optimal taxation approach." *European Economic Review* 49: pp. 1051–79.

Kragelund, Peter. 2008. "The return of Non-DAC Donors to Africa: New Prospects for African Development?" *Development Policy Review* 26 (5): pp. 555–84.

Ocampo, José Antonio. 2011. "Macroeconomic for development countercyclical policies and production sector transformation." *CEPAL Review* 104 (August).

Ocampo, José Antoniom and Stephany Griffith-Jones. 2007. "A countercyclical framework for a development-friendly international financial architecture." *DESA Working Paper* 39 (June).

OECD. 2011. *Aid effectiveness 2005–10: Progress in implementing the Paris Declaration.* Paris: OECD.

OECD. 2014. *Outlook on aid. Survey in donor's forward spending plans,* OECD (DAC), París: http://www.oecd.org/dac/aid-architecture/OECD%20Outlook%20on%20Aid%202013.pdf (accessed 9 July 2014).

Ravallion, Martin. 2009. "Do poorer countries have less capacity for redistribution?" *World Bank Policy Research Working Paper* No. 5046, September 2009.

Ravallion, Martin. 2012. "Benchmarking global poverty reduction." *World Bank Policy Research Working Paper* No. 6205, August 2012.

Ravaillon, Martin and Shaohua Chen. 2011. "Weakly relative poverty." *Review of Economics and Statistics* 93 (4): pp. 1251–61.

Sandler, Todd. 2004. *Global collective action.* Cambridge: Cambridge University Press.

Sandor, Elisabeth, Simon Scott, and Julia Benn. 2009. "Innovative financing to fund development: progress and prospects." *DCD Issues Brief* (November).

Spence, Michael. 2011. *The next convergence: The future of economic growth in a multispeed world.* New York: Farrar, Straus, and Giroux.

Subramanian, Arvind. 2011. *Eclipse.* Washington: The Peter G. Peterson Institute for International Economics.

Sumner, Andy. 2010. "Global poverty and the new bottom billion." *IDS Working Paper* 349, September, 2010.

Sumner, Andy. 2012. "Where do the world's poor live? A new update." *IDS Working Paper* No. 393, June.

Walz, Julie, and Vijaya Ramachandran. 2011. "Brave new world. A literature review of emerging donors and the changing nature of foreign assistance." *Center for Global Development Working Paper* 273.

World Bank. 2011. *Multipolarity: The New Global Economy,* Washington: World Bank.

World Bank. 2013. *Capital for the Future: Saving and Investment in an Interdependent World.* Washington: World Bank.

World Risk Report. 2012. Alliance Development Works: http://ehs.unu.edu/?ref=list/7302?t=human.

Zimmermann, Felix, and Kimberly Smith. 2011. "More actors, more money, more ideas for international development cooperation." *Journal of International Development* 23 (5): pp. 722–38.

Further Reading

Alonso, José Antonio, and José Antonio Ocampo (2012), *Development cooperation in Times of Crisis,* New York: Columbia University Press.

Alonso, José Antonio, Giovanni Andrea Cornia, and Rob Vos (2014a), *Alternative development strategies for the post-2015 era,* New York: Bloomsbury Academic.

Park, Kang-Ho. 2011. "New development partners and a global development partnership." In *Catalyzing Development. A new vision of aid,* edited by Homi Kharas, Koji Makino and Woojin Jung. Washington: Brookings Institution Press.

5

UN Development Cooperation

The Roots of a Reform Agenda

Bruce Jenks

This chapter provides a historical analysis of the radical changes over half a century that determined major characteristics of the UN's operational activities for development. Across a range of spheres, there has been a transformation in every aspect of the approach of the UN to development cooperation:

- The core mission of the UN's operational activities for development has changed.
- The UN's internal organization has undergone constant evolution.
- The financing arrangements have undergone radical changes.
- The governance of the system has been the subject of continuous debate.

The challenges that confront the mission, structures, financing, and governance of the UN Development System today are deeply rooted in its history.

Against this background, the chapter explores more recent developments impacting development cooperation and changes in the external environment over the last decade.

The chapter concludes by identifying and analyzing a menu of reform instruments available to meet today's challenges and makes a number of possible recommendations.

1 THE CONSTRUCTION PHASE

The creation of the UN Development System was a response to a unique historical period. Its sense of mission, structure of organization, governance arrangements, and funding allocation principles that were established all represent a remarkable response to the experience of the Second World War and the rise and fall of Nazism. This is perhaps best understood through the lens of functionalism, a philosophy that captured the essence of the strategic thinking behind the construction of the system (Jenks and Jones 2013).

David Mitrany argued that the world would be able to unite against commonly perceived problems. Mitrany considered that existing conditions had created "self-determining" (Mitrany 1975, 17–25) needs of a technical nature that transcended political and constitutional issues. He argued that if international organizations concentrated on providing those needs, they might succeed in instilling habits of cooperative behavior between peoples from different countries that could in the long run subvert national allegiances and put an end to classical national rivalries.

For Mitrany (1975) the experience of the war had created a "unity beyond politics." Functionalism is a reflection of its age in the specific sense that it is based on the assumption that a common will existed in the wake of the Nazi experience to go beyond traditional political rivalries. The concept of "self-determining needs" reflects this central assumption.

The mission and values of the system being constituted revolved around the application of expertise and skills in different areas of work. This was a period of numerous expert meetings and a plethora of expert reports. The role of experts and the publication of expert reports were to transfer skills and fill gaps. Universal principles were advocated and shared.

The UN system was designed around the concept of communities of practice that would create the building blocks to peace through their pursuit of common goals and interests. The International Labor Organization (ILO) had already been established in 1919 as a forum for issues related to labor and social justice. The Food and Agriculture Organization (FAO), United Nations Educational, Scientific and Cultural Organization (UNESCO), World Health Organization (WHO), and a succession of other agencies were created to allow communities of practice to build networks. Each of these agencies has its own governance structure, which ultimately is fully accountable for the activities of those organizations. The Economic and Social Council of the UN (ECOSOC) was given loosely defined coordination functions, but in practice these are autonomous organizations working within the framework of a common system. The Secretary General has no ultimate authority over these agencies.

The consequence of this design is that each organization is supported by its own constituency. These constituencies may align more with the international communities of practice embedded in each organization than with the foreign ministries of their own countries. This was precisely the intention of the functionalist founders of the system. Functionalist thinking was deeply suspicious of the tension between a policy process vested in foreign ministries and the building of global communities of interest. The strength of these constituencies is that they reflect a broad range of social forces and not just the government ministry involved.

The vision of a multi-stakeholder system defining and promoting common interests around communities of practice found expression in the early years in the political economy of the system. When the Expanded Program for Technical Assistance (EPTA) was launched in 1949, it was envisaged as a program that would provide support through the established communities of practice. Hence the financing available to the EPTA was distributed on the basis of percentage shares to the different specialized agencies so that they could manage programs in countries. A system whose formal governance arrangements was by and large reserved for governments produced a financial architecture based not on countries, but on the role of communities of practice in contributing to social and economic progress.

In retrospect what is clear is that the experience of the war was fundamental in creating the political space for leadership and innovation that characterized the "construction" phase of the UN. The construction of an enabling environment for building peace in the aftermath of the war could not be reduced solely to an administrative mechanism to facilitate intergovernmental exchange. Building a sustainable peace required expanding the space for international leadership, drawing on social forces to put in place and strengthen the building blocks to peace, and providing an inclusive form of governance that reached out to multiple stakeholders. The lynchpin of this vision remained the sovereignty of states, but it was a sovereignty embedded in broader values and principles. Anti-Nazism provided a common framework for the pursuit of these common values. This was the architecture that was constructed by the founders of the UN. It was not an idealistic project. Rather it was highly pragmatic, responding to the urgent need for action resulting from war's destruction.

2 PHASE 2: SERVICE TO MEMBER STATES 1950–90

The convergence of the reality of the Cold War, the emerging needs of developing countries, and the process of de-colonization led to a transformation in the authorizing environment in which the UN worked (Jenks and Jones 2013). Only a radical realignment in the UN's values and mission with this new authorizing environment could secure the UN's continued relevance. The space for international leadership, drawing on broad social forces and contact with multiple stakeholders, was challenged directly by the logic of both the Cold War and de-colonization. The Cold War, by dividing the world into two camps, severely curtailed the room for international leadership. With the acceleration of de-colonization, the international development agenda became focused on the fundamental process of national development. Throughout the

United Nations system there was a fundamental and radical shift from a vision of international leadership to one of service to member states.

The first victim of this realignment was the concept of the role and functions of the Secretary General. The Soviet Union questioned the very validity of the concept of an impartial, independent international force. This was a world in which all belonged to one of the two camps. There was no space in between. Khrushchev accordingly proposed that the leadership of the UN be replaced by a triumvirate reflecting the interests of the socialist, western, and non-aligned groups. The secretariat would revert to being of an intergovernmental character. This was echoed by de Gaulle. When invited to visit the Secretary General, he responded that the General Assembly was not meeting so he questioned what there was to visit. The implication was that the UN only had a meaning as an intergovernmental forum. Secretary-General Dag Hammarskjold's response was his robust defense of the original logic of the need for international leadership delivered in his Oxford speech of 1961 (Hammarskjold 1961).

The period from the late 1940s onwards saw the principle of state sovereignty be strongly affirmed, and throughout the UN system, the concept of service to member states became dominant. It is perhaps in the economic and social sectors that we can most clearly see the triumph of the concept of internationalism as an instrument of service to the member states. It was logical that, as vast new numbers of developing countries became members of the UN, the challenge of nation-building became the central focus of the UN's work in development. Economic policy stressed the virtues of government planning and the UN system focused much of its efforts to support the creation of national planning capacity. The importance of institution-building is cited regularly in the prevailing literature. The reports produced by the system at this time represented some of the first national reports and plans to come out of the new fledgling states.

A good example of the consequences of this shift is UNESCO's approach to education. Before the mid-1950s, education conferences were attended by technicians and experts and dominated by three central themes: the concept of fundamental education, the struggle for world understanding, and the revision of textbooks. International experts were drawing up international criteria to be followed by sovereign states. They were defining the nature of the objectives. During the 1950s there was a dramatic shift to an era of meetings of government education ministers discussing the role of education in national development. Education could no longer be isolated from national development policy objectives. UNESCO's mission changed dramatically to focus supporting national educational planning. The trip from expounding the principles of "Fundamental Education" to providing any services that may be required to ensure the success of respective national plans has taken a short decade.

This type of transformation occurred across all UN sectors. Hence Inis Claude's contention that the UN's function had actually become to support the "capacity of states to stay in business" (Claude 1964). The core vision for the mission of the UN Development System had been turned upside down: from drawing on communities of practice to bring states closely together, to building the capacity of states to develop and exercise their prerogatives as states.

This transformation marked a radical departure for the evolution of the UN system. At its inception, the coherence of the system was derived from the strength of its constituency roots. Now, coherence was a function of government policy. The coherence of development efforts lay within the realm of national government policy, not in the international development system as such. It was the member states that would establish priorities and the agencies of the system would be required to respond to the needs identified by member states. Already, with the creation of the EPTA in 1949, it was clear that responsibility was vested with governments. In 1952, resident representative offices were established with a view to facilitating country programming. By 1955, an early version of country programming had been adopted.

The creation of the United Nations Development Program (UNDP) and in particular the establishment by the General Assembly of the so-called indicative planning system for the allocation of UNDP's resources, marked the highpoint for the transformation of the system from functionalist to country-based principles (United Nations 1970). With the introduction of the Indicative Planning Figure (IPF) system, the allocation of development assistance moved for the first time from an agency-based system to a country-based system. Whereas previously each agency had been allocated a fixed share of total resources, now it was the countries themselves that were allocated resources based on a number of objectively defined criteria. The system had moved from an "agency entitlement system" to a "country entitlement system."

This transformation was matched with a fundamental shift in thinking about the nature and purposes of international cooperation. Originally, assistance had been seen as a means of transferring knowledge and skills. This knowledge had universal applicability, and it simply had to be applied by developing countries. The new approach saw international cooperation as a mechanism for transferring resources to newly emerging states.

Thinking about development in the 1950s and the early 1960s was dominated by the twin notions that growth constituted the essence of the development process and that its benefits would trickle down to all segments of the population. With growth, everything else would fall into place. Each country was to set its own growth rate; international measures were to be taken to support this. With this in mind, the General Assembly called for policies aimed at commodity stabilization, for measures to ensure countries an equitable share of earnings from the extraction and marketing of their natural resources by foreign capital, and for increases in the flow of both public and private resource flows.

Each of these measures was concerned essentially with mechanisms of resource transfer. International organizations were to play the role of facilitating the transfer of resources from one state to another. In this concept, there was very little or no sense of responsibility on the part of the system for the outcomes or the objectives that underlay the development process. Not only was this responsibility considered to lie exclusively with governments, but the very logic of trickle-down was to minimize the assumption of responsibility even by member states: growth was a natural process that should be allowed to take its own course. This approach fit very well with the two overriding features of the overall international authorizing environment. On the one hand, in the context of the Cold War, being a member of the alliance—not development performance—was the criterion for financial support. On the other hand, with de-colonization in full flow, there was a deep sense that the newly independent countries were entitled to these transfers.

3 THE SEARCH FOR IDENTITY: 1970–90

The need for more integrated and coherent approaches to development became one of the recurring themes of development thinking in the 1970s. Such language would not have been conceivable in the context of the development thinking dominant in the early 1960s. The evolution in prevailing conceptions was reflected in the numerous and varied qualitative objectives in the UN's Second Development Decade Strategy. The development process was no longer seen as the outcome of an automatic process. It required political, social, and economic choices to be made both at the inter- and intra-state levels.

It was against this background that the first great series of UN global conferences took place: environment (Stockholm), food (Rome), population (Bucharest), women (Mexico), employment (Geneva), and human settlements (Vancouver). Clearly the new commitment reflected in the agendas adopted by these conferences to the articulation of a broader set of development objectives had major implications for prevailing concepts of the mission and role of the UN, as well as the capacity of the system to adopt integrated and unified approaches. This found expression in the contentious debate on the need for a new international economic order (NIEO) on the one hand, and a basic needs approach on the other.

The search for a new sense of identity and coherence through the global conferences and debates about a new overarching framework were significant in that they asked more of the international system than simply serving member states. The call to serve newly emerging member states was a historical necessity and represents a critical layer in the UN's foundations, but in the long run, many considered that an exclusive preoccupation with this as the sole mission of the UN would condemn the UN system to marginalization. But defining the UN as a service provider was not just a response to de-colonization; it also aligned very well with the realities of the Cold War. The geopolitical situation made the prospects for a consensus around global objectives highly problematic. The prevailing system of political alliances continued to favor heavily a concept of international cooperation that was based on an inter-state transfer concept. Moreover, the process of globalization that would emerge so powerfully two decades later had not yet achieved a level that could provide legitimacy to the articulation of truly global problems, needs, and responses.

The reality of a highly restrictive authorizing environment is reflected very clearly in the repeated failures of a series of serious efforts to reform the UN system and give it a greater strategic capacity. Calls for a greater sense of cohesion and direction in the system multiplied during the course of the 1960s and 1970s.

The Report of the Ad Hoc Committee of Experts examining the finances of the UN and the specialized agencies emphasized the need for integrated planning, rational resource allocation, and further streamlining (United Nations 1966). The Report of the Enlarged Committee on Program Coordination argued for greater clarity of objectives (United Nations 1969a). The Pearson Commission, while avoiding institutional questions, focused attention on the need for clear development objectives (Pearson 1969). The Bertrand Report on Programming and Budgeting in the UN system argued that the system suffered from a total lack of method in its programming techniques (Bertrand 1969). It argued for a much more integrated and long-term approach to development planning. Later in 1974, Bertrand produced a second report on medium-term planning in the system, which argued the need for a global policy framework (Bertrand 1974). Perhaps the best known of this series of reports was the so-called Jackson Report, which advocated for an overarching direction for the system. This report deplored the absence of a centralized brain, and in this respect looked to the creation of a powerful Director General of Development (United Nations 1969b).

By the mid-1970s, the search for coherence and direction in the UN system had reached sufficient critical mass that it found expression in a specific high profile intergovernmental initiative. The General Assembly convened a Group of Experts on Restructuring with the aim of making the system, "fully capable of dealing with problems of international cooperation in a comprehensive manner" (United Nations 1974, paragraph 5).

The Group of Experts assessed the challenge they faced in 1975:

> "In its thirtieth year, the UN has reached a turning point. In one direction lies the prospect of new capacity to cope with the central issues facing mankind. In

the other lies the danger of decline in the effectiveness of the UN. Which direction the organization takes will be significantly influenced by the decisions on policy and structural questions which its member states take in the months and years ahead." (United Nations 1975, annex 3, p. 89)

The Group of Experts made five key conclusions:

- The role of ECOSOC was strongly affirmed.
- The post of Director-General for Development and International Co-operation was proposed.
- A joint unit established under the Director-General was to serve as a center for global analysis and as a system-wide planning bureau.
- An Advisory Committee on Economic Cooperation and Development under the Director-General was to bring all Agency heads together.
- All UN funds and programs for technical assistance were to be integrated into a United Nations Development Authority.

The proposals of the Group of Experts were referred to an Ad Hoc Committee, which was established to examine the restructuring of the UN system's economic and social sectors. In the end, the work of this Committee was heavily entangled in the debates around the concept of a new international economic order at that time. Consequently, very little from the original proposals was implemented.

Resolution 32/197 embodied the final outcome of this reform process:

- The UN General Assembly (UNGA) was unable to agree even on an annual ministerial meeting of ECOSOC, preferring the idea of periodic high-level meetings.
- The proposal for an Advisory Committee was abandoned.
- The proposal for a UN Development Authority was stillborn.

Only the proposal for a Director-General for International Cooperation and Development (DG) was realized. But the DG was left hanging in isolation as a structural abstraction—divorced from real authority and without access to resources. The DG was conceived as the icing on a carefully layered cake, yet all that remained was the icing. It was not to be the last time in the history of UN reform that the creation of an additional structure, in the name of restructuring, was to be a substitute for reform. The search for greater coherence simply added a superstructure largely disconnected from the existing multi-layered structure.

Failure to achieve greater strategic capacity was accentuated by the logic of the Reagan/Thatcher revolution in the early 1980s and the beginning of the Latin America debt crisis. This found expression in the emergence of the

Washington Consensus and the adoption of structural adjustment. The UN Development System found its role increasingly marginalized and any lingering appetite for a centralized strategic brain rapidly dissipated.

4 UN OPERATIONAL ACTIVITIES: TOWARDS A NON-SYSTEM 1990–95

Developments in the overall environment during the course of the 1990s were expected to generate another major push on the UN reform front. Towards the end of the decade this indeed began to occur. However, the first years of the decade saw a very different scenario evolve. This was the result of the very significant evolution that had taken place in the political economy of the UN Development System since the adoption of the Consensus resolution in 1970 (Jenks, Barcena, Civili, and Doryan 2006).

In the 1970s and indeed through most of the 1980s, UNDP remained essentially a funding agency, whose principal rationale was to transfer resources and skills to developing countries. The dominant paradigm was defined by the IPF system, which pre-allocated resources to countries on the basis of objective criteria. This "country entitlement system" had replaced the earlier "agency entitlement system." UNDP did not establish its own priorities. These were established exclusively by national governments.

This was the legacy of the Consensus Resolution. The legacy was founded on three core assumptions:

- UNDP responded to government requests on demand.
- Specialized agencies executed the program and provided technical backstopping.
- UNDP provided central funding for the system as a whole through the IPF system.

During the 1970s and 1980s, UNDP provided around 75 percent of the total technical assistance funds through the UN system, and 90 percent of UNDP's funding came in the form of core contributions. By the late 1980s each of these core assumptions were in play, and by 2000 there had been a complete transformation.

In 1990, UNDP's Governing Council for the first time established a number of priorities for UNDP support, in decision 1990/34. This was the first time an attempt had been made to identify priority areas beyond the idea that UNDP supported government priorities.

At the same time, the funding base of UNDP was undergoing a parallel transformation. Core contributions to UNDP peaked in 1992. The rest of the decade saw a dramatic decline in core funding, together with substantial increases in non-core thematic funding. The UN Development System was entering a new phase—the era of funding by goal.

Finally, the shifts in program focus and funding patterns found further reflection in a radical change of the method chosen for the implementation of the operational activities of the system. We have seen that, in the 1970s and 1980s, the great bulk of project implementation was undertaken by the specialized agencies. In 1990, a major review was completed of the arrangements that supported the implementation of operational activities (United Nations 1990). The study noted that, whereas in the 1960s and 1970s, agencies often had services to provide which were not accessible in the market, this was often no longer the case. The study recommended that agencies revert to being centers of excellence and that the system as a whole move towards the use of national execution. It was recognized that national capacities, both public and private, had increased substantially and were now often in a position to take responsibility for actual implementation.

The results were radical and transformed the political economy of the system. In the mid-1980s the six big agencies (World Health Organization, International Labor Organization, United Nations Industrial Development Organization, UN Systems Department for Development Support and Management Services, FAO, and UNESCO) accounted for 58 percent of total program delivery financed from UNDP, while national execution accounted for 6 percent. By 1995, the figures were 15 percent and 58 percent, respectively. The system ceased to have a central funding component. Each agency developed its own funding strategies. Each component in the system was pushed into branding itself, establishing itself in the market, and mobilizing funds earmarked for specific purposes.

The 1990 study saw specialized agencies evolving within a three-tiered framework. The agencies had a constitutional role derived from established mandates to generate norms and set standards in different areas. Secondly, the agencies had a consultative role to provide technical assistance and backstopping in areas commonly associated with their mandates. Finally, they had a contractual role which focused on implementation and the delivery of services often driven by resource mobilization opportunities. As we demonstrate below, the character of the next phase financially rewarded the contractors.

5 THE ERA OF GOALS

The end of the Cold War and the acceleration of globalization changed the rationale for the allocation of aid. In the early 1990s the international development community anticipated enormous growth in aid budgets as a result of the "peace dividend" that would accompany the end of the Cold War. In reality, the end of the primary foreign policy rationale for aid led to its rapid decline. By 2000, global aid in nominal terms was almost exactly the same as it had been around 1990 (namely, $54 billion). This meant a substantial decrease in real terms and compared in nominal terms with the doubling that had occurred during the decades of the Cold War.

Against this background, the mission and rationale for development cooperation had to be radically redefined. It was the series of global conferences held during the 1990s, culminating in the 2000 Millennium Summit, that crystalized the emergence of a new common development agenda.

The first of these global conferences in 1990, the Summit for Children, adopted a plan of action setting specific goals for the year 2000 for children's health, nutrition, education, water, and sanitation. It also gave a new impetus to ensuring universal ratification of the Convention on the Rights of the Child. This was followed by the UN Conference on Environment and Development, held in Rio in 1992. It adopted Action 21, which is the basis for a multitude of national commitments and programs. The conference resulted in four new international treaties involving major new international commitments: climate change, biological diversity, desertification, and high-seas fishing. The World Conference on Human Rights, held in Vienna in 1993, reaffirmed international commitments to human rights. The Conference on Population and Development in 1994 and the World Summit for Social Development in 1995 defined important new social targets. Finally, the Beijing World Conference on Women in 1995 established a five-year action plan that set specific targets and also gave renewed impetus to ratification of the 1979 Convention on the Elimination of all Forms of Discrimination against Women.

Most importantly, these conferences represented significant attempts to define clear goals and objectives to which the international community committed itself. While each goal needed to be translated into national action, the goals themselves are defined and established in global terms. This marks a radical departure from the previous paradigm, which had dominated thinking about development cooperation.

The shift to defining clear goals and setting measurable targets was the inevitable consequence of the need to provide a new rationale for development cooperation (Jenks and Jones 2013). In the absence of a clear foreign policy goal, performance and measuring impact became critical to remaking the case for aid. For the first time, legitimate global development goals were constructed around issues that voters in donor countries could relate to and support. This shift, which was conscious and deliberate, was first clearly reflected in the approval by the Organisation for Economic Co-operation and Development's Development Assistance Committee (OECD/DAC) of its document "Shaping the 21st Century" (OECD/DAC 1996). This document for the first time spelled out seven selected goals for further progress in the next 15–20 years. In turn, these goals were adopted by the millennial summit of the Millennium Development Goals (MDGs).

The MDGs do not represent an agreement on a global development strategy, but they do signify an extraordinary global commitment to meet a set of defined targets and a worldwide agreement that progress in development should be measured globally against a number of agreed targets. This standard, or norm, has been adopted worldwide in the development community: in the UN, the international financial institutions, regional fora, and in many countries nationally.

The alignment of the system behind a set of clear goals had radical implications for the way it was financed, the form the UN Development System was to take, and the way it was to be governed. We have already alluded to the growth of extra-budgetary funding that took off in the mid-1990s (see Figure 5.1). The graphs demonstrate that in less than a decade, the funding base of the UN Development System was transformed from reliance on regular contributions to a strong bias toward extra-budgetary financing.

This shift fit very well with the emerging culture of "goals" and "results," which put huge pressure on each agency to identify its specific comparative advantage and value proposition. Insisting on value for money from each institution made absolute sense, as the value of development cooperation was to be measured against specific benchmarks and targets. These targets were the basis on which donor countries would secure budgetary provisions for aid from their parliaments.

The problem was that from a development effectiveness perspective, the approach had a tendency to encourage further fragmentation. In due course, it

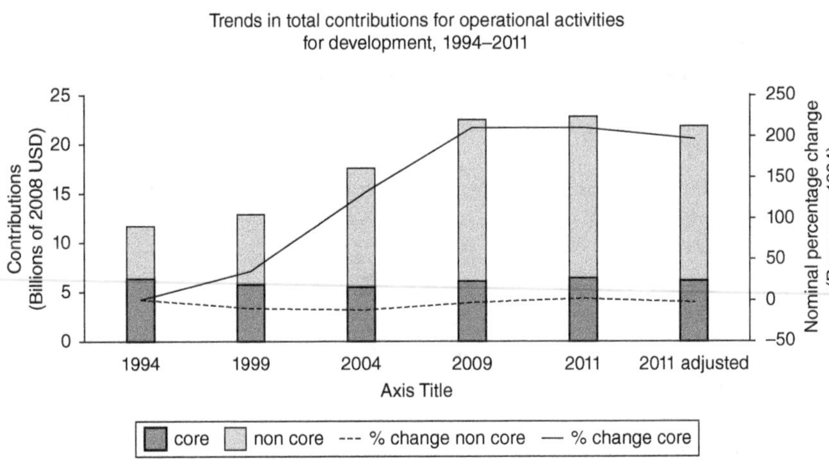

Figure 5.1 The growth of extra-budgetary funding in the mid-1990s

Source: A/66/79, 6 May 2011, Report of Secretary General on Funding of Operational Activities, p. 25

led to the inevitable reaction that the allocation of development resources had to be overseen and indeed decided upon by national authorities. Thus, in the wake of a wave of the proliferation and multiplication of vertical funds, there came the need for horizontal discipline and prioritization. The process had to be fully owned and led by the country and aligned with government priorities. This then led to a new focus on capacity development as the core of the substance of development cooperation.

The Paris Declaration in 2005 was the pinnacle of the counter-reaction to the victory of vertical funding. The Paris Declaration committed the international development community to a set of principles whose core purpose was to control the expansion of vertical programming and funding. Government ownership, alignment with national priorities, simplification, and harmonization were seen as critical to the future of development effectiveness. This was a commitment to the principle that a large part of the solution to supporting coherent development cooperation policies lay within the practices of the aid community itself. The key to reform could be found in operational effectiveness.

The irony of the Paris Declaration is that it identified as a core challenge a phenomenon whose time had already peaked, as captured by Severino's critique of the relevance for the future of the Paris Declaration mindset (Severino and Ray 2009a, 2009b). In his analysis, the Paris Declaration is largely irrelevant not only for a large group of middle-income countries, but also for countries in crisis and non-performing low-income countries, because it does not provide a credible framework for engaging in cooperation. In fact, the Paris Declaration provides a useful framework for only a small number of highly aid-dependent, well-performing, low-income countries.

6 THE ANNAN REFORMS AND THE SEARCH FOR COHERENCE

Within the UN Development System, the reform process that gained momentum in the mid-1990s was to follow a very similar logic and trajectory. The process started formally with Secretary General Annan's 1997 reform initiative, which was very much based on the assumption that the UN's external positioning in the overall development architecture required a strong focus on internal realignment (United Nations 1997).

With regard to its development activities, the realignment included two major components.

The first was the creation of four management groups, two of which were devoted to development matters. The Economic and Social Affairs Group (EC-ESA) was chaired by the Under-Secretary General/Department of Economic and Social Affairs (USG/DESA) while the United Nations Development Group (UNDG) was chaired by the UNDP Administrator. The groups were mechanisms to ensure proper coordination within their respective spheres. They were above all managerial instruments to strengthen internal alignment.

EC-ESA focused on the coordination of overall policy and brought together DESA, the Regional Commissions, UNCTAD, UNDP, United Nations Environment Programme (UNEP), the UN research centers, and other entities. Its aim was to bring coherence and common approaches to UN entities engaged in analytical work in the economic and social fields, particularly through a number of thematic task forces.

The UNDG was built around a group that had been formed earlier and consisted of the major programs and funds under the authority of the Secretary General, namely, UNDP, UNICEF, United Nations Fund for Population Activities (UNFPA), and the World Food Programme (WFP). The UNDG expanded this group to include virtually all the agencies, programs, and funds working in the sphere of development in the system. While this had the merit of inclusion, it also made it very difficult to take any binding management decisions. The idea of a small executive committee was therefore reconstituted with a view to becoming an effective management instrument.

The newly constituted UNDG focused its attention on a number of key operational issues:

- Expansion of the pool from which to select United Nations Resident Coordinators to the entire system
- Establishment of the UN Development Assistance Frameworks as the unified framework for UN country activities
- Establishment of the Common Country Assessment as a unified instrument for UN system on which to base programming
- Creation of common UN houses
- Promotion of joint programming

While these reforms represented important steps forward on the operational effectiveness agenda, they left unresolved two core tensions. Firstly, the split between UNDG and EC-ESA tended to widen the gap between the operational and normative dimensions of the UN's work in the precise time they needed to be working more closely together. Secondly, a trade-off within UNDG between a small group that could take effective decisions but could not provide system-wide coherence and a broad group that ensured the whole system was included at the price of lowest common denominator agendas, was not successfully secured.

The inadequacies of the earlier efforts led to a renewed effort at reform through the convening of the High-Level Panel on System-Wide Coherence (United Nations 2006). The major contribution of the Panel to be implemented was the Delivering as One Initiative. The approach was premised on the assumption that reform at headquarters level was politically impossible and that practical steps should be taken to strengthen cohesion at the country level. In this spirit the four ONES were launched:

- One UN leader at the country level
- One UN program
- One UN fund
- One UN office

We shall review in greater detail below some of the successes and failures of this approach. At this point, what is important is to note that the Paris Declaration and the Delivering as One Initiative were both tailored from the same cloth. They were both premised on the core idea that realignment within their respective businesses was the key to promoting their effectiveness and through that, the relevance of their enterprises.

Both the Paris Declaration and the Delivering as One Initiative certainly made significant contributions in their respective spheres of work. But the relevance of their businesses would be determined by the success with which they were able to align with the external, not the internal. By 2010, the world of development cooperation bore little resemblance to the world of 1990. The Annan Reforms made a useful contribution, in particular the reform initiatives relating to UNDG, Delivering as One, and the creation of the Development Cooperation Forum, but the pace of change demanded something more far-reaching.

7 DEVELOPMENT COOPERATION REVISITED

What, then, are the elements that make it appropriate to see the decade of 2000 onwards as revolutionary in its impact on development cooperation, as compared with the construction period, the period of service to member states (late 1950s through early 1980s), or the initial phase of the era of Goals in the 1990s?

Firstly, the extraordinary emergence of the growth economies in a historically remarkably short period of time has changed the fundamental character of the global economy, as the majority share of growth now emanates from the South (Bremmer 2012; O'Neill 2011). The emergence of the BRICS specifically reflects a corresponding major shift in the distribution of power between states.

There has been a significant evolution in the profile of poverty. A global middle class is emerging, which is having a dramatic impact on the nature and size of resource flows, the power of markets, and the role and positioning of Official Development Assistance (ODA). Today, the majority of the poor live in so-called middle-income countries. In 1990, 95 percent of the poorest in the world lived in the low-income countries. Some twenty years later, it is estimated that 75 percent of the poorest live in middle-income countries (Sumner 2011; Sumner and Carbonnier 2012).

The international community has seen the emergence of new challenges that are global in character. In the 1990s a broad range of development goals, which eventually culminated in the MDGs, was articulated through an exhaustive series of global conferences. This articulation of development goals, in its essence, took the form of creating a global framework (the MDGs) within which to pursue national objectives. What has emerged distinctively in the last decade or two is the identification of global problems that require collective action based on some agreed-upon allocation of national responsibility. How this is to be done is highly contested. The existence of these global challenges and the need to address them by and large is not. There is an important difference of substance between these two concepts. The consequence of the distinction can perhaps best be understood in the difference between the concepts of aid on the one hand and of global public goods on the other.

The growth in global markets has seen a transformation that many consider historic in the relationship of states, markets, and individuals. This has brought with it deep-rooted changes in the respective roles of the private and the public in the practice of development cooperation. The development landscape has been heavily influenced over the last two decades by a rapid increase in international private flows. It is important to recognize that there is a group of countries that do not benefit from these emerging private flows and remain heavily reliant on ODA. But the reality is that the group of low=income countries is a diminishing group, which is projected to decline to between 30–35 countries within the next decade (of which about 25 will be in Africa and two-thirds will be conflict or post-conflict states) (Chandy 2011).

The last ten years have seen a transformation in the development community's approach to working with the private sector. The critical importance of the private sector as the engine of growth was perhaps best captured by the World Bank in its World Development Report:

> "Private firms are at the heart of the development process. Driven by the quest for profits, firms of all types—from farmers and micro-entrepreneurs to local manufacturing companies and multinational enterprises—invest in new ideas and new facilities that strengthen the foundation of economic growth and prosperity" (World Bank 2004, 1).

The 1990s also saw dramatic increases both in the number of civil society actors as well as in the financial resources at their disposal. Civil society has been instrumental in moving forward the agendas on gender, sustainable development, and climate change. More people are employed in the NGO development sector than by the bilaterals and multilaterals combined.

The transformational impact that technology is having on the practice of development cooperation is already evident. The report "Disaster 2.0" chronicles the extraordinary impact that virtual communities had on the humanitarian response in Haiti. The World Bank's Open Aid Partnership mobilizes citizen cartographers, bringing engineers from around the globe together. Global Pulse is an initiative led by the Secretary-General's Office to support decision makers in using real time data to detect when populations are changing their collective behavior in response to slow-onset crises. Technology is changing the face of development cooperation. Notably, three out of eight of the microeconomic indicators used by Goldman Sachs in their influential Growth Environment Scores relate to internet/communications technology (O'Neill 2011).

The last decade has seen the emergence of a broad range of new institutional actors. These include new actors at the intergovernmental level, for example the G20 and the BRICS. These groupings have developed major agendas and policy formulation functions across a broad range of development issues. There has also been significant growth in the range of action of regional bodies and regional alliances.

Finally, there has also been a proliferation of increasingly influential foundations, such as the Bill and Melinda Gates Foundation, the Clinton Global Initiative, and the World Economic Forum. In the last several decades the number of foundations has tripled. Philanthrocapitalism has challenged many of the traditional ways in which development cooperation has worked, blurring the silos that have segmented the public from the private (Bishop and Green 2008). A number of these foundations not only carry significant financial weight but they have also developed major convening power, filling a gap that the UN appears to have filled unevenly.

The changes described above constitute a major transformation in the environment in which ODA and the UN Development System is working. In response to the changing development landscape, the OECD/DAC has engaged in a soul-searching exploration of how to understand and define ODA in the next decade. The World Bank for its part is now engaged in a major new reform initiative, which reflects an open debate about its changing mission. Similarly, G20 has emerged as a significant new intergovernmental forum in which to discuss development challenges.

In 2009, OECD/DAC completed a reflection exercise to consider its role in the future, an exercise that was undertaken for the first time in some 15 years (OECD/DAC 2009). Some 20 senior-level officials from OECD/DAC member states met for intensive discussions over a period of two years, and their conclusions were contained in the report, "Reflection Exercise: Investment in a Common Cause" (OECD/DAC 2009). This exercise reflected deep uncertainty about the future of ODA and its role in a rapidly changing world. On the one hand, a number of DAC donors were deeply concerned that reaching out to emerging actors and liberalizing the rules defining ODA would fatally undermine support for development cooperation in capitals traditionally among the strongest supporters of ODA. On the other hand, other DAC donors felt that maintaining OECD/DAC as an exclusive club would seal its fate over time as an increasingly marginal interlocutor.

The report did point to the future on two issues. First, it gave a positive nod to the desirability of OECD/DAC becoming more engaged in the emerging dialogue around global public goods. Second, it proved to be a stepping-stone to the Fourth High-level Forum on Aid Effectiveness in Busan (2011). Its outcome document does reflect the pressing reality of change. Para 28 states, "[W]e will rethink what aid should be spent on, in ways that are consistent with agreed international rights, norms and standards, so that aid catalyzes development" (OECD/DAC 2012).

The Busan Partnership document established a Global Partnership for Effective Development Cooperation. This replaced the Working Party on Aid Effectiveness which had its last meeting in June 2012. The new Partnership was to be supported by the OECD/DAC and UNDP and in this respect represented a new partnership between the UN and OECD on this agenda. The Global Partnership will be a ministerial meeting held every 18–24 months. A senior-level, 18-member Steering Committee representing different constituencies will be the interim decision-making body between GP meetings.

The ministerial level meetings will review progress in implementation of Busan commitments, ensuring continued political accountability. It will address key issues arising from country-level evidence and be a forum for sharing country-level experiences. The Steering Committee will steer the work of the ministerial-level meeting and provide overall support and direction to the implementation of the Global Partnership.

It remains to be seen to what extent this new mechanism is viewed as a legitimate and useful instrument by emerging countries, and how the work of the Global Partnership is coordinated with UN fora. In particular, there is an attempt to achieve synergy between the ministerial meetings of the Partnership and the UN's Development Cooperation Forum (DCF). The DCF is seen as the logical forum to pursue the mutual accountability agenda that is a core issue for the Global Partnership. The uncertainty surrounding the future of the Global Partnership is not an accident; rather it is an accurate reflection of the overall condition development cooperation finds itself in today.

The deep strategic review and self-questioning which OECD/DAC has been engaging in also characterizes current ongoing debate around the current and future role of the World Bank. On the occasion of the announcement of the retirement of Robert Zoellick as President of the World Bank, development experts were quite vocal in saying that in a world in which the World Bank plays less of a pivotal role in providing aid to developing countries, the institution is still looking for a definitive fresh direction. The new President of the World Bank, Jim Yong Kim, has launched a major reform to address this challenge. Early commentary suggests how difficult this might prove to be. The challenge is captured by an editorial leader in the *Financial Times,* "Restructuring hell at the World Bank" (Thursday April 10, 2014). On a more positive note, the opportunity provided by new leadership at the World Bank suggests real prospects for a strengthened partnership between the UN and the World Bank.

In sum, the emergence of new state actors has direct implications for the practice of development cooperation. The emergence of new global challenges raises questions about the core functions of ODA with respect to those challenges. The enormous expansion of markets, civil society, and individuals, all fueled by the power of modern technology, has changed the role of development cooperation. The emergence of new institutional actors has changed the playing field. All of these elements point to the need for a strategic repositioning of the role of ODA in development cooperation. This in turn requires the UN Development System to align itself with the broader development cooperation environment.

8 UN DEVELOPMENT COOPERATION REVISITED: REFORM STRATEGIES

Historical and recent debates about the UN Development System highlight a number of possible reform strategies. We conclude by examining each of these in turn and providing an analysis of the relevance of the strategies to the challenges the UN Development System faces.

8.1 Coherence Through Global Task Forces

As noted, the UN Development System was set up as a group of independent functional organizations deeply rooted in their own constituencies, loosely coordinated and with their own governance arrangements. The relationship of each specialized agency with its own constituency determined organizational relevance and performance. Creating issue-based task forces has proven the method of choice for attempting to increase overall coherence and capacity.

In this regard, the steps in the 2010s that have been taken by the Secretary General's office to promote selective new partnership platforms around a global public goods-type agenda have the potential to be transformative. The Secretary General has launched a number of major partnerships, including in particular the High-Level Task Force on Food Security, Sustainable Energy for All, and Every Woman, Every Child.

The High-Level Task Force on Food Security (HLTF) was set up in 2008 in response to the rapid increase in food prices. It was used to establish a common strategic position and way of working for the UN system as well as the World Bank, IMF, WTO, and OECD. Over the last few years, the HLTF has covered a broader range of emerging issues, as well as provided a common external face in a number of fora, in particular the G20. Sustainable Energy for All was established around three objectives: energy access for all, doubling the rate of energy efficiency, and doubling the share of renewable energy in the global energy mix. This initiative focuses on clear and measurable targets, reaches out to a broad range of stakeholders at a high level, and provides a common platform for advocacy and monitoring of results. In September 2012, the initiative was established formally as an independent entity. Every Woman, Every Child was launched in 2011 at the Millennium Summit with the objective of saving the lives of 16 million women by 2015. It reaches out to a very broad range of constituencies and provides a platform for shared advocacy and the monitoring of results.

These partnerships all share a number of key characteristics. They share some core strengths and constraints and a number of key questions hang over their fate. Each of these has been a strategic response to an external reality, which has created an opportunity that the UN has seized. The Secretary General's leadership in convening actors within and outside the UN Development System has been a critical element. The leadership of the Secretary General has imparted unique strategic leverage, an externally coherent message, and an ability to motivate stakeholders at the highest levels.

The UN has demonstrated a capacity to convene and provide a platform for a broad range of stakeholders. These are fully inclusive partnerships, which have demonstrated a willingness to go beyond the state-centric constraints that UN-led initiatives have often suffered from.

The major challenge facing these partnerships from a UN perspective is the extent to which they can go beyond taking the form of short-term ad hoc task forces and really drive a strategic allocation of resources within the system. How deep is the internal coherence? Are these One UN initiatives or are they very loosely formed coalitions? Is the monitoring of results and the accountability of stakeholders for their achievement credible?

8.2 Country-Level Coherence

The idea of focusing on country-level coherence was promoted by the Secretary General's High-Level Panel on UN System-Wide Coherence. The panel promoted the concept of "Delivering as One": this comprised in particular the "One programme," the "One UN leader," and the "One fund." This model assumes that it was politically impossible to implement major reform at the headquarters level. There is no doubt that the Delivering as One Initiative has demonstrated some success in particular with regard to improvements in operational effectiveness. Strong government ownership of Delivering as One Initiatives in a number of countries has enabled more coherent UN programs to be implemented.

However, it is difficult to see significant progress on broad issues of strategic repositioning. For the "One programme" to be implemented effectively, the contradiction between the need for strategic focus and the strong political pressures for inclusion have to be reconciled. More generally, this model assumes that the effective delivery of resources will remain the critical lever for the UN's development positioning. Given the rapidly declining share of ODA within total resource flows, this is an unlikely scenario. For the "One UN leader" to have real credibility would require a real transfer of at least some accountability from the vertical accountability lines that reach to agency headquarters, to a more horizontal based accountability with its roots at the country level. Some progress has been made on the concept of mutual accountability in the UNGA's 2012 Quadrennial review resolution, but it remains to be seen how the concept is implemented practically. The One UN funds attracted resources in the first several years, but as of end 2012, most of the resources allocated by donors for this purpose had dried up with little expectation of replenishment. Meanwhile the unwillingness in this scenario to tackle broader governance issues has created severe constraints, as the vertically-driven accountability system deriving from the current governance arrangements stands firmly in the way of implementing system-wide coherent governance.

The conclusion to be drawn is not to give up on the delivering as one initiative. On the contrary, this remains an important effort that should be supported. But expectations as to the scope and level of ambition of this initiative need to be put back in perspective. This is an initiative that principally will improve operational effectiveness. It does not represent the kind of strategic-level response that the transformation that has taken place in the last decade demands if the UN Development System is to retain its relevance.

8.3 UN "System-Wide" Governance

The governance architecture of the UN Development System is in many respects opaque. As discussed earlier, the governance of the UN Development System was by design deeply fragmented. The barrier to reform that this fragmentation represents resurfaced as a consequence of the Delivering as One Initiative, since there was no single location where a One UN document could be approved for the entire system. Consistent with the original design of the system, the UN Charter only provided for very loose coordination arrangements between ECOSOC and the specialized agencies. Subsequently, the establishment of specific Executive Boards for many of the programs further diluted ECOSOC's ability to exercise real authority. For decades, the reform of ECOSOC has been debated with little effect, and in the current structure, ECOSOC's value added remains unclear. The aborted proposal by the High-Level Panel on Coherence to create a Sustainable Development Board is a reflection of the deep-rooted resistance to institutional coherence. The futility of some of these governance structures is reinforced by the fact that in the operational sphere, the great bulk of the program approval process in reality takes place at the country level, consistent with the principles of the Paris Declaration.

The architecture is also characterized by enormous complexity and duplication. It is difficult to decipher the purpose and value added of each stage in the intergovernmental process as items progress from discussion in Executive Boards to the Joint Executive Board, through ECOSOC to the Second Committee and the General Assembly. Whether there is indeed a progression or rather a circular meandering is somewhat debatable. Another feature of the governance arrangements is that in many of the governance structures, representation comes from foreign ministries. Diplomatic interests often take precedence over development substance. This is far away from the original functionalist vision envisaged by the founders of the system. Similarly, the principle guiding the construction of the system that governance should be maximally inclusive with representation from a broad range of stakeholders remains a relatively exceptional practice.

A starting point in considering reform paths to pursue is to reflect on the ambiguity embedded in this extraordinarily complex structure, with respect to the purpose of these governance arrangements. Is it the oversight of operations, under the context in which UN operational activities represent an ever-decreasing proportion of total flows into the great majority of countries? In the vast majority of cases, the proper place for review and approval of UN country programs is in the country, with the full participation of government and all relevant stakeholders. Or is the governance function increasingly about monitoring trends and performance, sharing empirical data and knowledge, and providing high quality analysis? In this scenario, the governance arrangements would have to ensure the quality of the documents provided and the transmission of data and knowledge in a manner that would be useful to policy-makers. Participation would need to be substantive. The sharing of knowledge and lessons learned would displace the negotiation of intergovernmentally agreed text as the major output of the meetings. Or finally, is the governance of the future increasingly going to be about developing a common language and generating norms and standards? In this scenario the quality of the interaction between participants becomes the highest priority. Moreover if the purpose of the meetings is to share knowledge and generate norms, then governance arrangements in the future will have to successfully incorporate a much wider community of stakeholders than is currently the practice. Engagement with the private sector and civil society will need to be integrated in a more substantive manner.

One potentially significant innovation in the governance structure was the creation in 2007 of the Development Cooperation Forum (DCF) following the 2005 UNGA Summit Meeting. The DCF was established with the purpose of reviewing trends in international development cooperation, promoting greater coherence among different development partners and strengthening the normative and operational links in the work of the UN. Of particular importance in the ambitions for the DCF was its role in monitoring and reviewing trends and in representing a forum that could include all relevant stakeholders. Four DCFs have now been held (2008, 2010, 2012, and 2014) and they have generated good participation and active debate on a wide range of issues. Three areas appear to be emerging of particular interest: the monitoring of aid commitments, exchange on best practices, and increasingly, mutual accountability. Nonetheless it remains to be seen whether the DCF will be able to define for itself a significant and relevant role in the development architecture that will sustain high-level participation, or whether it will become another piece in a largely dysfunctional governance architecture. The future of the DCF will depend on the rigor with which its functions are defined.

Another recent innovation is the establishment of the High-Level Political Forum established at the Rio+20 conference in June 2012. The forum held its first meeting in September 2013. The purpose of the forum is to address and coordinate the entirety of sustainable development issues. In the words of John Ashe, President of the General Assembly, "The forum should be the home for concrete guidance in the review of sustainable development goals, their implementation and monitoring, as integration of the three dimensions of sustainable development by all actors" (United Nations 2013). The forum will meet at head of government level every four years and every year under the auspices of ECOSOC. It is too early to tell whether this forum will prove able to provide the kind of leadership on sustainable development that is needed.

8.4 Deep Integration

Intuitively, deep integration resonates as the proper response to deep fragmentation. There is no doubt that the current system is characterized by deep fragmentation, overlapping functions, duplicative mandates, and, in key areas, a real lack of critical mass. At the same time, the community of interests that form the nucleus of many of the different organizations in the UN Development System represents a powerful vision that has characterized the design of the system since the very beginning. A response to the current fragmentation, which led to bureaucratic centralization, does not provide a promising path forward. The brand recognition, commitment, and energy that come from entities supported by deep constituencies needs to be cherished and protected.

A policy of selective and strategic integration—rather than of deep integration—is what is required. A number of immediate challenges present themselves. The first challenge is the prevention of turf battles from throwing up roadblocks to emerging task forces and partnerships around defined agendas. The progress of the Global Food Security Task Force is a good case in point. The second challenge is for strong leadership to be exercised on a select number of priority agenda items where the UN needs to reorganize itself to create critical mass. The third challenge is to explore the various competing platform functions (presence, representation) performed by various organizations and to streamline them. The fourth challenge is to integrate administrative and operational functions, especially at the country level, to be able to refocus resources on emerging priorities. Finally, a much more rigorous approach is needed to decide on the trade-offs between creating new organizations to raise profiles on an important agenda, with the need for that agenda item to be mainstreamed throughout the work of the entire system. The lack of rigor leads to a process of further duplication and complexity, which detracts from the need for focus and profile. Both the creation of UN Women and the Peace-building Support Office encountered this problem.

8.5 Leadership

Historically, leadership has meant very different things at different times. In the construction phase, leadership was associated with great leaders in their communities—in science, education, health, labor, etc. These leaders were recognized by their peers and participated actively in the conferences and expert meetings of the fledgling organizations. As the system passed into the phase of service to member states, and as a multitude of new countries entered the world stage, leadership was very much associated with government leadership. In the 1990s, UN leaders were identified with the specific goals that the agency they were leading were advocating for. The 1990s was the time of Jim Grant on children, Sadako Ogata on refugees, and Gro Harlem Brundtland on global health.

Throughout this time, the need for institutional leadership of the UN Development System did not disappear. In practice the system navigated through a number of different options:

The first option was to create an additional layer on top of the agencies, programs, and funds that would provide overall leadership to the system. One expression of this was the creation of the office of the Director General in 1979. This was abandoned by Boutros Boutros-Ghali because it was seen as a superstructure with very little capacity and very limited value added. The creation of a superstructure in the absence of any real capacity to engineer coherence has led structural adjustments to substitute for real reform. Subsequently, Annan established the office of the Deputy Secretary-General. The portfolio of the incumbent has always included coordination in the economic and social spheres.

A second option was to follow a lead agency concept. Different agencies would take the lead depending on their prominence in different countries and on circumstances.

A third option was to reject institutionalized leadership and to opt for leadership through committee management. In practice this was often the preferred method because of the high value attached in UN decision making to consensus. While this type of approach may be useful at times, the price that is paid if this becomes the norm is heavy.

A fourth option was to turn to UNDP to provide leadership on the operational side as the major multi-sector program within the UN system. This flowed historically from a time when UNDP indeed was the central funding instrument for the operational system. With the transformation that took place in the early 1990s, the logic for this approach was weakened and this role became heavily contested within the system.

A fifth option was an adaptation of the fourth and was essentially endorsed by the High-Level Panel on Coherence in 2006. This scenario maintained UNDP's leadership role in the operational system but only under the understanding that there would be a clear firewall between UNDP's actions as a substantive agency and the functions it performed as manager of the resident coordinator system. The firewall would take care of the perceptions of conflict of interest that made UNDP leadership so contested throughout the system.

Finally, a broader source of contestation related to the emphasis given in many of these discussions to the UN's operational role at a time when once again the normative and standard-setting work of the UN system is seen as being of particular relevance.

It would be nice to be able to settle on one of these leadership options to point to the path ahead. In practice many of these options are not necessarily exclusive and different combinations of them will undoubtedly be required. Providing system-wide leadership in the face of institutional independence and proliferation, a vacuum in system-wide governance, and deeply competitive resource mobilization models is a challenging proposition.

Against this background it is easy to understand why many analysts and commentators stress that the quality of leadership will be the determining factor as to whether today's multilateral organizations can adapt and thereby maintain their relevance in today's world.

8.6 The Role of Financing

The financial model that lies behind the system will ultimately play a critical role in determining the path that reform takes. We have seen that over half a century, the system has been dominated by three models that could be characterized as financing communities of interest, transferring resources to member states, and allocating resources to goals. This last model has left the system today highly dependent on extra-budgetary resources and, consequently, project-driven.

The dominant response to this situation has been to call for a rebalancing between core and non-core contributions. Yet every indication is that the era of making large core contributions to institutions to enable them to implement their programs belongs to the past. There are many reasons for this, but one of the principal ones is the lack of trust in the governance arrangements in the UN Development System. Increasing core contributions could be a part of a solution, but it would need to be one part of a much more comprehensive approach.

One scenario that can probably be dispensed with is the idea of reverting to central funding. Most recently the High-Level Panel on Coherence showed interest in resurrecting the concept of central funding to impose discipline on the system. In the end, the diversity of funding sources that characterizes the flow of resources today and the strength of vertical funding make this option impractical.

Instead the panel turned to the idea of One UN funds at the country level to complement agency funding arrangements. The idea was that providing resources centrally at the country level to be managed by the resident coordinators would drive greater coherence at the country level. It became an integral part of the Delivering as One package. But just several years later, this financing instrument is drying up. In effect in a financial scenario where three types of funding were running side-by-side—core agency funding, extra-budgetary funding, and the One UN Fund—the One UN Fund would never be more than a residual source. This made it politically unsustainable as a major funding source.

By contrast, from 2004–2008, two new financial instruments were developed which have shown some promise. One instrument is the Multi-Partner Trust Fund (MPTF) facility. This established a UN system-wide window, so that donors could contribute to a UN system-wide program without having to decide which specific organization within the UN to partner with. Faced with a choice between the World Bank and 25 UN agencies, most donors preferred partnering with the World Bank. With a choice between a UN system-wide window and any other partner, many donors were interested in working with the UN. This was the situation that arose in immediate post-war Iraq, and from a financial point of view the UN-Iraq multi-donor trust fund performed above expectations. Since its establishment in 2004, the multi-partner trust fund office has development into a broad ranging facility with a portfolio of some $7 billion. It is noteworthy that in the case of country-level programs, the challenge of allocating resources within the UN system has been delegated to country-level steering committees. The experience with the MPTF suggests that the potential of the UN system when it gets its act together remains substantial. By the same token, it demonstrates that the fragmentation of the system is leading it to punch below its weight.

A second instrument is the Spain-UNDP MDG Achievement Fund. This instrument was established in 2006 as a result of a $720 million contribution from the Spanish Government. Spain was seeking a major partnership with the UN with the aim of making a significant impact on the achievement of the MDGs. They wanted to establish a MDG UN system-wide trust fund that would make a difference. In order to do this they wanted to entrust the resources to UNDP as the manager of the coordination of operational activities. They were insistent on the need for a credible and single management partner. The Spanish initially may not have been fully aware of the challenge they were posing the UN, as their proposal revealed the vacuum that a system-wide vision would inevitably encounter. UNDP welcomed this opportunity, but was well aware that their management of this facility on behalf of the system would be contested by elements within the system. It was confronted with the need to develop a new instrument that would meet the Spanish requirement of a single credible management partner as well as the Spanish expectation of a UN system-wide initiative. The dual structure created by UNDP consisted of a political-level strategic steering committee limited to Spain, UNDP, and thematic, agency-led steering committees to actually allocate resources. This structure represented a significant innovation. The flaw in the model relates to the fact that the source of financing was essentially a one-off contribution from a single donor.

Formal resolutions in the UN system have a well-rehearsed series of financing demands. They normally comprise four major demands: increase core funding, redress the imbalance between core and non-core, increase predictability, and improve burden sharing. Arguably, with respect to each of these issues, the rhetoric marks a harsh reality. Huge pressure on donor budgets has led to a decline in ODA commitments and is reflected in a significant cut in a number of UN agency budgets. Declining core resources makes the goal of practically redressing core and non-core income flows highly unlikely, and indeed the pressure to earmark contributions is only increasing. This has given rise to a new initiative to develop integrated budgets that would increase the flexibility provisions relating to non-core resources to make them more like core resources. Some progress appears to have been made in this respect in WHO. With regard to the issues of predictability and burden sharing, there is no evidence of movement in a positive direction, and again budget pressures in donor countries are only likely to compound current practices.

Comprehensive reform of the financing instruments at the disposal of the UN Development System remains the indispensable element of any credible reform proposal going forward. The desire to rebalance core and non-core contributions does not constitute a strategy; rather, it represents wishful thinking. What is required is a new viable political economy for the system that recognizes that different types of financing will be appropriate and feasible for different types of functions. Assessed budgets, core voluntary contributions, negotiated pledges, thematic trust funds, fees, and different types of earmarked funding are all likely to play a part in a new financial architecture. From a reform perspective, the critical challenge is to ensure that the new architecture provides incentives for the financing of those functions the international community wants the UN Development System to perform. There is no getting around the simple proposition that the international community will get the UN Development System that it chooses to finance.

9 SUMMARY REFLECTIONS

A lively debate is currently underway about the need for reform of the UN Development System. A good deal of the discussion focuses on reform of the governance of the system. The UN's role in development cooperation in its broadest sense and the governance of the system have evolved significantly over the last half century. This chapter attempts to demonstrate that a historical understanding of the evolution that has taken place can make a useful contribution to repositioning the system today to meet future challenges. This is all the more the case because embedded in the UN's structures today are layers of historical experience which provide critical insights into how the UN functions.

The first sections of this chapter (sections 1–6) trace the historical evolution of the UN Development System. The process of change can best be understood as an evolution with a number of distinct phases. Tracing these phases does not imply that with the emergence of a new phase, the old system is jettisoned; rather the new phase builds on the old. But with regard to functions, finance, structure, and governance, each new phase displays characteristics that are clearly identifiable and distinct.

The vision that lay behind the construction phase was deeply influenced by the experience of Nazism and the Second World War. The twin drivers of the Cold War and the process of decolonization led to a very different paradigm centered around the concept of service to member states. Both these drivers were strongly aligned with the supremacy accorded to the principle of sovereignty. In turn, the concept of service to member states led to fears about the increasing marginalization of the UN's work, and this led to an intensive period of what we have called a search for identity. The expansion of operational activities led to a further focus on attracting resources and increasing project activities. The political economy of the old system was replaced by something of a free-for-all, with intensive competition within the system for projects and the financing that went with them. With the end of the Cold War and the acceleration of globalization, ironically the political impetus behind development cooperation waned and called for a new rationale. This was provided by the new focus on Goals. But the focus on Goals did nothing to stem the trend towards increasing fragmentation, and in turn gave rise to the prioritization of the search for coherence, which in the last decade has become synonymous with reform.

Section 7 analyzes a number of the key elements that characterize the development landscape today. The chapter argues that the changes that are occurring are at least as profound as those that have marked previous transitions. The chapter explores some of the institutional responses to the challenges posed by these changes. It is difficult to escape the conclusion that all these elements point to the need for a strategic repositioning of the role of development cooperation more broadly, the role of ODA more specifically, and the role of the UN Development System in particular. The UN Development System needs to align behind a redefined set of functions.

Section 8 explores a number of the strategies for implementing reform that are currently under discussion. At one extreme lie attempts to provide coherence through the establishment of global task forces. These have the merit of having considerable agility and being able to align closely to issues and agreed functions. The question of long-term institutional sustainability remains. Another strategy focuses on strengthening country-level coherence, the path chosen by the UN with its focus on the Delivering as One Initiative. It has the merit of focusing on solving some very concrete problems, but lacks strategic ambition. A more ambitious strategy would be to seek system-wide coherence, but there is no indication that this can attract broad political support today. This still leaves deep integration and mergers as possible strategies to drive reform, but whether focus on structures is likely to generate reform in the political environment in which the UN works is doubtful. A final approach is to engineer more space for system-wide leadership to be exercised. Whatever the complications, revitalizing leadership throughout the system will have to be part of any overall reform strategy.

It is impossible to analyze the merits and pitfalls of these different strategies without understanding the historical layers that underpin the UN Development System today. Each strategy has a useful contribution to make, but none of them will provide solutions on their own. We are left with three overarching conclusions. The first is that the urgent need for radical reform must not lead to a reductionist logic that sees in complexity the problem to be rooted out. The UN has accumulated a rich historical legacy that in many respects is also its strength. Those historical roots need to be leveraged to promote change. The second is that for any reform process to be successful, it needs to follow the precepts of the founders of the UN: form must always follow function. Lastly, experience indicates that any credible reform process will need to take on the challenge of the financing system on which the UN Development System is based. Without radical reform of the financing instruments, reform will remain wishful thinking.

10 POSTSCRIPT. THE POST-2015 DEVELOPMENT FRAMEWORK: A NEW OPPORTUNITY?

The anticipated adoption in September 2015 of a post-2015 development framework anchored in Sustainable Development Goals (SDGs) lies at the heart of the new development agenda. The SDGs represent a new, unified and universal agenda. In this respect the new development agenda is being discussed as a transformative agenda—one that reflects the transformation in the development landscape that has taken place during the last fifteen years.

The adoption of a new transformative development agenda gives rise to the question of the longer-term positioning of the UN development system in the post-2015 development agenda. Is a business as usual UN development system fit for purpose to support the ambitious development agenda envisaged?

In December 2014, ECOSOC initiated a series of dialogues regarding the role of the United Nations Development System in the changing development landscape and the need to align the UN system to address emerging challenges. In this regard it requested analysis of the interlinkages among the alignment of functions, funding practices, governance structures, capacity and impact of the UN development system, partnership approaches, and organizational arrangements (Jenks and Aklilu 2014).

The dialogues will continue into early 2016 and will engage member states in intensive informal discussions on all aspects of reform. The ambition is to go well beyond the effectiveness agenda which has dominated reform discussions over the last decade and to take on core questions relating to the strategic positioning of the UNDS. Discussions in ECOSOC in December 2014 and 2015 reveal a great variety of views. However, there does appear to be a strong consensus about the need for radical reform. It remains to be seen whether this consensus will translate into concrete practical reform measures.

ACKNOWLEDGEMENTS

I am grateful to José Antonio Ocampo for his comments and guidance. I would also like to express appreciation to Sasha de Vogel for the editorial assistance.

REFERENCES

Bertrand, Maurice. 1969. *Joint Inspection Unit Report on Programming and Budgeting in UN family of Organisations,* Rep/69/7.

Bertrand, Maurice. 1974. *Joint Inspection Unit Report on Medium Term Planning and the UN System*, Rep/74/1.

Bishop, Matthew and Michael Green. 2008. *Philanthrocapitalism.* New York: Bloomsbury Press.

Bremmer, Ian. 2012. *Every Nation for Itself.* London: Penguin.

Chandy, Lawrence. 2011. *Reframing Development Cooperation.* Brookings Blum Roundtable Policy Brief.

Claude, Inis. 1964. *Swords into Ploughshares.* New York: Random House.

Hammarskjold, Dag. 1961. *The International Civil Service in Law and in Fact.* Oxford: Oxford University Press.

Jenks, Bruce, and Bisrat Aklilu. 2014. Discussion Paper on the Longer-Term Positioning of the United Nations Development System in the Post-2015 Development Agenda (9 December). New York: Department of Economic and Social Affairs, UN.

Jenks, Bruce, Alicia Barcena, Patrizio Civili, and Eduardo Doryan. 2006. "The case for a UN Development Pillar." Informal paper, available from authors.

Jenks, Bruce, and Bruce Jones. 2013. *UN Development at a Cross Roads.* New York: New York University/Center for International Cooperation.

Mitrany, David. 1975. *The Functional Theory of Politics.* London: LSE Robertson.

OECD/DAC. 1996. *Reshaping the 21st Century: The Contribution of Development Cooperation.*

OECD/DAC. 2009. *Reflection Exercise: Investment in a Common Cause. Development Cooperation in a Changing World.*

OECD/DAC. 2012. *The Busan Partnership for Effective Development Co-operation.*

O'Neill, Jim. 2011. *The Growth Map.* London: Penguin.

Pearson, Lester. 1969. *Partners in Development.* New York: Praeger.

Severino, Jean-Michel, and Olivier Ray. 2009a. *The end of ODA Death and Rebirth of a Global Public Policy.* Washington DC: Center for Global Development.

Severino, Jean-Michel, and Olivier Ray. 2009b. *The end of ODA: The birth of hyper-collective action.* Washington DC: Center for Global Development.

Sumner, Andy. 2011. *The New Bottom Billion.* Washington, DC: Center for Global Development Brief.

Sumner, Andy, and Giles Carbonnier. 2012. *Aid, Emerging Economies and Global Policies International Deveopment Policy.* Geneva: The Graduate Institute.

United Nations. 1966. *Report of the Ad Hoc Committee of Experts to examine the finances of the UN and the Specialised Agencies,* A/6289. New York: United Nations.

United Nations. 1969a. *Report of the Enlarged Committee on Program Coordination* (2 October), E/AC5/GR/25.

United Nations. 1969b. *Study of the Capacity of the UN Development System*, DP/5. Geneva: United Nations.

United Nations. 1970. *Consensus Resolution*, Resolution 2688 (XXV). New York: UNGA.

United Nations. 1974. *Special Session of the General Assembly devoted to development and international economic co-operation.* A/RES/29/3343. New York: UNGA.

United Nations. 1975. *A New UN Structure for Global Economic Cooperation Report of the Group of Experts.*

United Nations. 1990. *Report of the Expert Group on Agency Support Costs* DP/1990/9.

United Nations. 1997. *UN Renewing the United Nations: A Program of Reform,* A/51/950. New York: UNGA.

United Nations. 2006. *Delivering as One: Report of the High Level Panel on UN system wide Coherence.* New York: UNGA.

United Nations. 2013. *Remarks by H.E. John W. Ashe, President of the 68th Session of the United Nations General Assembly.* http://www.un.org/en/ga/president/68/pdf/statements/0924013Opening_of_HLPF.pdf.

World Bank. 2004. *World Development Report 2005: A Better Investment Climate for Everyone.* https://openknowledge.worldbank.org/handle/10986/5987

6

Multilateral Development Banks

Roy Culpeper, Stephany Griffith-Jones, and Daniel Titelman

In recent years, the valuable role that regional and multilateral development banks can and do play has received clearer recognition in wider and ever-growing circles. The positive role that these banks have played in providing counter-cyclical finance as private flows to developing countries collapsed during the North Atlantic crisis that started in 2007, is widely seen as valuable. Furthermore, the greater need for instruments to implement more long-term national or regional development strategies has been increasingly recognized.

The value of development banks, at a multilateral, regional, and national level, to help implement and finance development strategies and visions (by funding both the public and private sector) has thus received greater support. It is also interesting that the role of development banks has not just been highlighted as important in developing and emerging economies, but also in developed ones. Thus, as private lending fell, the European Investment Bank has played a prominent role in the provision of lending during the European debt crisis. At a national European level, Germany's public development bank, KfW, now the second largest commercial German bank, has played a very positive role in increasing lending counter-cyclically—for example to small and medium enterprises (SMEs)—during the crisis, as well as funding on a significant scale key sectors, such as investment in renewables. In Europe these actions are perceived and highlighted as a valuable model for other countries. France has just created a new public development bank and the United Kingdom is contemplating the creation of a similar institution.

Building on their successes to date, this chapter identifies four valuable functions that seem crucial for national, regional, and multilateral development banks: a) providing counter-cyclical finance, especially for supporting investment; b) supporting longer-term national development strategies; c) mobilizing increased resources, for example by leverage and blending; and d) financing the provision of public goods.

Prior to discussing these functions in greater detail, it seems important to stress that development banks should be conceived and analyzed as a system, where synergies and complementarities exist among multilateral, regional, and national development banks. That is the concept of densification at the institutional level, which implies a better articulation between multilateral development banks (MDBs) with regional and national development banks for the determination of development objectives and for the allocation of resources.[1] Regional and national development banks have—in broad terms—similar mandates to MDBs, which implies vast potential complementarities and synergies that should be further exploited. Thus, multilateral and regional development banks seem to perform far better their functions, including providing counter-cyclical finance and supporting productive development, if they work closely with national development banks. Similarly, national development banks can operate better if they have the financial and technical support of multilateral and regional banks. Thus, we need to think in terms of public-private financial partnerships, but also especially of multilateral/regional and national ones.

The changing global economic and social landscape highlights the need to find a consensus framework for financing for development based on pragmatism, that is, on identifying policies that suit the circumstances and conditions of countries that are profoundly different (Rogers 2010; Rodrik 2008). In this context, multilateral development banks as well as regional and national banks, can and must play an active role.

1 THE MDBS, SECTORIAL PRIORITIES AND TYPES OF LENDING

At present, the MDBs have objectives and priorities that range from providing finance for investment—both human and physical capital, with investment in infrastructure acquiring again renewed importance—to supporting productive and social development (via financing investment in health and education), supporting policy reform and capacity building, as well as financing climate change mitigation and adaptation, among other strategic objectives. Lending indirectly to SMEs, via global loans, is also an important area for MDBs, as we discuss below. In fact, priorities of MDBs have evolved through time, and are likely to continue to do so.

MDBs provide financial assistance to developing countries typically in the form of loans and/or grants, for investment projects and policy-based loans. Project loans can vary from large infrastructure projects to social projects including health or education initiatives. Policy-based loans on the other hand, provide financing to governments in exchange for a commitment by the latter to undertake certain reforms, or engage in certain sectorial policies (Nelson 2012).

MDBs usually operate through two lending windows or lending facilities. The first one is the non-concessional window, which provides financial assistance on market-based terms. The second window is the concessional one, oriented to give financial assistance at below-market terms.

Instruments used by MDBs in the non-concessional windows normally constitute loans, but also include equity investments and loan guarantees. Depending on the MDB, financing by this window is extended to middle-income governments, some creditworthy low-income governments, and the private sector in developing countries.

Typically, the capital of a Regional/Multilateral Development Bank (R/MDB) is financed by its member countries, and that allows it to borrow money from international financial markets at low interest rates, usually the same rates available to a developed country government in its domestic financial market. Then, the MDB uses its non-concessional window to lend these resources to the borrowers at lower interest rates than they otherwise should pay to commercial banks.

The concessional window differs from the former in the sense that it offers loans at significantly below-market interest rates and/or grants to governments of low-income countries. Funding for this kind of lending comes mainly from developed countries' commitments and contributions, typically through appropriations from their foreign aid programs, from the profits of the MDBs' operations through their non-concessional lending to middle-income countries, and from repayments of principal by recipients of previous concessional loans.

Table 6.1 summarizes the areas just discussed for six MDBs and describes the kinds of financing provided through the different windows (concessional and non-concessional) and the sectors (public and/or private) towards which financing is directed. For example, within the World Bank Group, the International Bank of Reconstruction and Development (IBRD) constitutes the non-concessional institution and offers loans and loan guarantees on non-concessional terms primarily to middle-income governments. Also within the World Bank Group, the International Development Association (IDA) constitutes the concessional window and offers concessional lending and grants to low-income governments while the International Finance Corporation (IFC) constitutes the "private sector window" of the group and provides non-concessional financing (loans, equity investment, and guarantees) to private sector firms in developing countries. In the same way, the African Development Bank (AfDB) lends on non-concessional terms to middle-income governments of the region, and to some creditworthy low-income governments and private firms, while the African Development Fund (AfDF) provides concessional loans and grants to low-income countries of this region.

Table 6.1 Characterization of different MDBs

MDB	Type of Financing	Type of Borrower	Year Founded
World Bank Group			
International Bank for Reconstruction and Development (IBRD)	Non-concessional loans and loan guarantees	Primarily middle-income governments, also some creditworthy low-income countries	1944
International Development Association (IDA)	Concessional loans and grants	Low-income governments	1960
International Finance Corporation (IFC)	Non-concessional loans, equity investments, and loan guarantees	Private sector firms in developing countries (middle- and low-income countries)	1956
African Development Bank (AfDB)	Non-concessional loans, equity investments, and loan guarantees	Middle-income governments, some creditworthy low-income governments, and private sector firms in the region	1964
African Development Fund (AfDF)	Concessional loans and grants	Low-income governments in the region	1972
Asian Development Bank (AsDB)	Non-concessional loans, equity investments, and loan guarantees	Middle-income governments, some creditworthy low-income governments, and private sector firms in the region	1966
Asian Development Fund (AsDF)	Concessional loans and grants	Low-income governments in the region	1973
European Bank for Reconstruction and Development (EBRD)	Non-concessional loans, equity investments, and loan guarantees	Primarily private sector firms in developing countries in the region, also developing-country governments in the region	1991
Inter-American Development Bank (IDB)	Non-concessional loans and loan guarantees	Middle-income governments, some creditworthy low-income governments, and private sector firms in the region	1959
Fund for Special Operations (FSO)	Concessional loans	Low-income governments in the region	1959
Development Bank of Latin America (CAF)	Non-concessional loans, equity investments, and loan guarantees	Middle-income governments, some creditworthy low-income governments, and private sector firms in the region	1968

Source: Nelson (2012). We also include the Development Bank of Latin America because it has become a de facto regional bank from its initial status of a sub-regional bank (the former *Corporación Andina de Fomento*), incorporating countries of the whole Latin American region. The IDB Group also includes two affiliates, the Inter-American Investment Corporation (IIC) and the Multilateral Investment Fund (MIF).

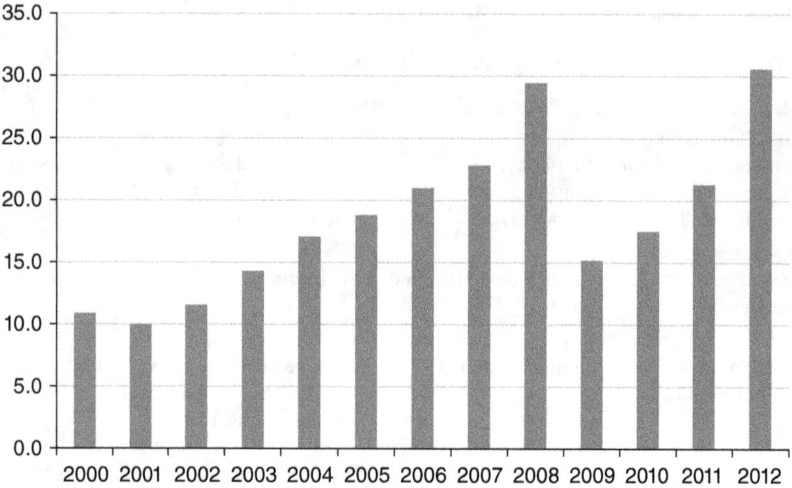

Figure 6.1 MDBs' loans to private firms in percent of total loans, 2000–2012

Source: ECLAC, Financing for Development Division on the basis of MDBs' annual reports.

Note: These figures are a weighted average of approvals to the private sector, as a percentage of total approvals of each bank. MDBs included are the IBRD, IDA, IFC, IADB (including IIC), and AsDB.

It is worth mentioning that in spite of the public sector predominance among MDB resource beneficiaries, the private sector has been gaining importance over time. As shown in Figure 6.1, at the beginning of the 2000s, the private sector accounted for only 11 percent of total lending by MDBs, increasing its share to nearly 30 percent in 2008, at the outset of the international financial crisis. However, this share fell quite significantly during the crisis, as has also occurred in previous crises. After the crisis recovery, MDBs' loans to the private sector also recovered to over 30 percent in 2012.

MDBs' private-sector finance traditionally took the form of direct-lending projects until recently when MDBs decided to redirect their funding towards the support of domestic financial institutions in developing countries (Curmally et al. 2005).

Indeed, the volume of lending by MDBs to domestic financial intermediaries—institutions that in turn lend to or invest in projects—in developing countries has been growing considerably over the last few years. As an example, in 2009 the financial services sector accounted for 40 percent of MDBs' loans to the private sector (up from only 15 percent in 2003) and for 60 percent of MDBs' equity investment in the private sector (up from nearly 30 percent in 2003) (Perry 2011).

The rise in the share of financing through financial intermediaries responds to the fact that it is a more efficient and effective way to channel funds, especially to SMEs as MDBs do not have the resources, manpower, and detailed knowledge necessary to service SMEs directly. In addition, financing

SMEs indirectly through domestic financial institutions can help develop the capacity of financial markets in developing countries (Curmally et al. 2005).

However, channeling a large proportion of resources through private financial intermediaries has some drawbacks. For one thing, it does not guarantee that development priorities of national governments are properly implemented and monitored. Also, it is hard to monitor whether the cost advantages of lending by MDBs (which typically have an AAA credit rating) are transmitted by private banks to the ultimate borrowers (for example, in their lending to SMEs). To achieve both the benefits of integrating national financial institutions more with regional and multilateral development banks, as well as ensuring national development priorities are funded and implemented, it seems clearly desirable to give a bigger role to national (or public) development banks. Indeed, national development banks are in many ways natural partners for regional and multilateral development banks, as discussed in the Introduction. This of course complements the role that private financial institutions perform; indeed public development banks can also support development of domestic capital markets, for example by introducing market-based counter-cyclical instruments, as we discuss below.

2 CHALLENGES AHEAD FOR MDBS: BALANCING THE AGENDA FOR STABILITY AND DEVELOPMENT

In recent years, stakeholders have come to recognize the different roles played by MDBs. Within the context of a post-2015 development agenda, MDBs can play several different roles and functions. These functions should combine and balance those directed towards supporting stability with those directed towards supporting development in the broad sense of the word and include: a) counter-cyclical actions to support macro-financial stability, as well as long-term investment; b) supporting national development strategies; c) helping mobilize increased resources, for example by leverage and blending; and d) financing global public goods.

These functions should be placed in a context of interconnectivity among multilateral, regional, and national development banks. Multilateral and regional development banks can improve the performance of their functions, including providing counter-cyclical finance and supporting productive development, by working closely with national development banks. Similarly, national development banks can operate better if they have the financial and technical support of multilateral and regional banks. Thus, it is important to think not only in terms of public-private synergies, but also in terms of multilateral-regional and national ones.

2.1 Counter-cyclical Lending, Especially for Supporting Investment and Sustained Growth

A first valuable function is development banks' counter-cyclical role when private lending falls sharply or collapses, especially during financial crises. This is particularly crucial to help maintain long-term investment, including in infrastructure, thus ensuring continuity of existing projects and helping new ones start, valuable both for short-term growth and long-term development.

The North Atlantic financial crisis showed that all multilateral, most regional, and a few national development banks of the developed and developing world significantly increased their total lending to developing countries in the years when these were most affected by the North Atlantic crisis (through the rapid expansion of existing mechanisms, as well as via specially created ones, like the World Bank's Crisis Response Window).

It is encouraging, as Table 6.2 shows, that the MDBs collectively increased their lending commitments to emerging and developing economies by 72 percent between 2008 and 2009, the year when private capital flows to these countries fell most sharply as a result of the global financial crisis. Their disbursements also grew significantly in the same year by 40 percent, though the increase was slower than commitments. This represented a major counter-cyclical response, which helped sustain investment in those countries, above levels they would have otherwise had. This lending by multilateral and regional development banks—as well as that of national development banks in developing countries (like the Brazilian development bank BNDES and

Table 6.2 MDB Commitments and Disbursements, 2007–2012 (billion dollars)

	2007	2008	2009	2010	2011	2012
Commitments						
World Bank-IBRD	12.8	13.5	32.9	44.2	26.7	20.6
World Bank-IDA	11.9	11.2	14.0	14.6	16.3	14.8
IADB	8.6	11.1	15.3	12.1	10.4	10.8
AfDB	2.6	2.8	8.8	4.0	5.7	3.2
EBRD	7.7	7.5	11.0	11.9	12.7	11.5
ADB	7.6	8.1	11.0	9.2	10.7	9.4
Total Commitments	**51.3**	**54.2**	**93.0**	**96.0**	**82.4**	**70.3**
Disbursements						
World Bank-IBRD	11.1	10.5	18.6	28.9	21.9	19.8
World Bank-IDA	8.6	9.2	9.2	11.5	10.3	11.1
IADB	6.7	7.1	11.4	10.3	7.9	6.9
AfDB	1.4	1.1	3.7	2.1	2.9	3.4
EBRD	5.7	7.4	7.7	7.9	9.4	7.8
ADB	5.2	6.5	7.9	5.9	6.3	6.8
Total Disbursements	**38.7**	**41.7**	**58.5**	**66.6**	**58.6**	**55.6**

Source: Annual Reports of the respective banks.

several national development banks in Asia)—also contributed to give continuity to trade finance in cases where private trade lines fell. In later years, when crisis was over or had mellowed, and especially after 2010, lending has declined in terms of both commitments and disbursements (see Table 6.2).

However, the counter-cyclical response of MDBs could be further improved, as it was proportionally far smaller for low-income countries than for middle-income countries, and it was also often slower for disbursements than for commitments (see Table 6.2 and for more details see Griffith-Jones and Gottschalk 2012).Thus, disbursements by World Bank-IDA to Sub-Saharan Africa hardly expanded in the initial years of the transatlantic crisis. Slowness in disbursements was partly due in some cases to the fact that much lending by MDBs is project-related. In order to enhance their counter-cyclical response, MDBs also need to address some of the constraints they face including the lack of flexibility of their investment portfolios. Disbursements to large, lumpy projects (e.g. infrastructure) may be difficult to arrange in a counter-cyclical manner, depending on the time-phasing of project execution. Large disbursements may not be possible in the cyclical downswing if such projects do not require them at that time. However, it may be much easier to disburse lending to smaller projects or companies (e.g. SMEs) in a counter-cyclical manner.

In order to enhance MDBs' counter-cyclical capacity, these should expand and make greater use of instruments that are used for this purpose. Some of the currently available instruments that can be used counter-cyclically include local currency loans or GDP linked loans, as well as less-discussed instruments like counter-cyclical guarantees or loans, which allow debt servicing holidays in the face of external shocks. The type of instruments that can be used include not just loans but also guarantees. In order to illustrate this point, an MDB could issue guarantees to private lenders that would take effect when lenders reduced their exposure to a borrower if, in the assessment of the MDB, the borrower's long-term fundamentals remain sound. When lenders resume their lending, such guarantees would lapse. A contingent guarantee facility of this nature would require MDBs to utilize risk assessment models that have a longer-term horizon than those employed by private lenders, and would need to be designed so as to avoid problems of moral hazard and adverse selection. A related idea would be to create regional guarantee agencies or funds to enable risk-sharing among neighboring countries with common interests, for example in infrastructure development. Such a mechanism, which could be supported by regional or sub-regional development banks, would be of interest to countries both considered less risky (as beneficiaries of the infrastructure development) and those considered more risky (which might otherwise be deemed not creditworthy) (see Griffith-Jones and Ocampo 2008).

Local currency loans are valuable as they avoid currency mismatches, which can be very damaging in the face of volatile capital flows or other external shocks; they also help countries develop their own domestic (local currency) bond markets, which provide a more stable source of local funding. Deepening local currency bond markets also provides opportunities for institutional investors to fund their own liabilities with long-term, fixed-income assets. The issuance by developing countries of local currency bonds has rapidly escalated since the East Asian financial crisis. East Asian countries in particular have sought alternatives to currency mismatches and volatile cross-border capital flows by developing their own domestic (local currency) bond markets, which also provide a more stable source of local funding for the public and private sectors (Griffith-Jones and Ocampo 2008). A viable domestic bond market also increases the latitude for governments to implement counter-cyclical policies and to better manage exchange rate fluctuations via sterilized intervention. In addition to reducing vulnerability to currency mismatches and sudden stops associated with foreign borrowing, deepening local currency bond markets also provide opportunities for institutional investors such as insurance companies and pension funds to fund their own liabilities with long-term, fixed-income assets. Local currency bond markets face similar general constraints to those discussed below for GDP-linked bonds, notably pricing and liquidity. However, in many developing countries the necessary domestic institutional and policy framework tends to be weak. These constraints span a range of issues from the technical (e.g. electronic trading platforms, clearing and settlement systems) to the legal and regulatory (information provision and transparency) to the institutional (lack of credit rating agencies and hedging instruments).

It will take time and considerable effort by developing countries to meet these institutional and policy challenges. The MDBs can make an important contribution in this regard. They could expand their own borrowing in local currencies, something the World Bank group, the IDB group, the CAF (now the Development Bank of Latin America), and the Asian Development Bank have all done to a limited extent in some of their borrowing member countries, principally to offer local currency loans to clients in the same country.

The World Bank Group has also launched two programs, the Global Emerging Markets Local Currency Bond Program (GEMLOC) and the Efficient Securities Markets Institutional Development Initiative (ESMID) to strengthen government and non-government bond markets, respectively. The specific objective of GEMLOC is to support local currency bond markets for governments in emerging markets to increase their investability and attract domestic and international investment. The program works with a leading global fixed income investment manager, PIMCO, to promote institutional investment in emerging market local currency bonds. It has developed a bond index fund, GEMX, covering sovereign local currency bonds in twenty-four countries, that weights these countries against indicators of market size and investability. Finally, GEMLOC provides advisory support to strengthen local currency bond markets to increase their investability and to attract new investments. However, it should be noted that external investment in domestic bond markets could generate pro-cyclical flows in a new form.

For its part, ESMID (managed by the Bank's affiliate IFC) focuses on developing non-government bond markets to finance sectors with high-developmental impact, such as infrastructure, housing, and microfinance. The program links development of the policy and institutional framework with specific demonstration transactions. Like GEMLOC, it also facilitates training and advisory services. It has launched two pilot projects, one in the East African Community and one in Nigeria. An innovative dimension of the East African Community project is its support for the regionalization of capital markets in the Community. This is important for smaller, low-income African countries whose market size is a limiting constraint on the development of capital markets at the national level.

Another counter-cyclical instrument that could be used by MDBs is GDP-linked bonds; these would serve to stabilize fiscal policy by curbing expenditures in times of rapid growth and providing "policy space" for higher spending or lower taxes during crises. Investors would find opportunities to take positions on countries' future growth prospects, and could diversify their positions across a number of countries with uncorrelated growth rates. GDP-linked bonds would help avoid the disruptions and uncertainties entailed in situations of debt distress and default for both borrowers and investors.

Once the viability of a market for growth-linked debt for countries in good times is established, it is quite likely that it would take off. This is why the MDBs can play a valuable role as "market-makers." They could do so directly, by developing a portfolio of their own loans indexed to the GDP of their borrowing members and selling the loans individually or securitizing the loans and selling these packages to investors seeking a diversified portfolio (Griffith-Jones and Ocampo 2008). Alternatively they could play a more catalytic role by coordinating the simultaneous issue of a critical mass of GDP-indexed bonds in international markets (Culpeper 2012b). Whilst initially, GDP-indexed bonds were thought of more for developing and emerging countries, the North Atlantic crisis that started in 2007 showed their potential value also for developed economies.

2.2 Support for National Development Strategies

One of the key roles for regional and multilateral development banks to play is in the provision of medium- and long-term finance. Over time multilateral banks basically provided direct funding to governments to help finance infrastructure, agriculture, natural resource development, and, to a much lesser extent, manufacturing. In those countries where capital markets have developed to include long-term finance or attract foreign investors, the role of multilateral banks has evolved to helping attract such flows, at sufficient maturity, for example by co-financing, guarantees, and other mechanisms. However, even in countries with developed capital markets, a role remains for public investment in supporting specific sectors that do not attract sufficient financing from the market. Infrastructure, for example, is typically under-financed, when commercial returns are lower than social returns, or where private markets do not want to commit to the length of maturities required. Where coordination failures exist, development banks can play a key role in helping to coordinate different actors, for example for putting together complex and large packages of private investors and lenders for financing infrastructure, e.g., hydroelectric projects (Spratt et al. 2013). This is especially desirable for intra-regional projects where different countries' regulations and laws are involved. As in infrastructure, other productive sectors, such as agriculture and manufacturing, are often under-financed. From the standpoint of private markets, the risks of investing in some activities in these sectors may be too high, and the private returns may be too low, to assure an adequate flow of financing. But from the standpoint of national development strategies, these sectors are usually key in underpinning national targets for economic growth, income generation, and employment, and are therefore associated with high social rates of return.

In short, for many sectors and countries, private investors/lenders may not be available at all to supply finance at sufficient maturity. In those cases, multilateral development banks have an important role to play by financing projects of strategic or national importance and working collaboratively with both national governments and national developments banks. In this, as in other cases, the rationale for regional and multilateral development banks lending is clearly justified because markets are either incomplete or non-existent. This becomes more of a problem after crises when, for example, private finance for infrastructure significantly declines or dries up. Additionally, where important externalities exist, such as in financing renewable, cleaner energy—implying social benefits exceed private benefits, due to lower carbon emissions, and projects do not yield a fully commercial return—development banks can play an important role, as will be discussed below.

A particular way in which MDBs can assist for national development strategies is helping to improve financial inclusion in those sectors traditionally excluded from the formal financial sector. Financial inclusion for households, and particularly for SMEs, is a prerequisite for productive development, innovation, and higher productivity. In non-inclusive financial systems it is normally small firms and poor individuals that do not have access to finance. This in turn is a mechanism that reinforces inequalities, since the latter will need to rely only on their own wealth and resources in order to get educated, open up a business, invest, or take advantage of promising business opportunities.

According to CGAP (2012), financial inclusion means that households and businesses have access to finance and can effectively use appropriate financial services. Such services must be provided responsibly, sustainably, and in a well regulated environment. As Reddy (2010) put it, this idea of financial inclusion should not be equated with aggressive lending of the sort that led to the sub-prime crisis in the United States, giving greater access to financial services a bad name.

In most developing countries, access to finance both by individuals and small firms is still an issue that calls for policy action. In general, financial systems in developing countries exhibit problems of segmentation and exclude broad segments of the productive sector such as small and medium-sized firms, as well as individuals at the lower end of the income scale, with obvious adverse consequences on poverty and inequality.

MDBs already have a means by which they can act to advance financial inclusion, notably the Consultative Group to Assist the Poor (CGAP),[2] which should be credited with the considerable body of work it has undertaken in the form of research, advocacy, and technical assistance. However, the members of CGAP (including not only the principal MDBs but also a number of bilateral donor agencies) will have to be convinced to take a broader view of financial inclusion, going beyond microfinance institutions to embrace the mainstream financial sector (including the state-owned banks) as well as community-based financial institutions.

Access to finance by SMEs constitutes a key policy concern among economies across the world since these enterprises are critical for sustainable growth and development at the worldwide level. SMEs play a crucial role in most market-based economies as providers of employment and income opportunities and as vehicles of innovation and growth. On average, SMEs account for 67 percent and 45 percent of total formal employment in the manufacturing sector of high-income countries and developing countries, respectively, as well as contributing to sizable shares of GDP (Financial Inclusion Experts Group 2010).

SMEs consistently report having severe obstacles in their access to finance in comparison to larger firms. In turn, the higher financing obstacles are reflected in their financing patterns as they tend to use significantly less external funding than larger firms for both working capital and fixed asset investment.

Cross-country evidence shows that the gap in access to financial credit between SMEs and large firms is much smaller in higher-income countries than in developing ones (see Figure 6.2), and among developing regions, access to a loan by large firms is twice the access of small ones (see Figure 6.3). Nevertheless, the Eurozone debt crisis has reduced access to private credit for SMEs, showing that even developed economies are not immune to cyclical downturns of such credit, requiring compensating actions by public development banks.

When access to external funding is limited, the production capacity of firms and their ability to grow and prosper is constrained as they have to rely on their own resources to operate. This creates a vicious cycle that maintains

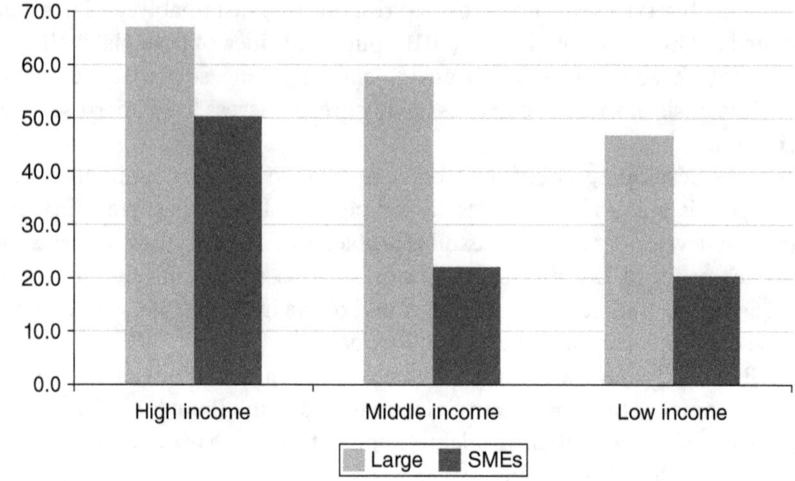

Figure 6.2 Percent of enterprises with an outstanding loan or line of credit

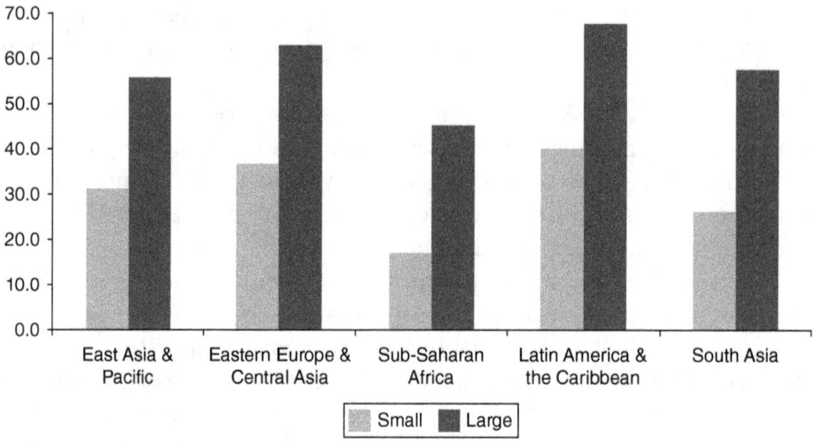

Figure 6.3 Percent of firms with a bank loan or line of credit

Source: ECLAC, Financing for Development Division on the basis of G-20 basic set of financial inclusion indicators database from World Bank (April 2013).

Note: Large enterprises are those with 100 or more employees and SMEs are those with between 5 and 99 employees.

smaller production units at a permanent state of vulnerability and low growth with large social consequences in terms of poverty and inequality.

A common rationale for development banks and similar institutions in industrial and developing countries alike is to provide financing for SMEs, which tend to be too small and risky to be of interest to most commercial lenders.

Many SME start-ups do not survive very long, yet generate benefits going beyond their lifespan. Private markets will thus tend to under-invest in SMEs.

State-owned banks that focus on lending to SMEs are designed to overcome this market failure by designing their lending and other facilities to meet the particular needs of their small business clients, for example through providing counseling and technical support.

Although lending to SMEs is risky, experience has shown that it can be done on a commercially viable basis. For example, the Business Development Bank of Canada (BDC) is required under federal law to return a profit to its only shareholder, the Federal Government, a requirement it has met annually for the past decade. It has been able to do so because it operates independently, at arm's length and without interference from government (Culpeper 2012a). Notable intermediaries focused on lending to SMEs in emerging market countries include the Small and Medium Enterprise Credit Guarantee Fund of Taiwan (Taiwan SMEG) and Small Industries Development Bank of India (SIDBI).

MDBs currently facilitate lending to SMEs in developing countries. Their activities could be expanded through new and existing mechanisms. First, they could fund intermediaries such as national development banks that have a good track record in lending to SMEs. Lending to SMEs would typically be in local currencies and provided on a medium- to long-term basis. In order to avoid currency and maturity mismatches, MDB financing of national development banks or other SME intermediaries could be made available in local currency, based on their own borrowing in the domestic market, and consist in providing long-term credit lines for SME on-lending.

Not all national development banks are necessarily well-positioned to meet the financial needs of small businesses. Some, like their private sector counterparts, are not adept at meeting the needs of an SME clientele. For others, the cost of servicing SMEs may undercut their target rate of return. In this context, other kinds of intermediaries such as credit unions and community-based banks may offer valuable insights and channels on how to meet the financial needs of SMEs.

For example, in Germany, the Sparkassen Finanzgruppe (Savings Banks Finance Group) has existed for 250 years with a mandate to serve lower-income residents. The savings banks are rooted in the municipalities and rural districts of Germany, providing loans and financial services to local SMEs, thus reducing information asymmetries. Particularly striking is the fact that, while their services (e.g. loans) are market-based and their operations commercially sustainable, they are not profit-maximizers. Their mission is both social and economic: surpluses are used to support social and cultural objectives of their communities.

Finally, MDBs and international bodies like the UN could use their convening power to bring together national development banks, credit unions, community-based banks, and other practitioners from industrial and developing countries alike to share lessons and best practices from providing financial services to SMEs. MDBs could also undertake research to identify modalities, institutional arrangements, regulatory frameworks, and policies that work best under different kinds of settings.

2.3 Helping Mobilize Increased Resources, such as by Leverage and Blending

One of the key advantages of channeling public resources via development banks is the positive multiplier impact of leverage. Governments finance the paid-in capital of new MDBs or the increases of paid-in capital of existing MDBs. This has to be qualified in two ways. Firstly, the actual capital paid-in is a small share of total capital, sometimes as little as 5–10 percent of total capital, implying an important multiplier or leverage effect in terms of impact on total lending increase. We will illustrate this with concrete numbers for the estimated impact of the recent increase in the capital of the European Investment Bank (EIB) that was recently agreed by EU member states. Only a very small proportion of capital (less than 10 percent) has been paid-in. Therefore if the total paid-in capital is being doubled, it would require only a total of €10 billion from EU member states. Rating agencies accept a leverage of eight of increased lending as ratio of paid-in capital for the EIB to maintain its AAA status. Because typically the EIB co-finances 50 percent of projects, with private sector or others contributing the other 50 percent, this would result in additional investment of €160 billion. This means a total multiplier effect, or direct and indirect leverage, of up to sixteen for the public funds contributed. (Griffith-Jones et al. 2012). Furthermore, to the extent that these development banks generate a profit and this profit is reinvested as expansion of capital (as has actually happened in the past), a large part of future capital increases do not require additional public funds. Therefore, the leverage, calculated at sixteen above, can be increased further if this dynamic dimension is added.

A second way of generating multiplier effects is, in the case of low-income countries or activities whose social returns are higher than the commercial returns, to use blending rather than grants. A previous issue in this context is whether it is desirable for donors to move along the spectrum from using a higher proportion of grants towards financing more concessional loans, through IDA and regional development banks (RDBs), soft windows to increase concessional loans to low-income countries.

Clearly this approach has the advantage of greater leverage of grants. This may be especially valuable when aid levels from Western donors do not grow, or even decline, as during the current crisis, whilst the needs of developing countries may expand, as a result of the same crisis or their long-term needs, such as financing infrastructure or investing in climate change mitigation and adaptation. Therefore, blending loans and grants have the advantage of "doing more with less." However, the risk is that there could be a build-up of excessive future debt servicing needs, which could lead to new future debt crises in the low-income developing countries. These risks can be reduced by two mechanisms. One is that the replacement of grants by concessional loans should be done, or done more, for relatively richer (such as lower middle-income) countries and less vulnerable developing countries, and less, or not at all, for very poor, more vulnerable economies. Indicators of vulnerability need to include not just existing debt burdens, which are important, but also variables such as economy size and diversification of exports. Secondly, the risk of debt crises should be moderated by counter-cyclical lending mechanisms, such as the Agence Francaise de Development Counter Cyclical Lending (which have debt holidays during years when such countries are hit by external shocks), but spread these mechanisms to MDBs and RDBs.

2.4 Financing the Provision of Global Public Goods

A final and extremely important area of engagement for the MDBs in the coming decades relates to combating climate change, perhaps the most crucial "global public good" of our time.[3]

The international community has defined preventing and adapting to climate change as a major new priority, given the great urgency of the subject. Indeed, the aim of "sustainable" growth puts environmental issues central to development strategies, so as to balance climate and environmental needs with economic growth.

While potentially very important, the role currently played by MDBs in the climate change arena is still small. To put the relative importance of the MDBs in perspective, recent estimates of the flows of climate finance to developing countries in 2009/10 suggest that of a total of \$97 billion,[4] most (\$55 billion) comes from private sector sources, \$21 billion from public budgets, and \$20 billion from bilateral and multilateral agencies (the latter including primarily the MDBs). However, the bilateral and multilateral agencies intermediate (channel) some of the finance from public and private sources and thereby allocate \$39 billion of the total. Most of this amount (\$24 billion) is allocated through bilateral agencies rather than multilateral (\$15 billion). Only a tiny proportion (currently \$1.1–\$3.2 billion) is channeled through dedicated climate funds managed by bilateral and multilateral agencies. In other words, currently MDBs and other multilateral organizations allocate slightly more than 15 percent of the current flow of climate finance (Buchner et al. 2011).

It should, however, be noted that the MDBs have demonstrated a considerable degree of cooperation with each other, exemplified by the Climate Investment Funds (CIFs) established in 2008 and administered by the World Bank, in partnership with the African Development Bank, Asian Development

Bank, Inter-American Development Bank, and European Bank for Reconstruction and Development. As of November 2013, the CIFs had received pledges of \$7.2 billion, including \$4.9 billion for the Clean Technology Fund and \$2.25 billion for the Strategic Climate Fund (ODI and Stiftung 2013).

However, because the MDBs bring the advantages of accumulated expertise, administrative efficiencies, and convening power, they should arguably be expected to do much more. They can help mobilize additional funding, design the necessary policy frameworks, and implement effective projects that can showcase the viability of certain green investment, as in renewable energy (see Spratt, Griffith-Jones, and Ocampo 2013). Above all they can help ensure that a sustainable climate policy is wholly compatible with and indeed facilitates the achievement of the post-2015 global development goals. Given these advantages, the following are offered as the principal elements of a strategy for the MDBs to combat climate change:

i) Mainstreaming Climate Change into Current Policies and Operations

To begin with, in conformity with the Hippocratic principle, the MDBs (and other development cooperation agencies) should first and foremost "do no harm." This is more than a platitude when it comes to otherwise meritorious development projects that nonetheless lead to, or do not try to limit, greenhouse gas emissions. The MDBs are in a key position to work with their developing country clients to pursue low-carbon options that also support poverty reduction and other development objectives. In this sense, the traditional financing role of the MDBs should be adapted to incorporate environmental externalities and to facilitate the introduction of required technologies, e.g., for renewable energy, even when this is less commercially attractive in the short term. Of particular relevance to developing economies, in relation to externalities, is the opportunity to "leapfrog" by immediate adoption of post-carbon technologies. Not only will this contribute to the adaption to and mitigation of climate change globally, but it will also avoid the transition costs that are being incurred by developed nations today and that would be required to be incurred where carbon-based technologies are adopted instead.

ii) Adaptation: Missing in Action

According to recent estimates on the uses to which the current flow of climate finance is put, \$93 billion of the \$97 billion total is allocated to mitigation; only \$4 billion is allocated to adaptation (Buchner et al. 2011).[5] An emphasis on mitigation initiatives is understandable—it seems more sensible to allocate resources to tackling the problem at its source, rather than to helping victims of climate change. More mitigation today could mean less need for adaptation in the future. But this rationalization does a grave disservice to developing countries as well as misunderstands the crucial importance of adaptation today.

First, much of the worst devastation caused by climate change will be visited upon the poorest countries and people, who are largely blameless for climate change. Second, "adaptation" is best considered as "building resilience" against climate change—that is, as a strategy to reduce risk, which is essential for all developing countries. Third, it remains true that climate change has been precipitated over the past two centuries primarily by the actions of developed countries, which should therefore bear the brunt of mitigation costs. The resources allocated to developing-country emission-abatement should not come at the expense of resources for adaptation. From the perspective of developing countries, the costs of mitigation should be borne entirely, or primarily, by the industrial countries. The more urgent need for developing countries is resources for adaptation, rather than mitigation, but even in this case, resources should be additional to current flows of development finance, because of the "causal responsibility" of industrial countries for climate change (Birdsall and de Nevers 2012).

These considerations point to the key role that MDBs (and perhaps other multilateral organizations) should play in spearheading climate change abatement initiatives. Being first and foremost financial institutions that support development objectives, they are in a position to advance a more coherent climate change policy agenda that meets the need of the global community without undermining the needs of developing countries. Such an agenda would recognize that mitigation has the characteristics of a global public good, the benefits of which would be universally felt, while adaptation has fewer aspects of a global public good and is more consistent with traditional support for development. But both are crucially necessary and, since the bulk is presently flowing into mitigation, more funding is crucially needed for adaptation (Ghosh 2010).

iii) Mobilizing Additional Funding?

Although the 2009 Copenhagen Climate Change Conference established a target of $100 billion in additional funding by 2020, there has been little progress toward mobilizing this amount during the current recession. Only $7 billion of $30 billion in pledges for the period 2010–2012 had actually been deposited in some form by mid-2011 (Birdsall 2012). Moreover, estimates of additional financing actually required range up to $200 billion for mitigation and $100 billion for adaptation, considerably above the Copenhagen estimates (Ghosh 2010).

In conclusion, if the MDBs are to play a much more significant role in combating climate change, as seems urgent, its members must agree to give them the mandate and the resources that they currently lack. One channel is to create a climate change affiliate in the World Bank Group with its own board and governance structure. If members are open to the possibility of a shareholding structure significantly different from that in the current World Bank Group, there could be a compromise that obviates the need to create an entirely new institution. Another possibility is to follow the "CG" model (as with the CGIAR and CGAP) by creating a "Consultative Group to Combat Climate Change." This would have the advantage of (potentially) being more inclusive (for example, all the MDBs could be members) and leveraging resources from a number of sources. But this CG would have to demonstrate that it would go beyond the incrementalism of the current "non-system" and make a dramatic difference in terms of resource mobilization and project implementation.

iv) Catastrophe Insurance

In addition to mitigation and adaptation, which can be considered "crisis prevention" strategies,[6] catastrophe insurance provides greater scope for "crisis management." Given that climate change is a palpable reality and that it will occasionally inflict devastation in some places no matter how effective are mitigation and adaptation efforts, the provision of catastrophic risk insurance is a necessary and important complement to "prevention" measures.[7]

The World Bank facilitated the creation of the Caribbean Catastrophe Risk Insurance Facility (CCRIF) in 2007 at the request of the Caribbean Community Heads of Government. The facility provides risk insurance to 16 Caribbean countries; in the event of pre-defined natural catastrophe, insured countries are given immediate access to liquidity to meet their emergency needs, obviating drawn-out requests for assistance requiring months to take effect. By spreading risk among a larger number of countries the facility was able to harness the reinsurance market, thereby lowering costs. An early review of the facility examined the sustainability of the CCRIF and concluded that it is one of the safest insurance facilities in the world (World Bank 2008). And the Caribbean example is replicable. However, care needs to be taken so that such an instrument is not excessively costly.

A similar risk-financing instrument offered by the World Bank is the Catastrophe Deferred Drawdown Option. This product provides immediate liquidity ($500 million or 0.25 percent of GDP, whichever is less) to IBRD members in the aftermath of a natural disaster. This facility provides more cost-effective insurance to IBRD members than conventional insurance, but is provided in the form of a non-concessional loan. Therefore it is of limited value to non-creditworthy low-income countries. Thus an insurance facility is needed that would be appropriate to the debt-servicing capabilities of the LICs.

Since MDBs have a global reach, they are in a position to help their borrowers achieve such risk-reduction benefits through global diversification (Perry 2009). Hence this is certainly one area in which the MDBs can utilize their current resources and convening authority to provide greater support to their borrowers against climate change (and other natural catastrophes).

3 CONCLUSIONS AND POLICY IMPLICATIONS

There has been an emerging consensus that MDBs and regional development banks (RDBs) have a crucial role to play in development finance. It has become widely recognized by the international community since the North Atlantic 2007/2008 crisis started that counter-cyclical lending by MDBs is crucial to provide official long-term finance when private finance contracts during and after crises, especially to maintain investment; indeed, such long term counter-cyclical finance by MDBs is the natural complement to counter-cyclical official private liquidity, as provided by the IMF for example. There has also emerged a growing recognition of the value of MDBs and RDBs to support productive public and private investment in all periods, as an instrument to finance and help implement a long-term vision and strategy of national and regional development. Furthermore, a clearer recognition has emerged of the need to finance investment in global and regional public goods on a significant scale, specifically climate change mitigation and adaptation, and the value of MDBs as a natural instrument to help achieve that.

In the wake of the North Atlantic financial crisis, and previous crises, much thinking is focusing on how the financial sector can better serve the needs of the real economy. Clearly, well-functioning and well-governed development banks have a key role to play, also because of the limitations of private financial institutions. Nevertheless, one of the key roles of development banks is to work closely with private financial institutions, especially with the aim of mobilizing broader resources. MDBs not only provide a blending of grants with concessional loans, which allows a greater scale of financing to poorer countries, but they are also able to generate a significant scale of loans with a relatively small amount of paid-in capital by leveraging government contributions made to their capital to raise money on capital markets. By co-financing projects with private banks, they are able to achieve additional leverage. Furthermore, close collaboration between development banks and private financial institutions facilitates lending funded by MDBs and implemented by national financial institutions, which are closer to the ultimate borrowers.

The synergies and complementarities that can be created by collaboration among multilateral, regional, and national development banks can be increased further to improve their mutual effectiveness. In this context, the concept of densification at the *institutional* level implies a better articulation between MDBs with regional and national development banks for supporting development objectives and for the allocation of resources.

By working collaboratively with national development banks, MDBs can, for example, help deepen local currency bond markets, thus mobilizing funds from institutional investors for corporate borrowers and helping to strengthen the infrastructure necessary to provide proper supervision and oversight in the market. They can also be "market makers" for instruments such as local currency and GDP-linked bonds to embed counter-cyclicality into market instruments. MDBs, RDBs, and NDBs (national development banks) can expand their joint work further to invest in projects of regional or national importance, such as in the infrastructure sector. The MDBs can also provide local- and foreign-currency funding to support the national development banks' lending programs, thereby supporting the national industrial strategy. In a word, MDBs can work actively to support developing countries' strategies through national development banks acting as partners and intermediaries.

Last but not least, there are vast unmet investment needs to help developing countries sustain growth. As emerging and developing countries have large savings and foreign exchange reserves, there is a strong case for the creation of a BRICS bank, which would complement the finance provided by the existing MDBs; it is therefore welcome that such a bank has been agreed by the BRICS countries.

The above analysis calls for growing public investment in existing (and new) MDBs as a necessary, indeed imperative, complement to a world of global private capital mobility. Such investment would both help ensure that global finance continues to serve the public good in a number of ways, as well as to provide insurance against the vagaries of global financial markets and their all-too-well demonstrated proclivity to frequent crisis and occasional breakdown.

Looking ahead, it is doubtful that the world will return to the relatively placid and crisis-free global environment of the early post-war decade. Regrettably, financial turmoil and occasional crises are to be expected, especially as private financial reform and reform of financial regulation will probably be insufficient to prevent a recurrence of the last crisis. That being the case, it would behoove the international community to have at its disposal a set of institutions in the form of well-capitalized MDBs that are able to help ensure that counter-cyclical finance and capital for long-run productive investment (commensurate with needs) is available and ready for quick disbursement.

NOTES

1. By densification we mean the increasing interaction and inter-linkages among financial institutions and instruments at global, regional, and national level. Densification can also involve taking advantage of complementarities between MDBs and private financial intermediaries. This can involve a better articulation at the

institutional level and also a larger densification at the instrument level by increasing the number and specificity of the financial instruments available for agents to manage different types of risks.

2. CGAP is a global partnership of 34 leading organizations that seek to advance financial inclusion (http://www.cgap.org).
3. There are a number of other global public goods, for example managing the global commons (biodiversity, desertification, deforestation, global health issues) in which the MDBs have taken a role. These are not discussed here. Some of them in any cases relate to climate change, which is perhaps the most urgent of global public goods issues.
4. While this amount appears to be close to the target of $100 billion in additional financing established at the 2009 UN Climate Change conference in Copenhagen, not much of the $97 billion was additional to what was already being spent. See Buchner et al. (2011) and Birdsall (2012).
5. Adaptation is defined as an "adjustment in natural or human systems in response to actual or expected climatic stimuli or their effects, to moderate harm or exploit beneficial opportunities" (International Panel on Climate Change—IPCC); see https://www.ipcc.ch/publications_and_data/ar4/wg2/en/annexessglossary-a-d.html.
6. Adaptation now usually means "strengthening resilience" against climate change. Thus the more resilient a country or region is against devastating droughts or floods, the lower the level of crisis.
7. Note that the risks covered go beyond extreme weather events, and include earthquakes, tsunamis, and all natural catastrophes.

REFERENCES

Birdsall, Nancy. 2012. "The World Bank and Climate Change: Forever a Big Fish in a Small Pond?" *CGD Policy Paper* 007.

Birdsall, Nancy, and Michele de Nevers. 2012. "Adaptation Finance: How to Get Out from between a Rock and a Hard Place." *CGD Policy Paper* 001 (February).

Buchner, Barbara, Angela Falconer, Morgan-Hervé Mignucci, Chiara Trabacchi, and Marcel Brinkman. 2011. "The Landscape of Climate Finance. A CPI Report." *Climate Policy Initiative* (27 October).

CGAP. 2012. *Advancing Financial Access for the World's Poor: Annual Report 2012.* http://www.cgap.org/sites/default/files/CGAP-Annual-Report-Dec-2012.pdf.

Culpeper, Roy. 2012a. "Financial Sector Policy and Development in the wake of the Global Crisis: the role of national development banks." *Third World Quarterly* 33(3): pp. 383–403.

Culpeper, Roy. 2012b. "Debt and Development in South Asia: Challenges and Opportunities." *South Asia Policy and Research Institute.* November 2012.

Curmally, A., J. Sohn, and C. Wright. 2005. *Multilateral Development Bank Lending Through Financial Intermediates: Environmental and Social Challenges.* World Resources Institute.

Financial Inclusion Experts Group. 2010. "Scaling-up SME Access to Financial Services in the Developing World." Washington DC: International Finance Corporation.

Ghosh, Anurabha. 2010. "Harnessing the Power Shift: Governance Options for International Climate Financing." *Oxfam Research Reports* (6 October). Griffith-Jones, S. 2012. "Exogenous Shocks; Dealing with the only Certainty, Uncertainty." Paper prepared for Commonwealth Finance Ministers meeting.

Griffith-Jones, Stephany and José Antonio Ocampo. 2008. "A Counter-cyclical Framework for a Development-Friendly IFA." In *Macroeconomic Volatility, Institutions and Financial Architectures: The Developing World Experience*, edited by José Maria Fanelli. New York: Palgrave Macmillan.

Griffith-Jones, Stephany and Gottschalk Ricardo. 2012. "Exogenous Shocks: Dealing with the only Certainty: Uncertainty." Paper prepared for the Commonwealth Secretariat September 2012, for the Commonwealth Finance Ministers' Meeting, Tokyo, 10 October 2012.

Griffith-Jones, S., M. Kollatz-Ahnen, L. Andersen, S. and Hansen. 2012. "Shifting Europe from austerity to growth: a proposed investment program for 2012–2015." *FEPS, IPD & ECLM Policy Brief.*

Nelson, R. 2012. "Multilateral development banks: Overview and issues for Congress." *Congressional Research Service.*

ODI andHeinrich Böll Stiftung. 2013. "Climate Funds Update." http://www.odi.org.uk/sites/odi.org.uk/files/odi-assets/publications-opinion-files/8685.pdf.

Perry, G. 2011. "Growing business or development priority? Multilateral development banks' direct support to private firms." *Center for Global Development* (April).

Perry, Guillermo. 2009. *Beyond Lending: How Multilateral Banks Can Help Developing Countries Manage Volatility*. Washington DC: Center for Global Development.

Reddy, Y.V. 2010. "Regulation of the Financial Sector in Developing Countries: Lessons from the 2008 Financial Crisis." In *Time for the Visible Hand*, edited by Griffith-Jones, Ocampo and Stiglitz. Oxford: Oxford University Press.

Rodrik, Dani. 2008. *One Economics, Many Recipes: Globalization, Institutions and Economic Growth.* Princeton: Princeton University Press.

Rogers, F. Halsey. 2010. "The Global Financial Crisis and Development Thinking." *World Bank Policy Research Working Paper* 5353 (June).

Spratt, S., Griffith-Jones, S. and Ocampo, J.A. 2013. "Mobilising Investment for Inclusive Green Growth in Low-Income Countries." Study prepared for Deutsche Gesellschaft für Internationale Zusammenarbeit (GIZ).

World Bank. 2008. *The Caribbean Catastrophe Risk Insurance Initiative: A Review of CCRIF's Operation after its First Season*. Washington DC: The World Bank (December 1).

Index

Tables, figures, and boxes are indicated by an italic *t*, *f*, and *b* following the page number.

The manufacturer's authorised representative in the EU for product safety is Oxford University Press España S.A. of el Parque Empresarial San Fernando de Henares, Avenida de Castilla, 2 – 28830 Madrid (www.oup.es/en or product.safety@oup.com). OUP España S.A. also acts as importer into Spain of products made by the manufacturer.

www.ingramcontent.com/pod-product-compliance
Lightning Source LLC
LaVergne TN
LVHW011800200926
848484LV00003B/745

* 9 7 8 0 1 9 8 7 8 5 9 4 1 *